CHASING NEOTROPICAL BIRDS

NUMBER SIXTY-ONE

The Corrie Herring Hooks Series

Chasing Neotropical Birds

Text by BOB THORNTON

Photography by VERA AND BOB THORNTON

UNIVERSITY OF TEXAS PRESS, AUSTIN

Requests for permission to reproduce material
from this work should be sent to
    Permissions
    University of Texas Press
    P.O. Box 7819
    Austin, TX 78713-7819.

∞ The paper used in this book meets the minimum requirements
of ANSI/NISO Z39.48-1992 (R1997) (Permanence of Paper).

Library of Congress Cataloging-in-Publicaton Data

Thornton, Bob, date
    Chasing neotropical birds / text by Bob Thornton ;
photography by Vera and Bob Thornton.— 1st ed.
      p.   cm. — (The Corrie Herring Hooks series ; no. 61)
    Includes bibliographical references and index.
    ISBN 0-292-70589-1 (hardcover : alk. paper)
    1. Forest birds—Latin America. 2. Forest birds—Latin America—Pictorial works.
I. Title. II. Series.
QL685.7.T56   2005
598.098—dc22   2004005930

*W*E DEDICATE THIS BOOK to the men and women of The Nature Conservancy, for both their commitment and their effectiveness in preserving critical habitat so necessary to the health and survival of the planet's unique flora and fauna. Science-based and partnership-driven, the Conservancy preserves special land the old-fashioned way—it identifies what's ecologically important, it buys it when it becomes available, and then it takes care of it. Even when critical land is not available for sale, the Conservancy works closely with landowners to nurture ownership pride and build good stewardship.

From tallgrass prairies and sweet, clean rivers to craggy mountain ranges and hardwood bottomlands, The Nature Conservancy has for the past fifty years provided visionary leadership in its mission to protect the earth's biodiversity. It has been responsible for saving over 100 million acres of the planet's most impressive and important landscapes and, in so doing, has become the largest private sanctuary in the world. One of the many beneficiaries of this massive conservation initiative has been the exotic birds inhabiting the rainforests of the Neotropics. From Belize and Costa Rica in the north down to Bolivia and Brazil in the south, the Conservancy has a splendid record in saving large-scale tracts of important wilderness that serve as the home to these magnificent creatures. So to The Nature Conservancy, we say, "Keep up the good work."

Contents

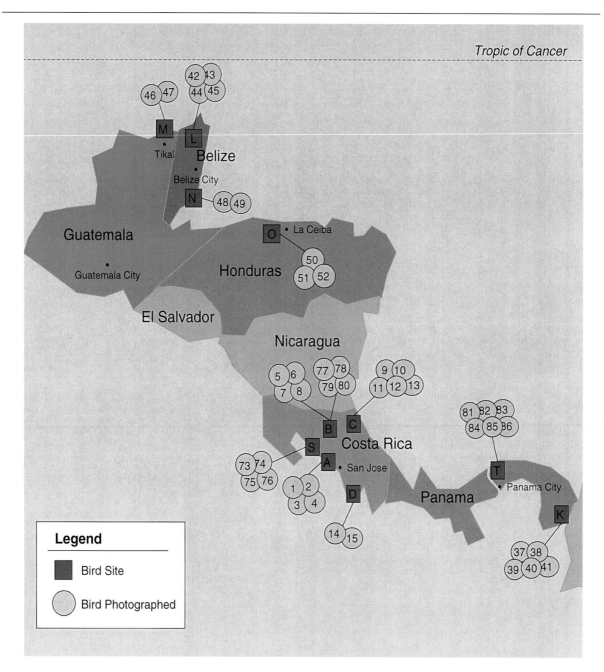

Legend

Bird Site

Bird Photographed

(A) Carara Biological Reserve, Costa Rica
(B) Monteverde Cloud Forest, Costa Rica
(C) La Selva Biological Station, Costa Rica
(D) Corcovado National Park, Costa Rica
(E) Trinidad
Asa Wright Nature Centre
Caroni Swamp
(F) Near El Pauji, Venezuela
(G) Río Grande Forest Reserve, Venezuela
(H) Hato Piñero, Venezuela
(I) Henri Pittier National Park, Venezuela

(J) La Selva Jungle Lodge, Río Napo, Ecuador
(K) Southern Darien Province, Panama
(L) Chan Chich, Belize
(M) Tikal, Guatemala
(N) El Pescador Punta Gorda, Belize
(O) The Lodge at Pico Bonito, Honduras
(P) Near Bocono, Venezuela
(Q) Itatiaia National Park, Brazil
(R) La Escalera, Eastern Venezuela
(S) La Ensenada Lodge, Costa Rica
(T) Canopy Tower, Panama

(U) Manu National Park, Peru
Cock-of-the-Rocks Lodge
Manu Wildlife Center
(V) The Pantanal, Brazil
(W) Chapada National Forest,
Brazil
(X) Western Slope Andes, Ecuador
Mindo Valley
Tandayapa Valley
(Y) Suriname

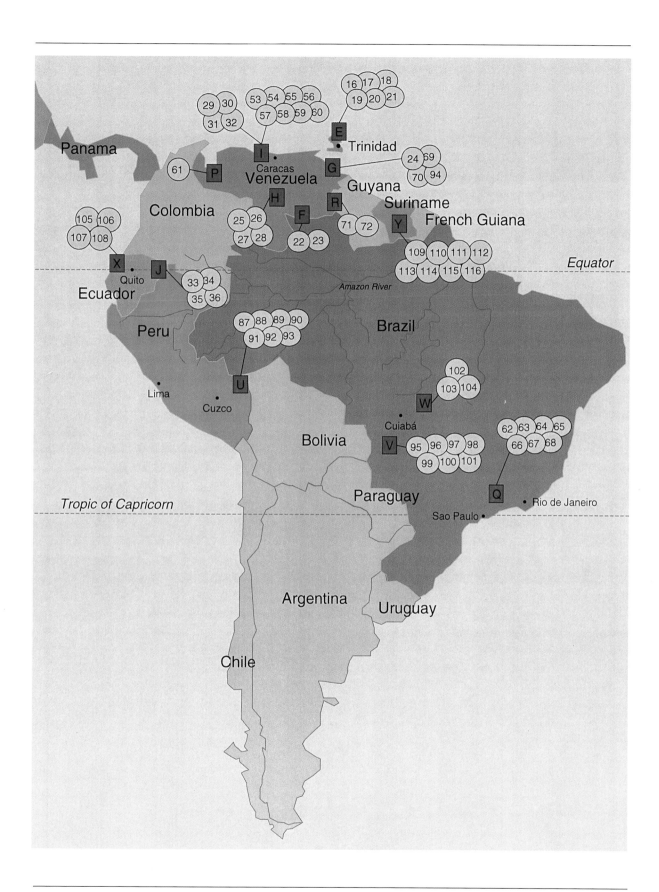

Bird Log

YEAR	BIRD NUMBER AND NAME	AREA
1987	1 Turquoise-browed Motmot	(A) Carara Biological Reserve, Costa Rica
1987	2 Scarlet Macaw	
1987	3 Boat-billed Heron	
2000	4 Baird's Trogon	
1987	5 Green-crowned Brilliant	(B) Monteverde Cloud Forest, Costa Rica
1987	6 Purple-throated Mountain-gem	
1987	7 Violet Sabrewing	
2000	8 Resplendent Quetzal (2)	
1988	9 Red-capped Manakin	(C) La Selva Biological Station, Costa Rica
1988	10 Gray-necked Wood-Rail	
1988	11 Scarlet-rumped Tanager	
1988	12 Masked Tityra	
1988	13 Broad-billed Motmot	
1988	14 Rufous-tailed Jacamar	(D) Corcovado National Park, Costa Rica
1988	15 Orange-collared Manakin	
1989	16 Purple Honeycreeper	(E) Trinidad
		Asa Wright Nature Centre
1989	17 Barred Antshrike	
1989	18 Tufted Coquette	
1989	19 Green Honeycreeper	
1989	20 Collared Trogon	
1989	21 Scarlet Ibis	Caroni Swamp
1989	22 Yellow-tufted Woodpecker	(F) near El Pauji, Venezuela
1989	23 Black-headed Parrot	
1989	24 Orange-bellied Manakin	(G) Río Grande Reserve, Venezuela
1990	25 Sunbittern	(H) Hato Piñero, Venezuela
1990	26 Snail Kite	
1990	27 Crested Caracara	
1990	28 Red-breasted Blackbird	
1990	29 Speckled Tanager	(I) Henri Pittier National Park, Venezuela
1990	30 Golden Tanager	
1990	31 Silver-beaked Tanager	
1990	32 Chestnut-crowned Antpitta	
1991	33 Black-fronted Nunbird	(J) La Selva Jungle Lodge, Río Napo, Ecuador

YEAR	BIRD NUMBER AND NAME	AREA
1991	34 Zigzag Heron	
1991	35 Long-tailed Potoo	
1991	36 Hoatzin	
1992	37 Bicolored Antbird	(K) Southern Darien Province, Panama
1992	38 Spotted Antbird	
1992	39 Chestnut-backed Antbird	
1992	40 Black-crowned Antpitta	
1992	41 Rufous-vented Ground-Cuckoo (2)	
1994	42 Agami Heron	(L) Chan Chich, Belize
1994	43 Ocellated Turkey	
1994	44 Tody Motmot	
1994	45 White-necked Jacobin	
1994	46 Keel-billed Toucan	(M) Tikal, Guatemala
1994	47 Collared Aracari	
2003	48 Slaty-tailed Trogon	(N) El Pescador Punta Gorda Lodge, Belize
2003	49 Gray-throated Chat	
2003	50 Keel-billed Motmot	(O) The Lodge at Pico Bonito, Honduras
2003	51 Golden-hooded Tanager	
2003	52 Vermiculated Screech-Owl	
1999	53 Blue-winged Mountain-Tanager	(I) Henri Pittier National Park, Venezuela
1999	54 Handsome Fruiteater	
1999	55 Orange-bellied Euphonia	
1999	56 Russet-backed Oropendola	
1999	57 Red-crowned Woodpecker	
1999	58 Cinnamon Flycatcher	
1999	59 Long-tailed Sylph	
1999	60 Wire-tailed Manakin	
1999	61 Spectacled Owl	(P) near Bocono, Venezuela
1999	62 Rufous-capped Spinetail	(Q) Itatiaia National Park, Brazil
1999	63 Black Jacobin	
1999	64 Dusty-legged Guan	
1999	65 Ferruginous Pygmy-Owl	
1999	66 Blue Dacnis	
1999	67 Saffron Toucanet	
1999	68 Blue Manakin	
2000	69 Black-collared Hawk	(G) Río Grande Forest Reserve, Venezuela
2000	70 Long-tailed Hermit	
2000	71 Ruddy Tody-Flycatcher	(R) La Escalera, Eastern Venezuela
2000	72 Capuchinbird	
2001	73 Black-headed Trogon	(S) La Ensenada Lodge, Costa Rica
2001	74 Orange-fronted Parakeet	
2001	75 Spot-breasted Oriole	
2001	76 Three-wattled Bellbird (2)	
2001	77 Long-tailed Manakin	(B) Monteverde Cloud Forest, Costa Rica
2001	78 Blue-crowned Motmot	
2001	79 Emerald Toucanet	

YEAR	BIRD NUMBER AND NAME	AREA
2001	80 Bare-necked Umbrellabird	
2001	81 Chestnut-mandibled Toucan	(T) Canopy Tower, Panama
2001	82 Great Jacamar	
2001	83 Western Slaty-Antshrike	
2001	84 Violet-bellied Hummingbird	
2001	85 White-whiskered Puffbird	
2002	86 Blue Cotinga (2)	
2001	87 Andean Cock-of-the-rock	(U) Manu National Park, Peru
		Cock-of-the-Rocks Lodge
2001	88 Bay-headed Tanager	
2001	89 Saffron-crowned Tanager	
2001	90 Versicolored Barbet (2)	
2001	91 Mealy Amazon	Manu Wildlife Center
2001	92 Red-and-green Macaw	
2001	93 Band-tailed Manakin	
2002	94 Harpy Eagle (2)	(G) Río Grande Forest Reserve, Venezuela
2002	95 Southern Screamer	(V) The Pantanal, Brazil
2002	96 Toco Toucan	
2002	97 Helmeted Manakin	
2002	98 Red-billed Scythebill	
2002	99 Bare-faced Curassow	
2002	100 Hyacinth Macaw (2)	
2002	101 Jabiru	
2002	102 White-eared Puffbird	(W) Chapada National Forest, Brazil
2002	103 Rufous-winged Antshrike	
2002	104 Coal-crested Finch	
2002	105 Club-winged Manakin	(X) Western Slope Andes, Ecuador
		Mindo Valley
2002	106 Violet-tailed Sylph	
2002	107 Toucan Barbet	Tandayapa Valley
2002	108 Plate-billed Mountain-Toucan (2)	
2003	109 Gray-winged Trumpeter	(Y) Suriname
2003	110 Thrush-like Antpitta	
2003	111 Ferruginous-backed Antbird	
2003	112 Wing-banded Antbird	
2003	113 Red-and-black Grosbeak	
2003	114 Guianan Cock-of-the-rock (2)	
2003	115 Yellow-billed Jacamar	
2003	116 White-plumed Antbird	

Neotropicals

*T*HIS BOOK TELLS A STORY of an adventure that extended over a fifteen-year period as Vera and I photographed some of the exotic tropical birds of Central and South America. It was inspired by an earlier project of ours to photograph all of a special family of U.S. nesting birds called wood warblers. That quest led us each spring through the temperate forests of North America in pursuit of those small, colorful birds and resulted in a book, *Chasing Warblers,* which was published by the University of Texas Press in 1999.

However, during several weeks of those very same years, and with no grand goal in mind, Vera and I began to probe the forests of the Neotropics to find and photograph the magical birds indigenous to those habitats. In a geographical range running between the Tropic of Cancer and the Tropic of Capricorn, we explored the rainforests of Belize and Guatemala in the north down to the coastal woods of Brazil and the Amazon Basin of Peru in the south. There were weeks spent high up in the cloud forests of Costa Rica and the Andes of Ecuador and others down through the Pacific lowlands of Panama and the Guianan Shield forests of Venezuela and Suriname.

In embarking on this Neotropical journey, Vera and I plunged into what was an enchanting and mysterious world of giant, ancient trees dripping bromeliads and wild orchids. We encountered cathedrals of vegetation with mosaics of green, impressive complexities of mosses and ferns, and fertile stands of bamboo that grow a foot a day. We patrolled riparian thickets and tropical savannas and elfin forests, finding along the way a stunning tangle of wildlife diversity. There were glorious great moths with "eyes" on their wings to discourage predators, brilliantly colored beetles of metallic rainbow colors, and poisonous dart frogs of bright red/blue and yellow/black harlequin markings. We saw Crab-eating Foxes, Bird-eating Spiders, and Fish-eating Bats. There were eagles that ate monkeys and sloths.

And there was adventure. We were charged by a herd of White-lipped Peccaries in Panama, attacked by a jealous tapir in southern Venezuela, and greeted by the deadly Fer-de-lance one night in the Caribbean lowlands of Costa Rica. Our excursions were charmed by moonlight canoe rides through Ecuadorian river forests and rattled by howler monkey troops moving through camp at dawn. We saw crocodiles and caiman, great otters, and anacondas, and were dazzled by special butterflies with reflective wings of a magic blue. We jumped both Jaguarundi and Ocelot, but never the magnificent Jaguar, "El Tigre," though we saw its tracks often and heard it cough one evening at the edge of a forest where it had dragged off young colts a few months before. We waded through army antswarms in the Darien of Panama, rope-climbed to the canopy of a giant laurel tree in eastern Venezuela, and at the La Selva camp off the Río Napo in Ecuador, shared a bathroom with a tarantula we named Sue.

There were crisp, cerulean blue days in the high Andes of Venezuela and blistering hot treks on the Osa Peninsula of Costa Rica. There were rainy-season marches in the Amazon Basin that nearly washed us away. And all of this exploration while weighted down with gear, but uplifted by a sense of wonder and an appetite for challenge as we stalked the exotic land birds of the Neotropics—with hopes of capturing photographs of which we could be proud.

For our adventure had always been about the birds, and the forests of Central and South America have more of them than any other place on the planet. The tropical latitudes of this hemisphere support over 3,700 different species, nearly 40 percent of all such avian creatures on earth. While North America might play host to perhaps 800 or so different varieties of birds, Costa Rica alone—a country about the size of West Virginia—can brag about having at least that many. Colombia and Peru have more birds than any other country in the world, with about 1,800 species apiece, each hosting more individual species than the entire continent of Asia. Their neighbors are also loaded: Venezuela, Ecuador, and Brazil—with over 1,500 birds per country—each claims more varieties than either India or China, and even the number posted by landlocked Bolivia exceed that of the entire continent of Australia. The reason for this abundance of riches has everything to do with the impressive calibrations of equatorial habitat that occur within a relatively compressed geographical area—from a high Andes tree line dropping quickly through a series of ecological zones to a humid Amazon Basin, sliced and diced and serrated along the way by ridges and rivers, cordilleras and canyons that have permitted the evolution of so many special and discrete species.

The Neotropics are inhabited by birds that are found nowhere else in the world—such as the toucans and antbirds, motmots and manakins, as well as the unusual members of the cotinga family like the umbrellabirds, bellbirds, and cocks-of-the-rock. These splendid creatures come in an assortment of colors and sizes and produce a marvelous range of songs and sounds. Some of the birds eloquently romanced us with their stirring melodies and flute serenades, while others barked like dogs or mooed like cows or screamed like cats. Some trumpeted, some hooted, some hissed, some moaned. And in addition to the celebrated and exotic birds we chased, the Neotropics support a great many more mundane species, like the ovenbirds and woodcreepers, and nearly four hundred different flavors of tyrant flycatcher.

These birds are accompanied by other "little brown jobs" like the leaftossers and woodhaunters, the gnateaters and streamcreepers, to which we were conspicuously inattentive and weren't able to devote much time.

As far as actually photographing tropical birds, Vera and I decided early on not to concentrate on any one family, as we had done with the wood warblers. Nor did we choose to showcase a representative bird from each family. Rather we pursued birds that we personally considered to be "special," a preferred Neotropical sampler of those species that either dazzled us with their beauty, or charmed us by their behavior, or, in a few cases, simply challenged us by the mystique of their rarity.

In selecting birds for elegance and beauty, we focused on the charismatic quetzals and hummingbirds of Costa Rica, brilliant honeycreepers found in Trinidad, and the extravagant tanagers common to Venezuela and Ecuador. In addition, there were jacamars and trogons, parrots and macaws, toucans and motmots, which defined, at least for us, the most glamorous birds the Neotropics had to offer. These were the stunners, the real showstoppers.

But we also targeted birds whose behavior and habits we found to be particularly intriguing, creatures that continually fascinated and often astonished us. This category was not about beauty, but behavior—although some of these birds were gorgeous in their own right. There were manakins displaying on their assembly arenas throughout the Neotropics, the cocks-of-the-rock in the woodlands of Suriname and the cloud forests of southern Peru, the "professional" antbirds stalking army antswarms in the Darien of Panama, and the marvelous bellbirds "bonking" throughout the day on the mountaintops of Costa Rica. There was also the incomparable and delightfully bizarre Capuchinbird.

And, finally, Vera and I were fortunate enough to photograph several birds that even the most discriminating Neotropical ornithologists might concede to be big wins—birds seldom seen and rarely photographed: the Black-crowned Antpitta, the Zigzag Heron, the Bare-necked Umbrellabird, the Long-tailed Potoo, the Rufous-vented Ground-Cuckoo, and, arguably one of the grandest of them all, the monkey-eating Harpy Eagle.

Trying to locate and photograph these birds in a rainforest environment, however, represented a huge challenge for Vera and me as we were, quite frankly, neither competent Neotropical birders nor broadly experienced wildlife photographers. In addition, we had committed ourselves from the beginning to capturing artistic images of these special birds rather than simply settling for obligatory photographic records of new birds encountered.

This, of course, made it harder and often required us to work within twenty to thirty feet of our targets, while striving at the same time to confiscate enough ambient light so that the picture would look as natural as possible. Consistently pulling this off, however, was difficult for us: many of our targeted birds hung out in forest canopies, and working close enough for a photograph was always a challenge. Or else they skulked in the dark interiors of the forest itself, where light is a scarce commodity on the brightest of days, and adequately flattering the subjects, even with the use of a flash, was often problematic. Our best-case scenario was a bright, overcast day, which spread a diffused light across the forest interior, but even then only 2 percent of the light reached the forest floor.

Another issue with rainforest photography is, of course—rain, which is what rainforests are known for even in the "dry" season. Many an otherwise promising day was literally washed out by the weather, and although tropical birds prefer rainy and foggy weather to sunshine, it's hell on photographers. We spent a lot of time wet.

Along the way we discovered that while a particular section of tropical forest might embrace many species of birds, there was not an abundance of individual birds to be found. The bird biomass was small, and even the most colorful of these birds on the brightest days of the year are often hard to see because they blend in so well with their surroundings. Many are sit-and-wait foragers, and even experienced ornithologists have difficulty spotting birds that perch immobile and mute amid thick, tropical foliage. The Neotropical woods can be both melancholy and expansively silent for long stretches of time, and many a wildlife photographer, dispirited by the inaction, has thrown in the towel early on to gratefully retreat stateside and resume shooting stationary waterbirds in good light. While there is no shortage of superb photographs of Roseate Spoonbills and Snowy Egrets and Great Blue Herons, flattered by the dappled glow of a South Florida lagoon, quality images of Neotropical forest birds are more difficult to come by. World-class photographs of some rainforest birds have indeed been taken by posing the birds in a controlled situation after they have first been mistnetted. Vera and I, however, "chased" our birds down, and our shots were taken in the field. Hence the title of the book.

In our pursuit of Neotropical birds to photograph, we initially sought whatever we could flush or spot as we moved ever so slowly through the forest, hoping to catch some small movement or even a snatch of a song or call note that would alert us to a bird's presence. We also attempted to locate areas where a targeted species of bird was known to consistently display, or call, so that we could try to maneuver close enough to it for a shot. At times we would use a tape recorder to play back the male's own song in an effort to draw him in curiously closer, but on other occasions we would simply remain motionless in the bird's area for long periods of time until it finally relaxed and resumed its routine.

Many of the birds we captured on film were busy and absorbed with feeding, and were often unaware of or unconcerned by our presence. There were berry pickers and insect snatchers; there were nectar drinkers and dead-leaf specialists. Consequently, jacamars diving after morpho butterflies, mixed-species flocks foraging up a mountainside, and squadrons of tanagers blowing into melastome trees provided us with some of our very best opportunities. Investing time looking for the right fruiting tree or the preferred feeding situation turned out to be our most useful strategy of all; these were the honey holes we attempted to locate in order to find the birds.

In the process, we learned that the insect eaters are far more likely to be specialists than the fruit eaters, and are more typically territorial as they defend their turf against competitors. We found many of the same birds in the same general area, day after day. Since insects are consistently harder to find than forest fruit, both parents are required to pitch in to keep a nest full of baby birds fully fed, and this has often encouraged monogamous pairings in some species.

The fruit-eating birds, on the other hand, have developed a different lifestyle, built around the luxury of having a relatively abundant food source available to them and lots and lots of time on their hands. After mating, this permits the female of many species to manage nest duties all by herself while rendering the male irrelevant to future family responsibilities.

In some species, these bachelor males congregate in display assemblies called "leks" and spend their days performing acrobatic and bizarre rituals, with repertoires often mystical in sweep, in order to convince the ever-so-choosy female that he is the one worth having. The female will eventually select the winner, and the two will proceed to mate. Afterward he will flutter back to his bachelor buddies to await another female, while she will pull herself together to fly off and tackle life as a single mother. A few members of the cotinga family, some hummingbirds, and a great many of the manakins operate in this fashion, and Vera and I delighted in ferreting out these display grounds for the dazzling male birds performing there.

Our exploration of the Neotropics, however, was not just about the creatures of the forest, but also the marvelously diverse and interesting people we met along the way. Many helped us immeasurably in locating some of the birds we were after, and they brightened our entire Neotropical experience. We learned from them, enjoyed their company, and some even became close friends. We also found it interesting to learn that many of the world's best Neotropical ornithologists are Americans who have for the last forty years been at the forefront of discovering, recording, photographing, documenting, and writing books about the birds of these remote regions. We spent some quality time with several of these experts, despite our own dilettante status, and were significantly influenced by their advice and insights.

There was the patrician Bob Ridgely, then representing the Academy of Natural Sciences in Philadelphia, and more recently affiliated with the American Birding Association. He and his collaborator, illustrator Guy Tudor from New York, are responsible for undertaking the definitive work on Neotropical birds, *The Birds of South America,* a four-volume tome of which the first two volumes have already been published. Ridgely also recently coauthored a new book with Quito resident Paul Greenfield, *The Birds of*

Ecuador, which was released in the summer of 2001. He is arguably one of the most respected Neotropical ornithologists in the world today and is even credited with discovering a new species of antpitta high up in the Andes of southern Ecuador as recently as 1998.

We also spent some time with Alvaro Ugalde, one of the principal visionaries in creating the splendid park system of Costa Rica that has become a working model for Neotropical ecotourism throughout the hemisphere. Toward the end of our journey, we worked with Raúl Arias, the enterprising Panamanian entrepreneur who built the Canopy Tower in the former Canal Zone as a focal point of ecotourism in his own bird-rich country.

There was Ted Parker, the most accomplished Neotropical ornithologist of them all and perhaps the greatest field biologist of the twentieth century until he was killed in an airplane crash in Ecuador in 1993. Parker's almost mythical genius for recognizing bird songs and call notes was so extraordinary that he had imprinted the songs and sounds of over 4,000 different tropical birds. It is part of his legend that once in some remote rainforest in South America, he identified by song a rare bird he had never seen or heard before simply because he knew by elimination what it had to be. He protected his ears and hearing much as concert pianists safeguard their hands, and his tragic death at the age of forty extinguished one of the great tropical resources of our time.

Following in Parker's footsteps, in addition to Ridgely, is the much respected Steve Hilty, the coauthor of *A Field Guide to the Birds of Colombia* and author of both *Birds of Tropical America* and the recently published *A Guide to the Birds of Venezuela.* There was the brother-sister team of John and Rose Ann Rowlett, founders of the highly regarded birding company Field Guides; Bret Whitney, one of the keenest birding talents and "ears" in the world; and Paul Coopsman, Kevin Zimmer, and Andy Whittaker, the renowned pros of Central and South American birding. We also corresponded with John O'Neill, the acclaimed ornithologist and wildlife artist from Louisiana State University, who had spent many years documenting the bird life of Peru. John is himself credited with the discovery of several new species of tropical birds, and the splendid book *A Parrot without a Name,* by Don Stap, chronicles one of those early adventures. A frequent partner of O'Neill's during those early years in Peru was John Fitzpatrick, formerly of Chicago's Field Museum and now director of the Cornell Laboratory of Ornithology. John himself co-discovered several species of birds new to science, including the Manu Antbird, and is additionally recognized as a world expert on tyrant flycatchers.

We were especially influenced by our close friend Victor Emanuel, founder and owner of V.E.N.T., one of the oldest and most successful ecotourism companies in the world. Victor's boyhood sense of wonder and his enthusiasm are contagious to all who meet him, and he is as responsible as anyone for exposing a whole new generation of birders to the Neotropics. Over the last twenty-five years V.E.N.T. has hosted trips around the world for more than 30,000 birders, and the destination of many of these tours has been the rainforests of Central and South America.

Through the years we would bump into many of Victor's guides in far-off tropical places, and they would help us however they could in trying to locate, or approach closely, or tape-call into view some particularly elusive species that we might have been pursuing. One such guide was David Wolf, who put us onto the Chestnut-crowned Antpitta in the Coastal Cordillera of Venezuela while his wife, Mimi, painted

its portrait for us several years after the original photograph was taken.

And there was also David Ascanio, the accomplished field ornithologist from Caracas who worked with us on some of the rare cotingas and located for us the majestic Harpy Eagle in the rainforests of the Río Grande Forest Reserve of Venezuela. Debra Hamilton and her extended family of researchers spent many hours with Vera and me in pursuit of both the Three-wattled Bellbird and the Bare-necked Umbrellabird in Monteverde, Costa Rica. Also in Costa Rica we visited the famous English naturalist and tropical photographer Michael Fogden at his summer retreat in Monteverde, and the redoubtable Alexander Skutch in the small patch of forest where he had lived and studied and written on the Neotropics and its wildlife for over sixty years.

In addition to these professionals, a whole separate cast of characters played an assortment of colorful cameo roles in our little adventure: "the Hummingbirders," the Randalls, "the Vertical Man," Bruno, "the Ice Cream Man," "the Germans," "the Harpy Man," and "Raymond the Maroon." And, of course, there was the unforgettable "Hatchet Tongue." You'll meet them all later.

But perhaps one of the most remarkable inspirations happened to be a woman who was the most accomplished birder of all—Phoebe Snetsinger. Of the 10,200 different bird species on this planet, Phoebe had managed to find and identify over 8,500 of them, exploring remote habitats in over one hundred different countries for twenty years to do so. Only one other birder has ever logged 8,000. Most believe her record is unlikely to be equaled, as future advantages accruing from increased access to rare birds in remote places will most probably be negated by the inevitable acceleration of species extinctions. And for Phoebe herself, it was no stroll in the garden. While battling cancer off and on over those exploration years, she fell off of a mountain in the Philippines, nearly drowned when her boat capsized off the coast of Irian Jaya in Indonesia, was gang-raped and left for dead in the highlands of Papua New Guinea, and was finally killed in the fall of 1999 in an automobile accident in Madagascar—hours after identifying yet again another rare bird to add to her list. She was sixty-eight.

Two months before her death, and the last time Vera and I heard from her, she wrote to compliment our book *Chasing Warblers* and the photograph of the Blackburnian Warbler on its cover. She said, "The first one I saw that magical spring over thirty years ago, and the impact of something so beautiful that I had never seen before, was strong and immediate—

and changed my life." Years earlier, Vera and I had ourselves experienced a spiritual reconnection with nature in much the same way during a "fallout" of Neotropical migrants on the Texas Gulf Coast. It was quite a moment, as birds of all colors dropped from the sky like holiday ornaments and began dancing at our feet as they feverishly tried to re-nourish. We could have reached out and touched them. It was magical. It was as if we had never before been dazzled by a sky full of stars until one crisp, clean night we were pulled by a strong premonition—to simply look up. And as we began our exploration of the Neotropical rainforests in search of the colorful birds living there, we knew that we were entering one of the planet's last sanctuaries of enchantment and mystery —and that inexhaustible opportunities for wonder were awaiting us.

Costa Rica—a Beginning

THAT IN 1987 we went to Costa Rica at all was itself a bit peculiar, as there was no destination south of Mexico that Vera and I had seriously considered before. Costa Rica wasn't even on the radar. Quite frankly, we weren't precisely sure where it was. If pressed, we would have likely characterized it as an unremarkable little country nestled somewhere between Mexico and Panama that was decidedly safer than Nicaragua, perhaps a bit better known than Belize. But that would have been about it.

We had no knowledge of tropical rainforests or pre-Columbian art or ruins to entice us south, and our growing interest in wildlife photography at the time had no direction—we wouldn't photograph our first warbler until later that spring. We were also in the process of making a return trip to Hawaii that February, but the thought of going back to Hawaii, as lovely as the islands can be, was leaving us a bit cold. It had begun to sound too predictable and structured to excite us that much—manicured beaches, horseback riding, tall fruit drinks, and the like.

So when our friend Andy Sansom casually suggested Costa Rica, we listened. Andy, then director of The Nature Conservancy of Texas and later the head of the Texas Parks and Wildlife Department, painted exotic images of parrots and monkeys and other colorful jungle creatures that sounded remarkably different from anything Vera and I had ever experienced. We took the bait, made some quick schedule adjustments, and in February 1987 simply took off—with just a map and a rough game plan. It was the beginning.

We arrived in the capital of San José midafternoon, picked up a rental car, and took off early the next morning heading west on a daytrip to the Carara Biological Reserve in the transitional forests of the Pacific lowlands. At the last minute, on the advice of Sansom, we had called up one of the most remarkable Costa Ricans of all to join us—Alvaro Ugalde, then director of the Costa Rican National Park Service and one of the principal architects of that country's marvelously preserved park system.

Others had briefly, and feebly, waved green flags for conservation in Costa Rica before, but they had wound up as just so much roadkill on the big agricultural interests' drive for arable turf. Then in the early 1970s, Ugalde, along with his mentor, Mario Boza, successfully spearheaded a conservation effort to set aside large tracts of forest for national parks. Their victory ultimately became the envy of all tropical governments and served as a strategic model for leveraging what was back then just some quixotic, economic concept: ecotourism. Although preserving biodiversity was their mission, sustainable revenue from ecotourism turned out to be their dividend. Boza was the strategist; Ugalde, the bulldog; and Karen Olsen Figueres—wife of José ("Don Pepe") Figueres, then president of Costa Rica—the catalyst and key ally as they fought to pass enabling legislation to put into place this massive conservation initiative.

And it worked, for today Costa Rica has set aside over 15 percent of its total territorial acreage in preserved and protected forests, while most of its neighbors have inadequately exploited what was once an equally remarkable opportunity. Costa Rica's splendid park system, its democratic form of government, and its high literacy rate have anchored the country as the "Switzerland" of the hemisphere and made it one of the truly remarkable countries in this part of the world. And we were running west to the bird-rich

Carara Biological Reserve (A) with one of the heroes who had helped make it happen.

When we picked up Alvaro that first morning, we were already briefed as to his reputation and the weight of his past accomplishments. But when we met him, he simply didn't look the part. He was a short, bald man in his mid-forties with a demeanor suggesting a mild-mannered history teacher, one clearly more suited to reflection than reform. But as the morning progressed, and as Alvaro began to outline his vision for conservation and his compelling moral commitment to it, Vera and I felt those flashes of intensity that indicated a man capable of being a formidable competitor or advocate or friend. And, of course, we would come to learn over time he could be all of these. Alvaro told us the history of a land once green that became ecologically wrecked when cut over for crops in a substantially impoverished soil—and of his eleventh-hour struggle along with his friends to save the rest of the best of his country. Driving along with him through the countryside that morning, we began to get a real feel for the implications of that victory.

Whereas this part of Costa Rica had once been a seamless green carpet of forest running all the way to the coast, it was now only a stained, yellow countryside of parched ravines and wounded hills, a pallet of fawns and golds with only odd mottecroppings of green. Although the clouds were plump and fleecy against a royal-blue sky, and there were glorious stand-alone Cortez trees, randomly dispersed along the way, with their springtime blossoms of bright yellow and soft rose, the destruction of the great forests had almost been fatal to the land's biodiversity.

Finally, we approached the Río Grande de Tarcoles, which separates the dry forest of the north

Turquoise-browed Motmot (1), Carara Biological Reserve, Costa Rica 1987

from the Pacific rainforest of the south, and Alvaro suggested we stop on the bridge to look for crocodiles, which were known to live on this river in impressive numbers. We counted thirty of them in all, either in the river or sunning themselves on the bank. They were big and fat, and several of them we estimated to run eighteen to twenty feet in length. It was our first wildlife experience in this new country and it was not a bad one, since there are not many places in this part of the world where one can observe so many of these large predators at any one time.

Thirty minutes later, while working the trail leading through Carara Reserve itself, we saw our first bird of the Neotropics, a Turquoise-browed Motmot (no. 1). Of course, we didn't know what it was at the time because we didn't know what anything was—all creatures were new and nameless. And Alvaro, quite frankly, wasn't much help since he preferred to stay focused on "big-picture" conservation issues and didn't intend to become distracted by the nitty-gritty of bird identification, similar to important humanitarians who make great gifts to mankind but don't like to be around people all that much. "A motmot of some sort" was the best he could come up with. But with a brilliant flash of turquoise, not so much on the bird's brow as on the racquet-shaped tips of its long tail feathers, the motmot flew up from the ground to a lateral branch not twelve feet high.

As the bird swung its tail slowly back and forth like a clock's pendulum, Vera and I fired twice each before it flew off. It was our first bird photograph of the Neotropics, and whether that would give the bird itself some significance it didn't necessarily deserve, the motmot would nonetheless come to symbolize—at least for Vera and me—what the romantic rainforest birds were all about. Over the ensuing

years we would photograph five different species of motmots, and we liked every one of them.

Ten minutes after the motmot photo was taken, we jumped one of the real specialties of this part of the world—the Scarlet Macaw. This brilliantly colored macaw is an exceptional bird—big and gorgeous, brassy and loud—but since we've seen so many of them so often in zoos and on TV nature shows, they somehow don't seem quite so special to us anymore. It's as if we've lived next door to them all our lives. The familiarity is misleading, however, because there aren't that many of the big birds remaining in Costa Rica anymore, although there used to be large numbers of them nesting here along the Pacific coast. Habitat destruction and victimization by the pet trade have been the principal culprits in the wholesale decimation of their numbers.

The pet trade specifically feasted on this great bird because of a culture throughout the Neotropics that prized the Scarlet Macaw as a status symbol, and a caged one thus became a much-coveted house pet for the locals as well as a lucrative export item for the international markets. This despite the fact that the big birds don't make particularly good companions—they are raucous and destructive and not very good talkers. But they are easy to get to and easy to harvest: one only has to find a tree in which they are nesting, chop it down, and take the babies. That's the way it's done. Their colorful feathers were also widely used for ornamentation, and feather-working tapestries once represented a religiously significant art form of the ancient cultures, with the Scarlet Macaw and Resplendent Quetzal being the providers of choice. In Costa Rica today one can find healthy populations of Scarlet Macaws only along the Osa Peninsula or here in Carara.

We saw six macaws in a single tall tree raising all

Scarlet Macaw (2), Carara Biological Reserve, Costa Rica, 1987

kinds of racket with their loud, hoarse squawks. Two of them, in particular, were erotically inflamed in a boisterous love fight of sorts, flapping and wrestling and tumbling through the air, then returning to a preening mode, side by side. These birds mate for life and can live to be up to fifty years old in the wild. It was an impressively colorful spectacle, with flashes of red, blue, and yellow intensified by the mid-morning sun. Afterward Vera and I would never think of these big, rare birds in the same cavalier way as we had before. Minutes later, one of the birds flew down just low enough for a decent shot, and the spectacular Scarlet Macaw (no. 2) became our second win of the day.

The last bird we photographed that first morning was as different from the first two as it could possibly be, the bizarre-looking Boat-billed Heron (no. 3), with a comically big mouth shaped like a flattened football. The photograph of this unique, frog-eating heron, sitting silently in the shadows of its roost, represented the ending to a big beginning for Vera and me on our first day in a Neotropical forest.

This was not, however, the last time we would be at Carara. Thirteen years later, while photographing bellbirds on the Pacific coast at La Ensenada Lodge, we dropped down for the morning to explore these woods once again. We couldn't tell that all that much had changed over the years—there were still the macaws and herons and motmots, but it was also clear that a special effort had been made to encourage the survival of the macaw by providing nest boxes high up in the trees around the compound to facilitate breeding.

About twenty minutes along the same trail we had taken years before, we heard a soft bark, and then we saw our first Baird's Trogon (no. 4). It was one of the prettiest trogons we would encounter,

but what made the moment memorable was simply this: there were eight males together, scattered low among the trees, and the birds were all just sitting, some softly calling. This was by no means a fruiting-tree situation—the birds weren't even feeding—and we had never seen more than three trogons together at any one time. We concluded this must be a mating-season gathering of bachelors hot on the scent of a female moving through the area. Vera and I watched them with fascination for ten minutes, photographing the closest bird at fifteen feet, then they were gone. It was quite extraordinary!

Several days after our visit with Alvaro, Vera and I headed for the famous Monteverde Cloud Forest (B), 65,000 acres of montane forest straddling the Tilaran Mountains about a four-hour drive from San José. It's two hours to the base of the mountain, and then a painful, rutted, two-hour climb the remaining eighteen miles to the top. The road then was mined with large boulders, as if to purposely discourage our intrusion, and we foolishly had not come prepared with four-wheel drive. It was like driving in an Arizona stream bed in August.

In a meadow at the base of the mountain, as we began our torturous climb to the top, we were surprised to see a gorgeous small bird of soft gray, with coral undersides and a strikingly long tail, sitting on a barbwire fence—a bird we actually recognized! It was a Scissor-tailed Flycatcher, so common to the fields and pasturelands back home in Texas. It was one of "our" birds, vacationing here in Costa Rica for the winter. We were surprised to see it, although we shouldn't have been. In fact, there's an old saying in Somervell County, Texas, that acknowledges, "The summer is over when the scissor-tails leave Glen Rose." Of course, when we were young, no one really understood what that meant, or where

Boat-billed Heron (3), Carara Biological Reserve, Costa Rica, 1987

the birds went, but today it's well recognized that as many as a third of our North American birds, 250 or so, spend their winters in Mexico, the Antilles, and Central and South America, returning only in the spring. The Scissor-tail Flycatcher is one of them.

This migration is massive and represents one of the marvels of nature. The Golden Plover of the north makes it all the way to the pampas of Argentina, the Golden-cheeked Warbler of the Texas Hill Country parachutes into Guatemala and Honduras, and the glorious Blackburnian Warbler—which we had admired so much in the boreal forests of Maine—can be found later cruising December cloud forests in northern Venezuela and Colombia. There would be Summer Tanagers moving into Belize

and Cinnamon Teal dropping into the marshes of southern Peru. These winged travelers by the billions —buntings, vireos, orioles, and hummingbirds— evacuate North America each fall and accompany the tanagers, warblers, flycatchers, and other insect eaters to the tropics for the winter. Our North American forests then fall silent until the following spring.

These travelers, oddly it seems to most of us, are considered to be actual citizens of the Neotropics since they spend most of their year living down there. Called "Neotropical migrants," they return to North America only in the spring —to nest—when there is an explosion of insect activity in the temperate zones and more daylight hours to feed baby birds. They fly by the millions most nights in March, April, and early May to get here, many

Baird's Trogon (4), Carara Biological Reserve, Costa Rica, 2000

launching from the Yucatan, to ride southerly winds over the Gulf of Mexico to Texas and Louisiana and Florida, where they will fan out and begin to make their way slowly north to their nesting grounds as spring unfolds, the trees start to bloom, and insect populations erupt. These migrants will then become—at least for a few months—"our" birds. And we will claim them fiercely.

After sighting our scissor-tail and then spending the rest of the morning inching our way up the denuded mountainside, in demoralizingly slow and painful degrees, we finally arrived at the isolated oasis of shrouded mists and low-hanging clouds that is Monteverde. In this rain-saturated atmosphere, the trees are heavily laden with mosses and ferns and bromeliads, and the pervading influence on this lush mountaintop is one of overriding dampness. At this elevation the humid air is always cooling, the fog always settling in, and this enchanted mountain always seems to be dripping from a wet wool blanket of green. A small group of Quakers came to settle here from Fairhope, Alabama, in the 1950s. They built the community of Santa Elena around their dairy farming operations and protected the tropical forests on top to conserve their water supply. Hence the preservation of the Monteverde Cloud Forest, one of the famous birding hot spots of the Neotropical world.

Vera and I found a dramatically different environment from the one we had experienced several days before at Carara; the first was dry and hot and low, this was wet and cool and high. And the birds were different, too, showcased by the famous Resplendent Quetzal—which we lusted to see—as well as bellbirds, manakins, and world-class hummingbirds. In late afternoon we checked into a Swiss-chalet affair called the Hotel Belmar, up from the cheese factory and down from the schoolhouse, and

the next morning we set off to run down some of the sparkling jewels of this famous sky preserve—the hummingbirds of Monteverde.

The New World is noted for its hummingbirds, with over 320 different species living all the way from Alaska to the bottom tip of Chile. They are the smallest warm-blooded creatures on the planet. They are also the gems of the avian world, as no other species of bird packs in more brilliance per ounce. They radiate colors of metallic magentas, sapphires, and rubies; they shimmer with their violets and purples and greens. They flash ornamental plumes and ear tufts; they flaunt streamers and beards. They can be small as a bee or large as a sparrow, and they advertise themselves extravagantly with names like "sabrewings" and "hillstars," "sun angels" and "velvet breasts."

With their remarkably controlled flight and high metabolic rate, hummingbirds are continuously in motion—always feeding, looking for food, or else aggressively defending their food source, usually favorite flowers with which they have evolved a co-dependence. A few that first morning even buzzed around Vera's head like large insects, undoubtedly attracted to her red lipstick, thinking it a flower blossom to which they held a particular fancy. They'll do that to red hats and red scarves, too. There were hummingbirds all over the place—pirouetting for tactical advantage, dive-bombing with attitude, vibrating with iridescence. The first three birds that Vera and I photographed at Monteverde were all hummingbirds—the Green-crowned Brilliant (no. 5), the Purple-throated Mountain-gem (no. 6), and the Violet Sabrewing (no. 7). Everyone loves hummingbirds, and Monteverde, we found, had some of the best.

But we had not come to Monteverde for just hummingbirds. We were here to engage the Re-

Green-crowned Brilliant (5), Monteverde Cloud Forest, Costa Rica, 1987

splendent Quetzal. This was the bird of myth, the "feathered serpent," the Toltec god—Quetzalcoatl. This quetzal is arguably the most glorious bird of the hemisphere and rivals even Papua New Guinea's birds of paradise as the grandest on the planet. The male quetzal is an iridescent, emerald-green member of the trogon family with a scarlet undercarriage and a three-foot-long rippling train of floating plumes that shimmer like streamers. The noted Costa Rican naturalist Alexander Skutch may have described it best: "The male is an extremely lovely bird; the most beautiful, all things considered, that I have ever seen. He owes his beauty to the intensity and arresting contrast of his coloration, the resplendent sheen and glitter of his plumage, the elegance of his ornamentation, the symmetry of his form, and the noble dignity of his carriage."

The quetzal takes its food in flight, plucking wild avocados in midair, just the kind of thing that Vera and I were hoping to observe. Although the Resplendent Quetzal happens to be the national bird of Guatemala—its currency is even named for it—the bird has become scarce in that country and is not easy to find there. From the time it was officially designated the "national bird," the quetzal automatically became a hot fashion item, and every household wanted one as a symbolic pet. They were substantially depleted in Guatemala within one generation.

Today two of the best-known places in the Neotropics to look for the quetzal are Costa Rica and western Panama, and one of the most predictable habitats in Costa Rica is the cloud forest in Monteverde. It's the star attraction of the country and serves as the poster child of the ecotourism business of Costa Rica. There are other great creatures in this country, to be sure, but the quetzal is the one that made it all happen. This bird started the whole ecotourism trend in this part of the world, and that's why Vera and I were on this mountain.

Walking down a dirt road late that first misty afternoon, in the last decent light of the day and with our binoculars partially clouded with condensation, we spotted what we thought might be the quetzal five hundred yards out across a large clearing in a small grove at forest's edge. There was a flurry of movement back in the trees, but we couldn't be sure. Then it got too dark to see. Not really knowing what else to do, we got up at four o'clock the next morning, retraced our steps in the dark,

crossed the meadow, and sat down under a stand of trees where we thought we had last seen the bird. And we waited. First light came and went, and then another hour passed. Nothing. Finally, Vera looked up in response to some small movement above, and there was a quetzal looking down at her. It had been there all along, fully camouflaged among the dense foliage, stone still, high up.

Then the birds became active all at once. There were five Resplendent Quetzals throughout the grove, two males and three females, and they all began to float among the trees. One male even performed what we would learn later was an in-flight

Purple-throated Mountain-gem (6), Monteverde Cloud Forest, Costa Rica, 1987

Violet Sabrewing (7), Monteverde Cloud Forest, Costa Rica, 1987

mating ritual by flying some one hundred feet up in the air, shimmering its streamerlike tail, then swooping back down in a graceful arc. Vera and I stood stunned as the morning light flashed on the green, red, and white of this graceful creature, spiraling downward back into the trees. It was a remarkable moment. Then the birds all flew away. We hadn't fired a shot. Although we predictably went back the next morning to the same spot to try again, they weren't there. And they didn't come, and it would be another thirteen years before we had any kind of a shot at another.

When we finally did return to Monteverde in the year 2000, the first thing we did was to organize ourselves to take another run at this famous bird. This time around things broke our way early on, and we located an active quetzal nest hole in an old, decaying tree not far off the trail that ran behind the reserve headquarters. We knew the nest was active because we could see the male's long, green tail feathers sticking out of the hole and shimmering in the breeze. At the end of the season these streamers can be beat up and frayed from the activity, and some lose their long feathers entirely, thereby rendering their appearance no more magnificent than an ordinary trogon, for which they are then sometimes mistaken. But that wasn't the case here; this male bird looked great.

Both the male and the female quetzal tend the nest, taking turns incubating the eggs and also feeding the babies once they hatch. Since they alternate nest duties, Vera and I were able to observe several baton passes between the two parents. Before the female would approach the nest, she would first call out to the male inside, which would then stick his head out of the hole, looking out at her between his two tail feathers. It should have been easy in such a controlled situation to get a decent picture of the bird, but it wasn't. The nest was sixty feet up in bad light, the birds moved in and out far more quickly and irritatingly than one would have imagined necessary, and the fog moved in both afternoons to kill whatever chance we might have had then. Our tactical plan was once again failing in execution, when during our last morning on the mountain the male flew to a nearby limb he occasionally used prior to his final flight to the nest site, and we were able to ambush him a couple of times there. The Resplendent Quetzal (no. 8) was now in the bag, but it had taken us a long time to land him. Of all the birds of the Neotropical forests, this "feathered serpent" is considered to be the most exotic of them all, and therefore represented a "must win" for my sidekick and me. We felt proud to finally have him.

Later that first evening in 1987 at the Hotel Belmar there was a slide presentation by one of the famous naturalists and wildlife photographers of the Neotropics—Michael Fogden, who with his wife Patricia had moved to Monteverde from England in 1978. They now spend six months a year on top of this mountain and combine their scien-

tific credentials (both have doctoral degrees in zoology) with their considerable photographic skills in publishing papers and books and giving presentations on this country they have come to care so much about. Michael's photographs of Neotropical birds are admired throughout the world, and his shots of the Sunbitterns, quetzals, bellbirds, and other cotingas are considered by many to be best of breed. They're that good. But the Fogdens' principal field of scientific interest, the subject that really turns them on, has to do with frogs and toads and snakes and such. They are crack herpetologists.

We didn't really know any of this when we bumped into Michael the next morning on a dirt path behind the reserve headquarters, and he enthusiastically invited us back to his house to "see his frogs." We thought he meant his photographs of frogs; he meant the real thing. So for the next half hour we became contentedly absorbed in playing with his three frogs and one Harlequin Snake out on the front lawn. Michael has such a keen ear for the night songs of these creatures that he can hear and recognize the various frog species singing high up in the trees. He then sends one of his local assistants scurrying to the top of the tree to deftly fetch them for his scientific collection. Michael asked us whether we had by chance run across the Golden Toad, an orange, "day-glow" rarity found only at Monteverde. We told him that we had looked for one but hadn't been successful. Nor would we be on that trip. Nor would anyone be much after that, since only a few of these toads were encountered in that year, only ten or so in 1988, one in 1989—and then they were all gone. Extinct.

Thirteen years later, when we were back in Monteverde, and the afternoon after our quetzal success, we went up to the Fogdens' house to say hello.

Resplendent Quetzal (8), Monteverde Cloud Forest, Costa Rica, 2000

Resplendent Quetzal, Monteverde Cloud Forest, Costa Rica, 2000

Patricia was out of the country working on a project, so the three of us sat on the porch, sipped cool drinks, and discussed the changes to their cloud forest since we had last met. Michael talked despondently of the dramatic climate change on the mountain over the years—how there were now twice as many dry days as there had been back then, and how several new creatures had begun to invade the cloud-forest zone to make this now drier environment their home. The immigration not only included ten new varieties of birds that were now competing with native residents for food and nesting sites, but also certain alien pathogens that could well have been responsible for the demise of the Golden Toad.

Of the frog species living at Monteverde when we had last seen Michael, 60 percent, he said, were now gone—and no one had seen a snake of any kind in five years. To a man who holds such a passion for these creatures, this crashing of their numbers had been devastating. His situation was not unlike that of a priest who has just watched his church burn to the ground, knowing in his heart that it needs to be rebuilt but knowing in his gut that it won't be. And the effect on Michael was apparent. Whereas his demeanor had once been cheerfully upbeat, we now found him subdued and visibly detached, seemingly absorbed in some desperate uncertainty as to how this whole global warming issue would play out. But he gamely concluded that he could see some renewed hope for Monteverde, as many of the dollars accruing from the dramatic increase in ecotourism here were now being plowed back into various conservation initiatives. He felt that this special place could well remain special for years to come.

After Monteverde, Vera and I flew over to Quepos on the Pacific coast to sample the Manuel Antonio National Park and its resident wildlife, but mainly to relax and enjoy the beautiful beaches there. We checked into a charming little hotel Mariposa, on the top of the hill overlooking the ocean, and for the next several days we ate well, slept late, and took leisurely swims in the Pacific. It reminded us of what Puerto Vallarta on the Mexican coast must have looked like forty years before—prior to the filming of *The Night of the Iguana*—with unspoiled beaches, tropical forests running to the sand, and an impressive scarcity of tourists. Except for us. We did see a bit of wildlife—a few more birds we couldn't name, some White-faced Monkeys, and one lonesome sloth.

Thus ended our introduction to the Neotropics. It had been a good experience, and Vera and I realized we were onto something big here—a whole new world now lay before us, a world of wild things and wonder, of new creatures to look for and new birds to photograph. But this first outing had admittedly been soft and slow-paced. We felt it was now time to step out a bit and try something more adventuresome.

La Selva/Corcovado

THE NEXT YEAR IN EARLY MARCH, upon the advice of Alvaro Ugalde, Vera and I returned to Costa Rica, this time to the tropical wet forests of the Caribbean lowlands and the La Selva Biological Station (C). La Selva is an important research site at the confluence of the Sarapiqui and Puerto Viejo Rivers, which is sponsored by the prestigious Organization of Tropical Studies, a consortium of U.S., Costa Rican, and Puerto Rican universities. The 4,000-acre preserved forest here is impressively rich in diversity, and the field station serves as a focal point for a wide range of research projects in tropical biology. Over twenty-five different research initiatives were underway, ranging from the feeding behavior of large vipers to the study of a rare orchid found only in the Caribbean lowlands to even an obscure field test to determine which specific minerals attract butterflies to the eye ducts of crocodiles.

We pulled into La Selva late one afternoon in a driving rain and were assigned a room commensurate with the status of our research credentials and the importance of our own project—which is to say, we were given the worst accommodations they had. This meant single-mattress bunk beds on the second floor of a deserted and distressed dormitory across the river, complemented by an open-air wash basin downstairs. We were the only ones there. This was the "Siberia" of La Selva, consigned to inconsequential drop-ins like Vera and me, but serving nevertheless as an interesting microcosm of biodiversity in its own right. Delightfully complicated moths appeared each morning in our sink as well as metallically fluorescent beetles with spots on their wings that glowed like "fire eyes." A little tribe of bats lived up the stairs under the roof overhang to our room, and a resident boa constrictor was an occasional visitor to the large washbasin downstairs across from the john.

That first evening it took us fifteen minutes to drag our old cloth duffel bags over the suspension bridge spanning the Puerto Viejo, down the muddy path, and up the stairs to our room. An aggressive mildew silently engaged our luggage and contents, and settled in with us for the length of our stay. The bags would mercifully be put to the torch a couple of weeks later. That night, along with the thirty accredited researchers also staying at La Selva, we had our first dinner of rice and beans. We would have that same food combination, with a little meat added now and then, for the next four days we were there. But Vera and I had no trouble adjusting to the menu, partly because we had grown up in an era and a part of the country known for the sophisticated fare of its field hands—where chicken-fried steak was the entree of choice, ketchup was put on everything that moved, and most of us were well into adulthood before we realized that macaroni-and-cheese wasn't a vegetable. And, of course, the only relevant food issues in a rainforest concern basic nourishment and basic health. If you need to "dine," you had better choose another hobby or another venue. No one puts chocolates on your pillow at night, nor do they offer a marmalade of Seville oranges for your perfect toast in the morning. You are not here for the quality of the food but rather for the magic of the wildlife. It's not complicated.

After dinner we struggled back to our room to unpack and attempt to get organized for the next day; when the generator shut down for the night, we carried on with flashlights. This punctuated yet another lesson of rainforest travel—everything runs on a gen-erator, generators shut down early at night, or fail altogether, and flashlights or candles rule after that.

The next morning early, from the second-floor railing of the dormitory, I noticed a variety of different birds flying into a fruiting melastome tree not forty feet from our room. Vera and I sprinted to retrieve our field guide and cameras to identify just what kind of birds they might be and perhaps even manage a photograph of some sort. We quickly determined one bird to be a Golden-hooded Tanager, but the other three species were all manakins—sprightly, small birds that are endemic to the forests of the Neotropics: the White-ruffed Manakin, the White-collared Manakin, and the Red-capped Manakin. These were the first manakins Vera and I had ever seen, although we would enjoy many experiences with these little acrobats and their complex mating displays over the years that followed. My sidekick, who has a well-documented capacity for astonishment, felt compelled to memorialize this little experience, and this otherwise unexceptional melastome became our "magical manakin tree." The only decent photograph we came away with, however, was a shot of the Red-capped Manakin (no. 9), clearly the most brilliant of the three and one of the prettiest of its entire family. It is a chunky little bird with a stunning scarlet-on-black costume augmented by another distinguishing feature—bright yellow thighs—which the male aggressively and proudly flashes to impress the ladies during mating rituals.

Later that same morning, from the suspension bridge spanning the Puerto Viejo and connecting "Siberia" to breakfast, we were startled by a racket overhead from a boisterous troop of Black Spider Monkeys moving noisily through the trees. At the same time we spotted a Three-toed Sloth moving ponderously out on a limb of a cecropia directly in the path of the advancing monkey troop. The sloth doesn't move so well; it's an unusually awkward creature, resembling some deformed monkey with a curious, vacuous smile. It also serves as a living pelt of sorts, with algae and many other little creatures actually using its body as their home.

As the monkey troop swung through, one young male peeled off and landed on the very limb of the cecropia occupied by the slow-moving sloth. Then, almost unbelievably, the monkey deliberately and spitefully pushed the sloth out of the tree! The sloth spiraled downward some sixty feet, crashing into a large clump of dense foliage below, and the monkey merrily danced away to rejoin his friends. It was a

daylight mugging of the most egregious sort, and we hoped the sloth had not come to an inglorious end. But the brush was too thick to see; we couldn't detect any movement from the spot where the sloth had landed, and we would never know. Then we crossed the bridge and went on to breakfast.

Throughout that first day, we explored much of the area, patrolled the paths winding through the preserve, and visited with the researchers about their assorted projects. In addition to photographing a pair of Gray-necked Wood-Rails (no. 10), sunning themselves at the forest's edge, and a brilliant Scarlet-rumped Tanager (no. 11) farther down a nearby slope,

Red-capped Manakin (9), La Selva Biological Station, Costa Rica, 1988

Gray-necked Wood-Rail (10), La Selva Biological Station, Costa Rica, 1988

we jumped a Snowy Cotinga as well as a Masked Tityra (no. 12). These latter two birds are stark white, contrasting so dramatically with the green backdrop of their surroundings that they appear to be especially vulnerable to forest falcons and other predator hawks looking for such an obvious target to take. But both birds have survived a long time in nature being white, and perhaps perching high up against a gray sky is not such bad camouflage for a white bird after all. Then again, while the predator field for young birds is extensive—from snakes and monkeys to other birds, like toucans and jays—it narrows quite significantly for adult birds to include only a few hawk, owl, and eagle species. Consequently, if a bird is able to survive infancy in a rainforest, its chances

for a relatively long life are surprisingly good, despite its color—be it white or yellow or scarlet red.

That night after dinner Vera and I decided to take on another challenge—looking for venomous snakes along the paths around the compound proper. La Selva is famous among herpetologists for supporting an impressive density of Fer-de-lances and Bushmasters, the two deadliest snakes of the Neotropics, and nighttime is the best time to find these serpents since they are on the move then, looking for food. The compound paths serve as productive game trails for these vipers as they attempt to ambush small mammals looking for food themselves. However, it's many times easier finding a rattlesnake in West Texas than one of these deadly

Scarlet-rumped Tanager (11), La Selva Biological Station, Costa Rica, 1988

snakes in the rainforest, and many a tropical birder and researcher has gone years without seeing one. Vera and I knew that if we ever wanted to find one ourselves (and we concluded with some understandable qualifications that we did), La Selva might well represent our best shot. We had actually done a little homework on the subject at the Dallas Zoo, which at the time supported one of the finest herpetology research operations in the country and was indeed the first zoo in the United States to breed Bushmasters in captivity. We had wanted to be able to properly recognize these deadly reptiles should we happen to stumble across one in the field.

Now looking for large, poisonous snakes at night in a dark rainforest might seem like a pretty dumb

thing to do, but it isn't as reckless as it first might appear, since we were working the paths very, very slowly, and the paths themselves were well worn and uncluttered. We could see where we were stepping. Also, it's far easier to detect a moving snake at night with a flashlight than a daytime snake off trail, coiled and camouflaged in the leaves. But no matter, all jungle creatures are a bit scarier at night; it was pitch black, and we had never attempted this kind of thing before. We were edgy.

We combed the area thoroughly for about forty-five minutes, with no action whatsoever, before we decided to call it a night and head back to the room—with Vera out in front. Then it happened, and it happened fast. As we cut back to the path

Masked Tityra (12), La Selva Biological Station, Costa Rica, 1988

that led to our dormitory, Vera shrieked and lurched backward, causing me to stumble backward myself, both of us nearly losing our balance. We recovered quickly, however, and moved forward to better see what had so startled her in the first place. It was a Fer-de-lance, and it was big, and it was slowly moving across the path not six feet from where she had been. We stood motionless, spellbound, as we watched this imposing viper move on off out of sight through the brush. The snake had a sinister beauty of a grayish fawn color with large, diamond

markings on its body, and we estimated its length to be over five feet. That's a nice size for a Fer-de-lance. We were both shaken but thrilled to have observed one of these deadly creatures up close and in the wild.

It is also part of the Fer-de-lance brief that, in addition to the toxicity of its venom, this snake is unusually aggressive and prone to go out of its way to attack. But this rap seems questionable, since La Selva hosts a large population of these vipers as well as numerous researchers regularly in the bush among them; yet at the time of our stay in 1988, there had been only two documented bites from a Fer-de-lance over the previous forty years. What "aggressive" most likely means in this context is that the snake will react vigorously if provoked and will not quickly flee if challenged. What it probably does not mean is that it would automatically go for you should you happen to walk near one. No matter, our nighttime experience with it was all we needed for the moment and we weren't anxious to

go out again at night looking for another one. So we didn't.

The next afternoon we drifted over to a small gladed area called the "arboretum." Here, over a period of years, more than 1,300 different varieties of trees had been planted for tropical study. We reasoned that this might be a good place to look for birds, and soon we spotted a Broad-billed Motmot intermittently feeding its mate out on a limb some thirty feet up. They repeated this feeding pattern

Broad-billed Motmot (13), La Selva Biological Station, Costa Rica, 1988

CHASING NEOTROPICAL BIRDS

several times until we inched close enough to one of them for a shot. We were successful with our second motmot photograph of the Neotropics—the handsome Broad-billed Motmot (no. 13).

Before we left the arboretum we were in for another treat as we spotted a bright red/blue poison dart frog about three-quarters of an inch long out on the mossy root of a large tree. The Choco Indians of Colombia used the poison from the sweat glands of these frogs for their blowguns, and the poison is so virulent that it can kill the equivalent of a hundred people should the toxin get into the bloodstream. This little frog, like some other of the poisonous creatures of the forest, flaunts its bright colors to signal would-be predators that it is neither a tasty nor a safe thing to eat. It has another curious habit: the female will carry her tadpoles on her back, one by one, high up into the trees where she will place each of them in a different rain-filled bromeliad for safety. Every other day or so she will climb the trees, remembering in just which bromeliads she has put her offspring so that she can then deposit unfertilized eggs to feed them.

By day four, Vera and I had covered La Selva fairly well and concluded that it was time to move on to our next stop at Corcovado on the Osa Peninsula near the Panamanian border. Curiously, I was beginning to sense an odd wariness from the same researchers who had been friendly enough to us only days before. It was the beard thing, I suppose. On my arrival at La Selva, I had decided to grow one, part of the jungle experience I had reasoned. But it had now reached that peculiar stage of development that had left me looking—at the most flattering—slightly contagious, and even, I was told later, a little bit dangerous. Those we bumped into during the day would continue to engage my sidekick warmly enough, it seemed, but now nodded

nervously in my direction, making only fractional eye contact as they did so. Conversations also tended to end abruptly whenever I approached. It was time to head for Corcovado.

The year before, when we were in San José with Alvaro Ugalde, we had met fellow Texan Larry Gilbert, who ran the Zoology Department at the University of Texas. Over that next year, Vera and I visited Larry and his wife, Christine, several times in Austin. One icy December morning we even toured Larry's "butterfly collection" atop the zoology building of the campus—a "collection" consisting of seven different greenhouses filled with more than 1,500 Neotropical butterflies that he had been breeding for several years. Larry also urged Vera and me to visit his "rustic" little research station in the Corcovado National Park (D) on the Osa Peninsula of Costa Rica. The park represented, he said, the last remaining tract of primary lowland rainforest on the Pacific coast. He promised we would be impressed by the diversity of its wildlife as well as the remoteness of the outpost.

The facility itself, known as the Sirena Station, was circumscribed by three rivers: the Río Claro, the Río Pavo, and the Río Sirena, whose mouth was known to be aggressively patrolled by Bull Sharks that drifted in from the sea. Due to the richness of the soil at Corcovado, the primary habitat there is also known for its cathedral-like forest, which supports twice as many species of trees as the United States and Canada combined.

To reach Corcovado, we chartered a prop plane to fly us down the Pacific coast to the Sirena Station, which was no more than a grassy swath cut through a section of dense forest running to the beach. The flight in was a series of pitches and yaws, the landing awkwardly rough. We deplaned, however, with a lively sense of purpose and crossed the

Rufous-tailed Jacamar (14), Corcovado National Park, Costa Rica, 1988

grassy airstrip to the research compound itself. There was an issue of significance, however, that— had we known of it at the time—would have substantially dampened our enthusiasm: the high grass on the airstrip at Sirena is renowned throughout the tropics for its impressive chigger population. We would have our first scratch the next night, the whole experience would last three weeks, and it would not be fun. We were covered up. A year later we learned of something far more serious—the very same prop plane that had just bounced us onto this grassy strip would overshoot the same runway in a rainstorm three months later, killing all aboard. The crash would be attributed to pilot error.

The research compound consisted of an open-air laboratory, a screened wooden dormitory (under repair and thus unavailable for use), a corrugated-roofed kitchen with two small tables, and a charming little outhouse next to an open-air shower. There was, of course, no electricity and no hot water. However, two of Larry's research students were on the premises, a young primatologist who was studying Squirrel Monkeys and would take Vera and me with her occasionally as she followed her monkey troops through the forest, and a botany expert specializing in canopy epiphytes.

We spent the first night in a small, one-person tent pitched on the floor of the open-air research area. It quickly turned dark, the generator expired, and Vera and I wrestled with our gear under flashlight as we shoe-horned ourselves into the one-person tent. The night was exhaustingly hot and humid, with no breeze at all, and our new home was fully stuffed by the two of us—and a family of small ants. It was the Night from Hell, and on more than one occasion, Vera, in an almost uncontrollable state of panic, unzipped the tent to flee into the night—before she despondently concluded that there was simply no place for her to go, since nighttime in the tropics is when the snakes are out hunting and big cats are king. My sidekick had a tough time of it, and so did I. But we sweated it out.

By the following afternoon I had discovered a much larger tent stowed up in the rafters, which I positioned on higher ground out in the open to catch what little breeze there happened to be, and we were actually not all that uncomfortable from then on out.

As dawn broke and the Mantled Howler Monkeys began their roar, we felt great relief, for we knew we could now escape the tent and go hunt down some coffee to kick-start a brand new day. The Costa Rican coffee being brewed in the cooking shed that first morning was filtered through an old sock directly into the pot by a perky little lady who sang cheerful messages to some higher spirit as she did so. It was the best coffee we had ever had anywhere and, as it turned out, would ever have after that.

When breakfast was over, we set off on a three-hour early-morning walk down a fairly open path to the river. We saw parrots and trogons, and at least twenty different Scarlet Macaws, which thrive at Corcovado in what is one of the largest populations of this grand bird left in Central America. We also heard the "bonking" of several Three-wattled Bellbirds deep in the forest, though we spotted not a one. Their bonk seemed less robust and complete than those we had heard at Monteverde, and Vera

and I assumed they were young males in the green grip of adolescence practicing their pitch. It would be many years later, however, before we learned that these bellbirds of Corcovado were a separate subset of sorts with a distinctly different dialect.

As we headed back from the river about ten o'clock, the sun had risen high with equatorial swiftness, and there was no shade at all out on the open path to shield us from the direct rays. It was an exhausting, desperately humid trek back to camp, and after a quick lunch of rice and beans, we lurched to the tent exhausted and eager for a siesta.

Later that afternoon, we jumped another handsome bird of the tropics, the Rufous-tailed Jacamar (no. 14), which in flycatcher fashion sallied forth from a small branch ten feet overhead to nail a morpho butterfly in mid-flight. He then used his long bill to negotiate away the troublesome wings before he tackled the sweet part of his prize. This was also the first jacamar Vera and I had ever seen, and although we would encounter several different species of jacamar in the years that followed, we would always like this one the best.

But Corcovado was not just about the birds; it hosted an important variety of mammals. Early the next morning a troop of about ten Mantled Howler Monkeys came roaring through the camp at dawn; after lunch a group of up to sixty Red-backed Squirrel Monkeys did the same thing; and then in the late afternoon we encountered a marauding band of Spider Monkeys that threw sticks and orchids at us from the tree tops. There were monkeys of one kind or another all over the place, but there were also other grander mammals like the White-lipped Peccary, Baird's Tapir, and Jaguar, which are found at Corcovado in impressive numbers.

We heard the tapir thrashing outside our tent the second night we were there, heard the tell-tale "cough-cough" of the Jaguar a couple nights after that, and found its tracks with some regularity along the banks of the Río Claro nearby. And since the forest here collides with the ocean on the Osa, the water yields an extra form of protein in the form of sea turtles, which the Jaguar captures on the beach at night to supplement its normal diet of peccary and tapir. This area, we were told, is able to support one of the greatest densities of the big cat in all the Neotropics.

Larry Gilbert, who has been coming to Corcovado for thirty years, has never seen a Jaguar here, although his graduate students see them with great regularity and tease him relentlessly over his inadequacy. The locals gave up raising horses at Corcovado a few months before we arrived because

El Tigre kept dragging off the colts not fifty feet from where we had pitched our tent. The year before, one of Larry's graduate students observed a Jaguar wading and playing mid-stream in the shallows of the Río Claro and, for reasons absurdly naïve, tried to shoo him away as if he were some annoying and troublesome tabby cat. I suppose some Jaguars don't shoo well, and this happened to be one of them. In a flash the big cat charged him full bore across the stream and screeched to a halt several feet from where the student stood rooted to the ground. The cat looked him up and down, then slowly walked away. It was quite a moment in the young man's life as he limped back to camp, badly shaken, with wounded pride and wetted pants, to sputter out a story that would quickly become an anecdotal part of Corcovado lore.

Orange-collared Manakin (15), Corcovado National Park, Costa Rica, 1988

As for the photography, we had some wins and we had some losses. We ran down many different species of birds at Corcovado, but our biggest missed opportunity came when I returned alone one afternoon to the creek behind the research station where I had photographed the jacamar on that first day. After waiting with no luck for the jacamar to return, I was about to leave when I saw one of the grandest of all of the Corcovado birds, a male Great Curassow, moving right in front of me not thirty feet away. It was a big black bird similar to a female turkey in size and shape, with a black, curly crest and a bright, yellow-knobbed beak. Curassows are rare, especially in areas where there are people around, since roasted curassow is a delicacy. Consequently, this was an extremely unusual bird to be able to observe up this close. But it was a black bird on a black stream bank deprived of all daylight, and my flash at the time just didn't have the horsepower to get there. The photograph was developed pitch black with a faint yellow spot in the center. A great opportunity missed.

On the other hand, Vera and I did have some luck with a special chickadee-size bird of the Pacific lowlands here, the Orange-collared Manakin (no. 15), performing at its lek along a trail about two hundred yards from camp. These manakins are small puffs of feathers, with minimal tails, wearing what appears to be little baseball caps. We heard them first, as you most always do, because their "firecracker" reports are sharp and distinct and are made by the mechanical snaps of feather shafts. It sounds like the snapping of one's fingers, except much sharper and louder. There were about seven males on this lek ricocheting from one sapling to another over a clearing on the forest floor. They dazzled us with their energy as they jumped back and forth in a frenzy of motion from twig to branch. Then they would all be quiet for a while, until a female would suddenly reappear and each male would once again go crazy in order to impress her so that she would fly off with him to mate. They would quiver and growl, chirr and whirr like some giant grasshoppers in order to catch her attention. These little acrobats had accumulated a lot of practice with their courtship ritual, and since these birds can live to be up to fifteen years old, they had most likely been using this particular display site for a long time.

Vera and I moved off the path near the lek area and simply sat down quietly to wait. Once the birds became accustomed to our unthreatening behavior, they resumed their performance, permitting us to take away some shots with which we were pleased. Vera's photograph of the Orange-collared Manakin, in particular, its head cocked back alertly, and with attitude, captured the unique personality of the species, and this photograph progressed with us all the way to book form. Manakins-on-lek are one of the most irresistible wildlife treats of the Neotropics, astonishing all those who witness them, and represent an almost unmatched opportunity to get close-up photographs of a special rainforest bird. It simply doesn't get any better than a manakin lek for what we wanted to do, and we were always on the lookout for these multiple-male display arenas wherever we went.

Corcovado was to be our last stop in Costa Rica. It had been a rewarding experience with some physical challenges, to be sure, but we came away impressed by the remoteness and wildness of the Osa Peninsula, and thankful that it has been preserved in its natural and pristine state. We would, however, not return to Costa Rica for several years, as we had other countries and forests to explore. South America was next on our list.

Hatchet Tongue

ALTHOUGH VERA AND I were eager to probe the rainforests of South America, we hadn't a clue about where to begin, since we didn't know anybody who had ever been in one before. Said another way, and as unlikely as it may seem today, there was no one in Dallas, Texas, in 1989 to whom we could turn for guidance on anything remotely related to the tropical forests of this continent. So one day we simply picked up the phone and called Venezuelan Audubon in Caracas. We were put through to its then director, a seasoned veteran of Venezuelan birding named Mary Lou Goodwin, who had coincidentally written a small book titled *Birding Venezuela* several years before. We were elated to have uncovered such a resource and felt certain she could put us on the right track.

We told Mary Lou of our limited Costa Rican adventures with hummingbirds, motmots, manakins and such, and explained that we wanted to explore new tropical terrain for similar creatures to photograph. She couldn't have been nicer and said she knew of a wonderful place down in the southern part of the country near the small community of El Pauji on the Brazilian border. Mary Lou said that it was the best place in Venezuela for the birds we were after, and a romantically remote setting from which to operate. She also suggested that we join her in a couple of months to explore this habitat and stay with her and her friends at their rustic, three-cabana camp called Shailili-ko, where she was going to tape-record the numerous antbirds in the area. This sounded too good to be true—exploring the rainforest with a birding professional who had even written a book on the subject.

And, as it turned out, it was. But more on that later.

Before Shailili-ko and our adventures with Mary Lou, the sidekick and I had planned a four-day visit to a special mountaintop oasis on the island of Trinidad some seven miles off the Venezuelan coast. We had recently heard about Trinidad (E) and the famous Asa Wright Nature Centre there, but when we arrived at the Piarco Airport in Port-of-Spain in February 1989, we thought we had backed into some ugly mistake. Not only had Vera's luggage been mysteriously diverted in Miami to the Dominican Republic, but the atmosphere we now encountered was ripe with the associated rhythms of a Caribbean beach culture rather than the forested nature sanctuary we had been expecting. But we quickly negotiated transportation, gave Asa Wright as our destination, and climbed the narrow switchbacks up the mountain for an hour to the preserve itself.

A former coffee and cocoa plantation, the twenty-two acres at Asa Wright are high center to a lush tract of preserved rainforest that dominates the high elevations of the island. Vera and I found a dazzling floral spectacle of giant elephant ears and bamboo stalks fifty feet high throughout a landscape smothered with sandbox trees and heliconias, the likes of which we had never seen before. In an environment that receives over ninety inches of rain a year, we were told that over four hundred different species of birds have been listed here as well as nearly six hundred types of butterflies. And commanding the top of the Arima Valley was the Asa Wright Centre itself, now owned by a government trust but once managed by the prestigious New York Zoological Society.

The lodge is an old plantation house surrounded by papaya and banana trees that looks manicured enough today, but when the grounds were originally cleared years ago, over fifty Bushmasters were eliminated in the process. The screened-in veranda, where the hallowed custom at Asa Wright is afternoon tea,

Purple Honeycreeper (16), Trinidad: Asa Wright Nature Centre, 1989

Barred Antshrike (17), Trinidad: Asa Wright Nature Centre, 1989

represents what might well be the most civilized setting in the tropical world for observing so many different species of rainforest birds—without ever leaning that far forward from your rocking chair. This is because Trinidad is a fertile island so near the Venezuelan coast that many of the bird families of that country are represented here.

From the elevated veranda itself, and on the grounds immediately around the lodge, Vera and I saw many interesting new birds and even managed photographs of the stunning Purple Honeycreeper (no. 16) and the noisily curious Barred Antshrike (no. 17). There was also the delightful Tufted Coquette

(no. 18), a miniature hummingbird with its colorful cheek plumes flying rakishly to the side, theatrically punctuating its unique beauty. Three terrific birds before lunch! It was a superb start. That same afternoon we observed a colony of Crested Oropendolas maneuvering artfully around their pendulous nests not thirty yards away, along with a pair of Blue-crowned Motmots dancing near the fruit trays out front. Vera and I were energized by so many colorful birds all around us, many of which we were actually able to photograph.

The next day, and for three days after that, we were guided by a Trinidad veteran of Asa Wright, Jogie

Tufted Coquette (18), Trinidad: Asa Wright Nature Centre, 1989

Ramlal. He and his East Indian family members had served as official guides of the center over the years and had acquired an uncanny feel for the wildlife of the area. Our first stop with Jogie was Dunston Cave, not that far from the lodge itself, to look for one of the most unusual birds of the tropics —the Oilbird. This mysterious bird nests in a few known cave colonies in South America, with this particular one in Trinidad being one of the most famous and accessible. They are called Oilbirds because the babies are stuffed with fatty fruit for so long by the parents that they grow to be

plump butterballs; throughout history they were prized for food and cooked down for oil by the locals who found them. With our flashlight we were able to see a few of the birds up on ledges deep in the cave, but a photograph in this pitch-black environment was out of the question.

Later that evening under a full moon that enchanted the valley in a silvery glow, we walked down from the center along a road overrun by white flowers. They had opened for the night to receive the bats and moths that pollinate them and at the same time were putting forth a perfumed fragrance that was both stimulating and delicately sentimental—like the overpowering sweetness of summertime honeysuckle on warm Texas nights. The air was clear and unpolluted, and the moonshine so bright that it literally hurt our eyes to look skyward, as if we were somehow closer to the moon here than any other place we could possibly be. We had never been moon-blinded like that before, nor have we been since. Vera and I hardly recognized the clear, clean air for what it was since our daytime skies back home were always seen through the soft haze of a first-world economy; the glow of suburban TVs had long since snuffed out the magic of fireflies, and our downtown city lights reach up nightly to flick off the switch to the stars. The ex-

perience punctuated a much-overlooked fact of third-world Neotropics—that despite its other unenviable forms of pollution, the nights here can be crystal clear, the sunny-day skies a cerulean blue.

Halfway down the stretch was a large fruiting tree where Jogie had suggested we might be able to photograph the Oilbirds during their night feeding activities. We saw flashes of movement in and out of the tree, to be sure, but we couldn't seem to spot any of the birds feeding in the branches. And with good reason. These amazingly strong birds, with their three-foot wingspans, take their food on the fly, simply plucking off the fruit as they swoop in and out. The Oilbird, we would come to learn later, is the only nocturnal fruit-eating bird in the world.

Green Honeycreeper (19), Trinidad: Asa Wright Nature Centre, 1989

Collared Trogon (20), Trinidad: Asa Wright Nature Centre, 1989

Scarlet Ibis (21), Trinidad: Caroni Swamp, 1989

Our last couple of days on Trinidad we spent with Jogie outside of the preserve proper working the Blanchisseuse Road, where we encountered jacamars and euphonias, along with a Green Honeycreeper (no. 19) and a Collared Trogon (no. 20), of which we came away with nice shots. Then, fifteen minutes later, Jogie put us right on the edge of an especially active lek of about seven or eight White-bearded Manakins. These fluffy, chickadee-size performers, impeccably clad in black skullcaps, bounced from sapling to sapling, with firecracker-like snaps, and would occasionally protrude their throat feathers out front like a "beard," for which they are known and named.

On the last afternoon of our stay, we visited the fa-mous Caroni Swamp, a complex system of mangroves and mud bars and shallows, to witness one of the most staggering wildlife spectacles of this part of the world: the late-evening roosting of the Scarlet Ibises (no. 21) as they spiral into the mangroves here by the hundreds. At one time there used to be thousands of these birds roosting each night, but today the event, while still stunning, apparently pales in comparison with what it had once been. At least that's what the old-timers say.

The next morning we flew to Caracas to hook up with Mary Lou Goodwin for what turned out to be a colorful and memorable experience of a completely different sort. It was easy to spot Mary Lou, as she was the only person in the Caracas airport who looked even remotely like a birder—with her wide-brimmed hat, binoculars slung around her neck, and a T-shirt that screamed, "Venezuelan Audubon." She was a short, late-fifties brunette of high energy who immediately began shepherding us through baggage claim and customs in sharp, abbreviated sentences intended, it seemed, to establish early on her credentials for decisiveness and a sense of urgency. We would come to learn that she was not only an enthusiastic birder but also a feverish environmentalist, an eco-warrior so combative in style—with an arsenal of all sticks and no carrots—that she was known in both government and conservation circles as "Lengua de Hacha," or "Hatchet Tongue." And it was a label that she didn't mind at all. She had reached such an intense level of personal commitment to save the environment that she could no longer respect, or even tactfully accommodate, those who were not as fully pregnant with the cause as she. And while others might try education and persuasion and compromise to advance their environmental agendas, it was always Mary Lou who was the first to lead the charge to stop a dam, or save a special patch of forest, or publicly rail against a government logging program that she felt to be harmful. Never one to be discouraged by the prospect of a glorious but doomed crusade, she had, over the years, become all clinched teeth and sharp elbows—but that's the way she liked it. She was "Hatchet Tongue."

The three of us flew together that same afternoon to Ciudad Bolívar on the Orinoco River, where we spent the night, and then the next morning early flew again for two hours to Santa Elena de Uairen on the Brazilian border. Before setting down at Santa Elena, however, we made one stop at the modest airstrip at Icabaru. There the pilots deplaned for an unexplained thirty minutes while additional passengers began to

appear mysteriously out of the woods to pile onto the aircraft. After casually strapping their luggage into the forward hold, they proceeded to fill the seats and aisles until there was standing room only. When the plane took off for Santa Elena, it was the airborne equivalent of some flying subway. That it got off the ground at all was quite remarkable.

At Santa Elena, as Mary Lou had originally written, we were to be met by the Shaili-ko staff for a "scenic two-hour drive through thick Amazonian jungle to the lodge," which Mary Lou had recommended as the best place she knew in Venezuela for rainforest birds such as trogons, motmots, antbirds, and manakins. We had planned to stay five days. We were met by a young Venezuelan from Shaili-ko named David, who seemed to be more comfortable in the local coffeehouses than slogging down dark forest trails.

Our drive to the lodge wasn't two hours long, as advertised, but nearly four. More unsettling, however, was the fact that there was no "Amazonian jungle" along the way at all; there weren't even any trees. It might as well have been Iowa. For all along that boulder-rutted road, the full length of our drive that day, and as far as the eye could see, was a vast rolling terrain of yellow-stained grasses and scattered, lonely hills. Mary Lou said that the land had changed a lot since she had last been there and admitted that it had been some time.

We dragged into camp near the small community of El Pauji (F) about dusk, met both proprietors with the softly upscale names of Philippe and Archimedes, stowed our gear in one of the treehouse cabanas, and set out to explore the area before it got dark. The camp was anchored in a scruffy clearing surrounded by a small knot of trees where the Gran Sabana had petered out and a tropical forest—which had long since been cleared—had once stood. We were the only guests at the camp, and we would soon come to understand why: Shailili-ko would be closed within a year due to a crippling lack of interest. We crossed a dry creek bed and climbed up to a grassy field where we spotted a few unremarkable seed-eating birds and also observed what was a beehive operation of impressive commercial scope. There were bees all over the place.

When we returned to camp, clearly dispirited by our situation's escalating lack of promise, we learned that we were fortunate not to have been stung by a large commercial colony of Africanized bees, which were extremely aggressive and attacked with little provocation. We soldiered on.

Mary Lou, Vera, and I then had dinner and went to bed. We were hoping the next day would be a bright and altogether different experience. But it wasn't. We awoke the next morning to a heavy rain, and after the showers had ended, we set off on our first hike to look for birds to photograph. But then again there was no forest in which to find them, and we simply spent two hours walking down a lonely dirt road through the cleared countryside. Then we turned around and walked two hours back. The sun was high by then, it was blisteringly hot and humid, and we hadn't fired a shot. We hadn't even seen a bird. Mary Lou apologized for the lack of action.

Before lunch, however, we had an unusual visitor to camp—a 300-pound male tapir, the awkward, long-snouted rainforest equivalent of a hippopota-

Yellow-tufted Woodpecker (22), near El Pauji, Venezuela, 1989

mus. The tapir was a frequent guest to the campsite and was more or less a celebrity throughout the area from the time poachers had killed his mother several years before. He would come and go at will, and sometimes many days would pass before he was seen again. Why he hadn't become an integral part of some tapir stew long before now was a mystery to us all, as these animals are known to be pretty good to eat. On his periodic visits to the camp, however, the tapir took a certain shine to the sidekick and would actually go out of his way to approach and even nuzzle her a bit.

Later that same afternoon, as Vera and I were hiking through a stunted sand forest not far from camp—looking once again for birds that weren't to be found—we heard a thrashing noise of sorts, only to look up and see our tapir bearing down on us at full speed. He blew past Vera and, as ridiculous as it seems in retrospect, tried to run over me. I dodged the lumbering beast by stepping quickly aside, and he then thundered off into the brush. We didn't know what to make of this bizarre behavior, so we simply continued on down the path. But no more than ten minutes later, here he came again. Once more I sidestepped him, and once more he lumbered off into brush, obviously intent on setting up yet another ambush a bit farther down the trail. When he came the last time, I struck him hard on the flanks with my monopod as he rumbled by. He gave a short grunt and was through for the day. Another up-close-and-personal experience in the Neotropics—charged by a jealous tapir. But we never saw him again.

Still later, just at dusk, we had a brief flurry of bird activity in the camp compound itself. We saw an exotic Paradise Tanager high up, arguably the most multicolored of its species, and were even able to get photographs of two other birds that were working

the camp area at the same time: a Yellow-tufted Woodpecker (no. 22) and a Black-headed Parrot (no. 23). But that was it—four days in Venezuela and two photographs. We were reaching a turning point of some kind, and after a short, sterile walk the next morning, it came.

It all began with "the case of the missing sunglasses." Vera had set them down someplace around camp not thirty minutes before, and now they were gone. This was a greater loss than it first might appear because in the tropics, with the intense sun, sunglasses are a necessity, and good ones are almost impossible to replace in the field. These were good ones—designer items, as I recall. So all six of us looked up and down, high and low, for over an hour to find them but without any success. Just what had happened to the glasses became a source of spirited conjecture, and several suggested—with a straight face—that our tapir probably had slipped into camp when no one was looking and eaten them. With the prospects of replacing them slim at best, and otherwise dispirited by our experiences before this time, Vera and I decided it was time to cut our losses, so we had a heart-to-heart with Mary Lou about the urgency of devising an alternate plan. We needed to make a change. And to her credit, she responded impressively and produced from the small Bohemian settlement down the road at El Pauji a beekeeper named Hugo, his serviceable Toyota Land Cruiser, and a reasonably coherent strategy to explore the fertile Río Grande Forest Reserve (G), which was a day's drive to the north. And so it was that we bade farewell to Shailili-ko and headed out toward the Gran Sabana with our compass set for the Río Grande— the unlikely foursome of sidekick and me, "Hugo the Beekeeper," and "Hatchet Tongue."

We made Santa Elena by nightfall and took off the

Black-headed Parrot (23), near El Pauji, Venezuela, 1989

Orange-bellied Manakin (24), Río Grande Reserve, Venezuela, 1989

next morning to cross the marvelous Gran Sabana. We were greatly impressed with the rolling green plains, dotted by Moriche Palm groves, and the sheer-sided, table-topped mesas of sandstone called "tepuis," which explode from the Sabana floor to heights up to 10,000 feet, shrouded in clouds and mists, and are stunningly ribboned with cascading waterfalls. This region is considered by many to be the most beautiful in all of Venezuela and was the reference point for Sir Arthur Conan Doyle's science fiction dinosaur novel, *Lost World,* and H. H. Hudson's surreal fairy tale, *Green Mansions.* There were no signs of civilization for hundreds of miles around. This land is only sparsely occupied by small, scattered populations of Pemon Indians, whose young males periodically burn the savannas—partly perhaps to keep back the forest.

We stopped at midday to look for a Scarlet-horned Manakin in a particular wooded ravine not far off the road, and then realized, for reasons that remain unclear to this day, that we had taken off that morning on what was to be a fourteen-hour drive without any food or water, all the while knowing there would not be even one tiny refreshment stand or gas station anywhere along the way. It became hot, and we were thirsty. It was then that we seemed to enter some sort of twilight zone as Mary Lou, with her signature decisiveness, suggested that we slake our thirst by drinking from the small stream that trickled neatly nearby. At this suggestion, the sidekick let Mary Lou know, with a certain longshoreman's clarity, that she was fed up with what had clearly become an "endurance test," and one she had personally not signed on to take. Voices were raised, opinions were shared—all of which, in retrospect, didn't reflect particularly well on anyone involved.

Mary Lou, however, stoically drank her water from the stream while Vera, the beekeeper, and I toughed it out for an additional three hours until we limped into a truck stop in the mining town of Las Claritas, where we bought bottled water and some cooked sausage to save the day. However, in one of the lingering ironies of our little adventure, we would come to find out some ten years later that the stream water that Mary Lou had drunk was in fact safe and clean—and most likely purer than even the bottled product we consumed so eagerly in hygienically challenged Las Claritas.

And so it went. We made Upata by nightfall and for the next three days explored the Río Grande Forest Reserve, set amid the low Serranía de Imataca hills, a western extension of the great Guianan rainforests. Despite its designation as a "reserve," the area was hardly pristine since it had been heavily harvested under timber concessions approved by the government itself, and logging roads sliced it vigorously throughout much of its range. We nevertheless managed to see quite a few good birds, in addition to a splendid Jaguarundi that darted across the road early one morning as we entered the reserve proper. We even bagged a nice photograph of a handsome Orange-bellied Manakin (no. 24) feeding in a melastome tree on the last day we were in the area. When it was finally over, Vera and I concluded that our first tip to Venezuela had been an unusual but interesting experience, as we had seen some diverse and even beautiful areas of the country in a most unconventional way.

As for Mary Lou, Vera and I saw her only once after that, some thirteen years later as we were arriving in Las Claritas to run down the Crimson Topaz, rumored to be in the area. Her car had broken down and she was saying good-bye to friends prior to being towed five hours north to Puerto Ordaz for repairs. We spoke to her briefly in passing, but it was clear that since we had seen her last, she had softened and slowed. She barely recognized us. Mary Lou was then about seventy, and we were told she was soon to retire and leave the country. But she had clearly paid her dues to Venezuela, and even though some might still have referred to her as "Hatchet Tongue," her friends and supporters here knew her affectionately as "La Madre Verde"—"Green Mother"—in warm acknowledgment of her love for their country and the good fight she had waged for so many years to help preserve some of the best of it.

Singing "Pittas"

ALTHOUGH OUR MAIDEN ATTEMPT the year before to explore mainland Venezuela had been a confused and poorly managed affair that had taken the better part of a week, covered hundreds of miles, and yielded acceptable photographs of but three birds, the sidekick and I decided to give it another shot—but this time with some semblance of focus and structure. We had recently made a new friend in Victor Emanuel of Austin, Texas, and had signed up for a two-part trip in January 1990 with his renowned ecotourism company, Victor Emanuel Nature Tours (V.E.N.T.). The first was to visit Hato Piñero, a cattle ranch of seasonal marshes and savanna woodlands in the high *llanos,* known for its impressive numbers of waterbirds; the second, to explore a famous cloud forest on the Coastal Cordillera of northern Venezuela, the Henri Pittier National Park, distinguished by its colorful variety of mixed-species flocks.

Vera and I had never traveled with a group before, and we were understandably concerned that we would be too restricted in our movements to permit any kind of acceptable photography. But Victor reassured us that we would have plenty of superb opportunities for photographs and that this particular trip, encompassing two completely unique habitats of Venezuela, was one of his absolute best for that purpose. There were to be twelve of us in all—including a lawyer, a college professor, a ranch foreman, a mortgage banker, and a neurosurgeon—and from geographic areas as diverse as New York to Minnesota, Michigan to Maine. Plus two other Texans. As it turned out, they were an interesting and compatible group to run with, and we enjoyed them thoroughly. They didn't cramp our style, and I don't think we cramped theirs.

Sunbittern (25), Hato Piñero, Venezuela, 1990

Our leader for the trip was a cheerfully intense and experienced naturalist from Nacogdoches, Texas, acknowledged by many to be one of the best birding guides in the business, and one who had been associated with Victor from the very beginning. His name was David Wolf, and we would come to know him through the years that followed as both a great guide and good friend. Vera and I would be with him a year later on the Río Napo in Ecuador; we would stalk Worm-eating Warblers with his wife, Mimi, in East Texas three years after that; and in 1996, once again with his help, we would locate and photograph the elusive Louisiana Waterthrush on its linear territory along the Angelina River not far from his home.

We all met in Caracas and then proceeded the next morning to a 200,000-acre cattle ranch called Hato Piñero (H) in the llanos of west-central Venezuela

near the little town of El Baúl. This important region of Venezuela represents a grassy savanna-floodplain of both the Orinoco and Caroni Rivers, similar in many respects to the Florida Everglades. In the rainy season it's flooded; during the dry season—which is when we were there—it's a land of island woodlots and rolling pastures dotted with ponds stuffed with long-legged waders like ibises and storks, herons and egrets, which have become magnetized to the few remaining, shrinking pools of water.

Hato Piñero itself is a working ranch that has been managed by the Branger family for over a half a century, and since hunting has been prohibited over the years they have owned it, the wildlife is understandably tame. Our group slept in the bunkhouses, and each morning we took our coffee down to the corrals to watch the *llanero* cowboys saddle up their horses for the day. At night we would often hear the same men settle down after dinner with their smokes and their music, the latter primarily from the *cuatro,* a small, four-string guitar.

During the day we explored the ranch in flatbed trucks with seats and wood railings to best view the birdlife, and encountered seven different species of ibises and five different kinds of kingfisher as well as tiger-herons and rails, screamers, and crakes. On several of the mornings, we motored softly down a small, winding stream, replete with wildlife, that was narrow enough in some sections to give us close shots of some of the important birds working the shoreline. We were able to capture a displaying Sunbittern (no. 25) flashing his colorful wings on a rock near the banks, and though the shot was a good one, we were nevertheless reminded of the one Michael Fogden had taken many years earlier—on its nest, with wings fully flared. It still represents the best photograph of the bird we've ever seen.

Another great sighting that day was the rare and illusive Agami Heron, arguably the most beautiful of the New World herons. But it's a hard bird to see and photograph because it prefers to skulk and then "freeze" in the deep shadows on the banks under foliage that hangs out over the water. We were lucky to get a glimpse of this one out in the open. Also adding to our take on this stream was a handsome Snail Kite (no. 26), which we found to be fairly common along this stretch of inland water.

But there was much more at Hato Piñero than just the waterbirds. We saw Scarlet Macaws and Yellow-knobbed Curassows and Red-capped Cardinals, and even one Aplomado Falcon patrolling an open pasture behind the compound. We were also able to sneak improbably close to, and photograph, the handsome Crested Caracara (no. 27) sitting on a

fence post behind the bunkhouse as well as the Red-breasted Blackbird (no. 28) perched on a strand of barbwire not far away, the latter looking like some equivalent of a black meadowlark with a breast painted an orangy-red instead of yellow.

In addition to the birds, we were impressed with the variety of other wildlife at Hato Piñero, beginning the first afternoon we arrived. About dusk we were patrolling the banks of a large pond, looking for things to photograph, when we saw a couple of field workers pulling a large submerged structure by rope slowly to the surface. What was being hoisted obviously required great effort and looked at first to Vera and me like a medium-size boat that had presumably sunk and was now being lifted topside for repair. But as more and more of this structure was brought visibly to the surface, we observed that it just happened to have a tail and a long snout with teeth. It was in fact a giant Orinoco Crocodile that had recently been captured and now was being encouraged to make this pond its home. And it was immense, certainly in the eighteen- to twenty-foot range, and seemed to be twice as big in girth as the twelve-foot alligators we regularly encountered back home in East Texas. Although there are caiman all over Venezuela, these big Orinoco Crocodiles are today extremely rare, with estimates of no more than several hundred breeding pair left in the wild. It was a thrill to see one this large, and up close.

As it started to get dark, we were also startled by another creature we had never seen, or even heard of, before—the Fish-eating Bat, several of which were dive-bombing the water for finned food. These bats fish entirely at the surface of the water and have impressively strong hind feet, which equip them well for the heavy lifting required. We even saw several make a score and fly off with fish for dinner.

Snail Kite (26), Hato Piñero, Venezuela, 1990

Crested Caracara (27), Hato Piñero, Venezuela, 1990

Red-breasted Blackbird (28), Hato Piñero, Venezuela, 1990

The waterholes and streams of the llanos are often beautiful and clear and therefore seductively inviting as swimming holes, except for the fact they are populated with harmful creatures that make going in the water an extremely dangerous thing to do. In addition to the crocodiles and caiman, there are other such lovelies as anacondas, piranhas, and electric eels, all of which have the potential of substantially ruining your day. But there is one such aquatic denizen that is the most consistently troublesome of them all—the Freshwater Stingray. Its sharp, venomous barb is so painful, and the effects of its attack so incredibly damaging, that we actually know of a female manager of a similar ranch in the low llanos who foolishly took a dip, was stung, and after three years of rehab still walks with a troublesome and ugly

limp. We're told she had once been a beauty queen in Caracas.

The only other dangerous creature Vera and I ran across in the llanos was a bright yellow Tropical Rattlesnake that we encountered one afternoon, but jumped back from in plenty of time. As for the mammals, we regretfully never saw either an anteater or a Jaguar, but we did have a number a great experiences on our night rides each evening with multiple sightings and drop-dead views of Crab-eating Foxes, Red Howler Monkeys, and even the elusive and much-coveted Ocelot, to the delight of us all on the last night we were there.

Our second destination in Venezuela embraced the lush cloud forests of the Coastal Cordillera and the 250,000-acre Henri Pittier National Park (I). The park is anchored by the famous Rancho Grande Biological Research Station and was once a mountain retreat of the dictator Juan Vicente Gómez in the 1930s. Subsequently it became a research facility where the celebrated naturalist William Beebe once worked and wrote. The station has been in various stages of disrepair over the last twenty years, although it remains officially connected in some ill-defined way to the Maracay branch of the Central University of Venezuela. Despite the station's dilapidated condition, which makes it unsuitable for overnight stays except for the most desperate of young researchers, the cloud forest is one of the most impressive in Venezuela and one of the most accessible and productive birding environments in all of South America. The area has recorded over 500 species of birds. That's huge.

Vera and I will long remember that first morning out on the balcony of the station itself, feathered by shadow and sunlight, when a cool, wet cloud downdrafted the entire terrace in an enveloping mist, making it difficult to see five feet in front of our faces. When the cloud lifted fifteen minutes later, we were in the midst of one of those stunning spectacles for which this cloud forest is famous—a mixed-species flock of what seemed to be forty or fifty different birds working frenetically up the mountainside on one of their foraging runs. It had all of the frenzy and magic of one of those celebrated fallouts of Neotropical migrants on the Gulf Coast of Texas. There were tanagers and antbirds, flycatchers and woodcreepers, as well as several other varieties of birds, all part of an extended family, many members of which had been

Speckled Tanager (29), Henri Pittier National Park, Venezuela, 1990

Golden Tanager (30), Henri Pittier National Park, Venezuela, 1990

Silver-beaked Tanager (31), Henri Pittier National Park, Venezuela, 1990

Chestnut-crowned Antpitta (32), Henri Pittier National Park, Venezuela, 1990

foraging together for a lifetime on this same mountain. The action was fast and furious all around us for about ten minutes, and then it was over. They had moved on through and were gone. Nevertheless, our stateside experience with photographing wood warblers, which never stay still themselves, served us well, and we were able to focus quickly on these fast-moving birds to capture shots of three colorful tanagers: the Speckled Tanager (no. 29), the Golden Tanager (no. 30), and the Silver-beaked Tanager (no. 31).

But the highlight of our trip to Henri Pittier didn't come at Rancho Grande, or even on any of the trails that run deep behind the station, but rather on a small obscure path running off the switchback some thirty minutes down the mountain. Our group had been birding slowly down the road, hoping for more foraging flocks to move through, but Vera and I and David Wolf had somehow lagged behind. I had

drifted away to make a pit stop on a small trail off the main road when a medium-size bird, which looked remarkably like a large, vertical brown egg on sticks, took a short hop onto the path and then scurried rapidly across it not ten feet from where I was walking. And then it was gone. I had no idea what it was, and Vera was of no help either. But David said without hesitation, "Chestnut-crowned Antpitta," a bird considered to be one of the most legitimately prized of the area. Vera and I didn't even know at that point what an antpitta was, but we would come to realize over the ensuing years that finding an antpitta—any antpitta at all—was a highlight of most trips, and that managing a photograph of one represented a special kind of victory.

David, Vera, and I went back to the path, sat very still, and waited—while David tape-played its three-whistle song. And the antpitta responded. It sang back and began to move progressively closer to where we were now crouched. Then in a small clearing in the forest, not fifteen yards away, we actually saw it. And it was elegant—an eight-inch-tall, cinnamon-colored bird with relatively long legs and brown streaks on a cream-colored breast. It jumped up on a small log and began to sing back to us, its throat moving up and down as the registers would rise and fall. We stood frozen, afraid to twitch a muscle for fear that the spell might be broken, its magic lost.

But it was not over. Almost immediately—and incredibly—a second antpitta suddenly jumped up on the log next to the first and began singing also. It was the female; they sing, too. Duetting antpittas, side by side on a log serenading us, a flash of wonder and en-

chantment so rare that we would later learn that few birders had ever seen anything like it. The two antpittas sang for nearly a minute, then jumped off the log together, with one heading away back through the brush, while the other approached us ever so slowly. As this second antpitta edged out of some thick brush that had blocked our view, it hopped across a clear spot in the forest not twenty feet from where we were standing. I fired one shot, and then it was gone. But I had hit it good, and the resulting photograph of the Chestnut-crowned Antpitta (no. 32) would always remind the sidekick and me of "the morning of the singing pittas," as she would romantically brand it, a morning that represented one of our most memorable Neotropical experiences in all the years we were at it.

Río Napo

No SAMPLING OF THE NEOTROPICS would be complete without some accommodation to the mighty Amazon River, or at least negotiation of one of the many big rivers that feed it, and drain the astonishingly bird-rich Amazon Basin. Vera and I decided early on, however, not to navigate the big river itself, though nothing sounded wilder or more adventuresome. Even the Congo River of deepest Africa doesn't evoke the same degree of mystery as does the Amazon with its reputation for deadly crocodiles and ravenous piranha, cannibals, and giant anacondas—all of which are capable of eating a man, and occasionally do. Tour promoters today still wax gushy and prattle on about all of the exotic wildlife to be seen on this river and hype expectations of viewing the elusive Jaguar resting on a log, or large, colorful birds foraging at the forest's edge, or even caiman sunning on a sandbar waiting for meals to swim by, like large river turtles or freshwater dolphins. But that's not the way it is on the Amazon anymore, nor has it been for a long, long time.

Yet the importance of the Amazon River cannot be minimized. It's one of the planet's most significant and majestic forces of nature and is responsible for producing over a fifth of all the fresh water in the world. And what begins as a clean trickle 18,000 feet high up in the snow fields of Mt. Mismi in Peru gathers force and volume from over a thousand streams and rivers that drain the Andes and feed it along the way—ten of which are bigger than the Mississippi River itself—to finally empty four thousand miles later on the other side of the continent as a sprawling brown monster two hundred miles wide with an island in its mouth the size of Switzerland.

But for the purpose of photographing exotic birds, the Amazon River is not where you want to be, for the river is wide and brown and includes many of the aesthetic characteristics of the New Jersey Turnpike. Indians living along this big river, because of the fertile soils from the annual floods, have long ago shot for food most of the large and interesting mammals and birds that once patrolled its banks. Though the Amazon is unquestionably the mother of the Amazonian ecosystem, there are other rivers that flow to it that are less densely inhabited and traveled. Some of these extend to remote stretches of rainforest where the wildlife has remained relatively intact. The Río Napo is such a river. It was in fact on the Río Napo that Francisco de Orellana of Spain first traveled on his way to discovering the Amazon River itself, a trip during which he presumably battled a group of fierce women-warriors who ultimately became the stuff of legend, the "Amazons."

The Napo, however, is no clean mountain stream. It's also big and muddy, gooey and brown, and throbs with commerce moving up and down it as it connects with the Amazon nearly six hundred miles farther east from its own source point in the mountains of Ecuador. But a mile in from the river's edge, in a productive stretch of seasonally flooded forest (*varzea*) in the eastern part of the country, there is a remote jungle lodge called La Selva, on a oxbow lake named Garzacocha, which has the reputation of supporting some of the most interesting and diverse wildlife in the Amazon Basin.

You can reach the Río Napo, and the La Selva Jungle Lodge, only by first flying to Quito, Ecuador, the capital of a country about the size of Colorado, where Vera and I stayed for several days. Even though Ecuador is a third-world country, Quito's high elevation at nearly 9,000 feet and cool temperatures inure you a bit to its poverty, and the city is additionally charmed by a mixture of colonial and Indian cultures, which gives it texture and flavor. There are sparkling new office buildings shadowing four-hundred-year-old churches; there are mountain Indians in brightly colored serapes selling baskets to businessmen in Italian suits. Quito was a pleasant and visually stimulating place to spend time.

But our next stop on the way to La Selva, after a short flight from Quito, was not. It was Coca, an oil-service town of stunning ugliness at the eastern foot of the Andes that supplies logistics and equipment to the significant drilling operations downriver. Coca whines with activity and is scarred with streets composed of oil runoff, mud, and the accumulated defecations of the unmolested mongrel packs roaming the town. It is squalid and treeless, and its one-story buildings have a patina of grime and smoke. There are roughnecks and roustabouts and doorway debutantes, all of whose financial circumstances are indirectly but inextricably tied to the price of crude oil on world markets. We gratefully fled Coca an hour later to embark on our trip downriver to La Selva in the heart of Ecuadorian Amazonia called El Oriente.

Our mode of transportation was a fifty-foot motorized canoe, propelled by a two-stroke engine connected to a six-foot shaft. The pilot of our little vessel was skilled in speaking the special language of the Napo and knew the eddies and sandbars, the deadfalls and drops, all along this stretch of water for several hundred miles. He had once apprenticed under his father for several years, and he told us that he would also take his own son into his one-boat business when he too came of age.

Before La Selva, however, we stopped for an afternoon and night at the Limoncocha Biological Reserve at an oxbow lake on 10,000 acres of *varzea* forest an hour or so downstream from Coca, and one of the largest oxbows to be found in eastern Ecuador.

Black-fronted Nunbird (33), La Selva Jungle Lodge, Río Napo, Ecuador, 1991

The next morning we continued downriver for an hour, and when we finally disembarked, we maneuvered our luggage and equipment another twenty minutes down a slippery-planked boardwalk through a Mauritia Palm–swamp forest. Then we reloaded our gear onto a long dugout canoe for yet another twenty-five minutes across the Garzacocha Lagoon until we reached the dock of the La Selva Jungle Lodge (J) itself. We finally hauled our luggage up the stairs to a planked walkway that connected each cabana, and then dragged the bags the remaining distance to our assigned room.

Vera and I were relieved to have landed at last, and it felt good to unpack and drop down. But we were not alone. We quickly discovered we were sharing our bathroom with an imposingly large tarantula that made its home in a wall crevice about two feet from the john. This presented the obvious problem. Of course, we could have tried to eliminate the little beast, but that seemed a bit unwarranted and mean-spirited at the time. Or we could make an effort to work around the problem. So we chose the gentler alternative, and for no particular reason that I can remember, we named her Sue. The three of us then settled in for the length of our stay and early on negotiated the terms of our relationship: when Vera or I entered the bathroom, we would gently knock twice on the wall. Sue would then scurry back into her little crevice. When we finished our business and left, she would scurry back out. No harm, no foul. But in the evening after we shut off the kerosene lamps, a different issue surfaced—nighttime is feeding time for large spiders. They're on the prowl then, out on the town looking for prey. And the only thing worse than finding Sue late at night by the john was not finding Sue late at night by the john. But things worked out amicably, and our only adrenaline rush came to the sidekick early one morning toward the end of our stay when something jumped on her in low light. But it was only a frog.

As for the bird action, we were right away alerted to the exceptional wildlife possibilities of the La Selva area as we quickly managed a photograph of a Black-fronted Nunbird (no. 33) working the grounds of the compound proper. This sit-and-wait forager is a dark gray bird with a bright orange bill, and although it's a member of the puffbird family, it behaves very much like a motmot as it swings its tail back and forth.

Also, less than thirty minutes after our arrival and well before lunch, the local guide, José, directed Vera and me to see a Zigzag Heron, a chunky little forest heron with barred plumage that skulks quietly inside its wooded-swamp surroundings. The inaccessibility of its habitat and the shyness of its behavior have made this little heron highly coveted by serious birders and one of the most sought-after targets of the Neotropics. La Selva has the reputation of being one of the best spots in all of Amazonia to find a "Zigzag," and although they are often difficult to locate, their froglike grunts can regularly be heard at dawn and dusk throughout the breeding season.

For us, observing the little heron was easy, as it was perched on a log, off trail and not sixty feet away. We spotted it immediately. Getting a photograph of it, however, was a different kind of challenge since there was brush all around the little bird, blocking any chance we might have for a clear shot. So we slowly began to crawl toward it, thinking at any moment that it would flush and be gone. When at last we cleared the remaining overhangs fifteen feet away from the bird, we couldn't have wished for a better opportunity: the sidekick took a shot at point-blank range that filled the frame. Then we slowly and carefully backed out of the bird's area. It hadn't moved an inch. The Zigzag Heron (no. 34) became our second win at La Selva, and the morning was still young.

Zigzag Heron (34), La Selva Jungle Lodge, Río Napo, Ecuador, 1991

Almost immediately, José produced for us another significant opportunity not five minutes farther down the trail. It was a bird called a Long-tailed Potoo (no. 35), and Vera and I knew it as yet another prized bird of the Río Napo. We, of course, had never seen one. We would learn later that this potoo was an extreme rarity, almost impossible to find, and that La Selva once again was one of the few places in the world where high-octane "listers" had a reasonable chance of running one down. It is a large potoo with a long tail, handsomely plumaged in rich rufous and browns. And there was also a dividend because this particular bird had an offspring, and mother and chick were welded vertically together on their nest in a tree not twenty feet up. We snapped several photographs and declared another victory. It was quite a start.

Late that same afternoon on a canoe ride around the lagoon we came upon one of the most unusual birds of all: the Hoatzin (no. 36). Everything about this creature is bizarre. To begin with, it is large and clumsy and acts chronically confused, always crashing out of control into the trees along the streams where it likes to roost. Additionally, these birds have long, loose crests that spike outward, giving them a painfully startled look, as if they had mistakenly stuck a claw into some wall socket. Then there's their diet—they are able to eat leaves that are too toxic for other birds to handle because they have an extra stomach chamber like a cow that produces a bacteria to facilitate digestion. Also their babies hatch with little reptilian claws on their wings so that they can pull themselves out of the water and onto a bush after jumping in to avoid predators. All this has given the Hoatzin some significant and distinct advantages for survival, and that's why they are plentiful in the gallery forests they inhabit: they are far too ugly and noisy to be attractive to the pet trade, they have an exclusive food source that other birds won't touch, and the special bacteria they produce for digestion makes them smell bad and taste awful. In fact, no smelling creature wants to be anywhere near them. The Hoatzins have their neighborhood all to themselves, and they most likely have whatever neighborhood they want.

Early the next morning we walked the trail from our cabin for about fifteen minutes to reach a 135-foot emergent kapok tree in which had been constructed a multilevel treehouse with stairs to the top. It was the first time Vera and I had been privileged with a canopy experience, and we were able to observe at eye level many of the high-perching birds—like the fruit crows, nunbirds, and guans as well as the tanagers and antbirds. But our principal quests, the birds for which we lusted the most, were the high-perching members

Long-tailed Potoo (35) and baby, La Selva Jungle Lodge, Río Napo, Ecuador, 1991

Hoatzin (36), La Selva Jungle Lodge, Río Napo, Ecuador, 1991

of the glorious blue cotinga family, which are difficult to observe adequately from the forest floor—specifically the Spangled Cotinga and the Plum-throated Cotinga, both in eruptions of turquoise and aquamarine, magenta, and rose, which glisten and explode with color. We saw them both, often and well, but getting a photograph turned out to be a nonstarter because the birds were simply perched too far away. We did, however, have one brief opportunity at the Spangled Cotinga; it blew into our kapok tree one morning, and we fired several times quickly. But the bird was blocked in part by leaves, the shots were slightly out of focus, and there was a napkin-white sky as the background—rendering the color of this gorgeous bird no more vibrant than slate gray. These shots would thereafter rank as the worst photographs of the most beautiful bird of the trip. And there would be no more chances at these cotingas, or at anything else for that matter, because it suddenly started to rain, and it rained steadily for three days.

Rainforests are known for rain, and the rainforests of La Selva seem to have as much of it as anyplace. For photographers, this complicates what is already a challenging situation, and while there are admittedly a lot of things one can do in bad weather, consistently sharp photography is not one of them. The noted wildlife photographer and outfitter Leonard Rue, after a week at the La Selva Jungle Lodge a few years earlier, said that he was able to come away with acceptable photographs of only several flowers. He managed no photographs of any birds at all and later remarked that his "camera was the most useless piece of equipment" he had along with him.

Our experience was not altogether different since the next several days of steady rain rendered our outings a bust from a production standpoint. We went scoreless for the rest of the trip. One dark, stormy afternoon on our last full day on the Napo, we explored some of the river islands to tease out of the foliage several bird species that are unique to these kinds of microhabitats. We were not successful.

Later that same afternoon we circled one small island in our motorized canoe for over an hour, hoping to see another one of the great cotingas of the tropical forests here, the Amazonian Umbrellabird, as it flew back to the island for its nightly roost. We saw it all right, but this jet-black bird glided in high over the trees at deep dusk in a blinding rain like some little dark cloud blowing quickly through, and it was all over before we knew it.

But as we later returned to our canoes to cross the lagoon, we had one of those enchanting experiences we wouldn't soon forget, and it had nothing to do with the birds. It was all about the moonlight and the increasing brightness of the night and of a forest that had suddenly grown silent and still. For the rain had stopped and the moon was rising, and as Vera and I slowly eased our shallow craft through the palm-studded lagoon, with the moonlight shimmering off its partially submerged trees, the only sounds we heard throughout the entire forest came from the ever-so-slight drippings from our own paddles. We felt the moment to be ghostly evocative—with the pull of some nameless emotion so strong that it filled the air. It was a slightly eerier version of our romantic moonlight walk that night in Trinidad, but this time we were gliding through a forested lagoon off the Río Napo in Ecuador.

We left the Napo the next morning after a four-hour trip back upstream to begin the second leg of our Ecuadorian adventure: some high-altitude birding in the rich forests of the Andes. But our adventure got off to a poor start when the ferry broke down near Coca, delaying us for over half a day. We spent that first night in a little room above the Tena River and awoke the next morning to a Spanish serenade right outside our window, over by the dining room. As I went on to breakfast, Vera veered off to greet our morning singer but couldn't seem to locate him, until she finally heard the song once again right near her—up in a tree. It was a Yellow-crowned Amazon that had been hanging around camp for several years and had picked up song fragments from cheerful local laborers who sang while they worked about the premises. This colorful green parrot turned out to be our morning serenader.

After breakfast we began to work the roads for the resident birdlife, but the tanagers and mixed-species flocks were all moving high and fast and were hardly suitable for satisfactory bird watching, much less photography. And by the time we wanted to change our approach and explore the other side of the mountain, our little adventure aborted for good. It was, as it turned out, a form of political season in Ecuador, and the Indians had decided on a political protest over some lingering grievance. And the way they like to do this in Ecuador is to declare a strike, then chop down trees to barricade the roads, stopping all traffic in both directions for days at a time. Game over. We had a helicopter fly in to pick us up, took a van ride back to Quito, and then made our flight back to Dallas. It was unfortunately to be our last trip to Ecuador for some time, but Vera and I knew we had left a lot there unseen, especially the mountain-toucans and hummingbirds of the high country, and we were determined to get back one day for another shot at them.

Army Antswarms

ANY WHO HAVE NEVER been to the Republic of Panama associate it only with the Panama Canal. But the country is much more than that: it's a slender land bridge of staggering biodiversity that separates two oceans and links two continents. And covering the southern flank of Panama, running all the way to Colombia, is an impressively large, unspoiled tract of the Pacific watershed called the Southern Darien Province (K). It's one of the wildest stretches of habitat left on the continent.

This isolated region is where the Choco Indians, who had drifted over from Colombia many years before, perfected the use of poisonous dart guns with lethal toxins sweated from the glands of small frogs. They still live there. But they might not for much longer if the Pan-American Highway, designed to connect Panama to Colombia by bridging the Darien Gap, plows through this region as is planned—for the forest would most likely be gone thirty years after that. This last piece of linkage, however, has been temporarily forestalled because Panama has wisely come to realize that the thick jungles of Darien serve as a useful buffer from unwanted imports in the form of drug-trafficking Colombian guerrillas and the hoof-and-mouth disease carried by South American cattle.

When Vera and I first explored the area back in 1993, it was pristine, remote, and hard to get to. Our focal point was Cana on the eastern slope of Pirre Ridge, one of the most isolated places in Central America. There had once been an important gold-mining operation in the area that had been abandoned several years before, and only a relic in the form of a grassy airstrip remained. The nearest civilization was three days north by foot on the Boca de Cupe Trail. Cana was a hundred miles from the nearest road.

Vera and I hitched a ride on a prop flight along with a V.E.N.T. tour and dropped down at the grassy strip at Cana one blazing hot morning a couple of days before New Year's Eve in 1993. In addition to the birding group from V.E.N.T. and the two of us, there was a well-appointed couple from Hamburg, Germany, who were also in Panama for the first time. They pretty much stayed to themselves, however, and we never did learn their names. We knew them only as "the Germans."

Our accommodations were simple. Most slept in tents, but Vera and I, by prior arrangement, had weaseled superior treatment. We had two cots in a dilapidated toolshed with a shelf and a candle and a little colony of bats that made their home in the wall two feet from our head. The bats served as our alarm clock each morning as they returned at dawn from their nightly hunt, chatting anxiously among themselves to greet each new arrival.

There was also a central cooking shed where the meals were prepared, and despite the ruggedness of the surroundings, the food was tolerably good. "The Germans," however, cleverly supplemented the prepared food with private stores of their own, and it became increasingly apparent, by the most delicate of degrees, that they were far ahead of the curve in most every way. While the sidekick and I struggled with 35 millimeter cameras, they cruised with video, explaining that they liked the tropical movies to get them through their miserably cold Hamburg winters. While we ineptly battled the mosquitoes that drifted through the open window at night, they had brought back-up mosquito netting of their own to comfortably protect them. And as we strained to examine ourselves at the end of the day to see if we had picked up any ticks in the woods, they were calmly equipped with magnifying glass and tweezers, as required. We were always bumping into them in some remote section of the forest as we set about our business of looking for birds to photograph, and somehow they always seemed to have arrived at the best spots first. "The Germans" simply had their game together while Vera and I, by comparison, were always struggling to figure it out.

This wild and remote region of the Darien supports a number of interesting and endemic birds, and although there is a particular warbler and a hummingbird and a bush-tanager that can be found only on the upper slopes of Cerro Pirre, and no other place on the planet, Vera and I decided early on not to invest the full day it would take for this side trip. We wanted to concentrate on the significant opportunities in the immediate area, including four different species of macaws and five different species of antpittas. The macaws were particularly stunning, always squawking and flying in pairs near the large trees that abutted the airstrip.

On New Year's Eve, Vera and I celebrated with champagne under a clear, starry sky, enthusiastically agreeing that there was no place on earth we had rather be, while acknowledging that our more civilized friends were most likely saying the same thing on some country club dance floor back home.

But all this was in the form of preliminaries, the main event was yet to come, because when you talk to knowledgeable Neotropical birders and you mention Panama, they think of the Darien and its army antswarms, the most impressive to be found in the Neotropics. They are referring to the massive swarms of a medium-size black ant with a big bite, *Eciton burchelli,* and the diverse number of bird species that follow these ants when they are on the move and hunting. For it's these unique and interesting birds, not the ants, which draw serious birders to the Darien, much like those who venture to the Gulf Coast of Texas for the spring migration of Neotropical migrants, or to Hawk Mountain in Pennsylvania to take in the fall migration of raptors. That was the reason Vera and I had come to the Darien; "the Germans" too, I suspect, though they didn't say so.

These huge Darien antswarms can contain a million or more ants and spend as much as 60 percent of their time on the march, especially during the rainy season when they are aggressively searching for insects and arthropods to take back to the queen and larvae. They blanket the forest floor in a seething front up to a hundred feet wide, going up and down trees, over logs, and in and out of holes and crevices, creating havoc in their relentless search of prey. There is also a steady stream of ants coming back the other way with dismembered victims that they have vanquished along the way.

At night the ants lock their long legs together in a solid mass, sometimes the size of a beach ball, enclosing their queen and her brood in a suspended bivouac under a log or an expanded root system, until they are ready to begin hunting the next day. When legions of these ferocious ants are on attack, scouring the forest floor, every small creature is panicked to get out of the way; and as preposterous as it may seem, the locals are known to open their doors to let an antswarm rage through, knowing that all of the other little uglies living there will soon be flushed out and gone, one way or another. They simply shut the door behind the ants when the dirty work is done and the swarm has moved on through and out. No pesticides required at all.

And with the ants come the special, fascinating birds—not to eat the ants, but rather to ambush all of the spiders and roaches and beetles that are scurrying to get out of their way. It's not all that different from the hunting tactics of Cattle Egrets following cattle, or tractors, to get at the little creatures spooked by something larger. Although several species of tropical birds are attracted to antswarms, the stars of the show are actually the antbirds themselves. These little guys are not fashionably colored, as they are usually decked out in some combination of rufous and white, gray and black, but they are handsome nevertheless and are loaded with energy and fascinating behavioral traits.

Of the 240 or so species of antbirds living in the Neotropics, about 30 are considered "professional" antswarm followers and are dependent on the hunting rhythms of the ants themselves to find and flush their meals for them. These "professionals" have evolved well-developed leg muscles and large, strong feet that allow them to tenaciously grip small vertical stems directly above the swarming ants, thus giving them a competitive edge in capturing spooked prey. The antbirds are part of a family in which couples mate for life, and they also seem to be among the most vulnerable of birds to the effects of forest fragmentation. They won't cross streams or roads, and when the forest becomes sliced into a series of isolated patches, you won't find any of the antbirds left.

One of the defining highlights of a Neotropical forest is a seething river of *E. burchelli* with its attendant antbirds and other camp followers in tow. Sometimes you discover a swarm by simply stumbling across one while hiking through the forest, but more often than not, you will hear the attendant antbirds first. They chirr and whistle, they call and scold. One of the real leaders of the Central American antbird patrol is the Bicolored Antbird, and if you see or hear this bird, army ants are likely to be nearby. It was, in fact, a Bicolored Antbird that attached itself many years ago to the venerable naturalist Alexander Skutch, and it would follow him through his Costa Rican forest to pounce on any small, tasty thing Skutch happened to kick up while hiking. For a couple of years, every time Skutch would go out for his daily walk, this little antbird

Bicolored Antbird (37), Southern Darien Province, Panama, 1992

would find him, and they would spend their mornings hunting together.

So when a birder rushed into camp early one morning and screamed, "Antswarm!" we all jumped up and ran down the trail in hot pursuit. Fifteen minutes later we found it, a pulsing mass of marauding ants relentlessly moving through the leaf litter and terrifying every small thing in its way. Vera and I had on rubber boots, up which these ferocious ants fortunately wouldn't crawl, so intent were they on the ant scent laid down before them and apparently so texturally unappealing were the boots themselves. As long as we didn't lean against the trees, where the traffic at times was also heavy, we were perfectly safe from them. Vera moved into the swarm somewhat gingerly but with grace; I stumbled in with considerable less style, prompting V.E.N.T.'s local guide,

Willie Martínez, to more or less good-naturedly refer to me as "El Tapir."

Willie was a charming and knowledgeable Panamanian, who was extremely proud of the fact that he could identify and imitate the songs of over three hundred different local birds. Around the table in the evenings he would tell marvelously engaging stories of the region, and of his own particular exploits in the field, which Vera and I felt at times he tended to overvalue and which we would come to learn later were occasionally true and nearly always unverifiable. Willie's stories were mostly about Willie, and he told them big.

After Vera and I had maneuvered to the head of the swarm where the rampaging ants were advancing, we crouched like cats and waited for the antbirds to return to action. And when they did, we were ready. The birds clung to slender stems, not two feet above

Spotted Antbird (38), Southern Darien Province, Panama, 1992

Chestnut-backed Antbird (39), Southern Darien Province, Panama, 1992

the ground, alertly waiting to exploit the chaos that the ants were creating. They pounced on beetles, they squeaked and chirped, they scolded each other, they wrestled for prey. We were operating in some invisible observation zone as the birds remained oblivious to our agenda, preoccupied as they were with their own. This presented an exceptional opportunity for close-up photographs of these energetic little hunters, although it was admittedly difficult for us to keep the constantly flitting birds in focus.

We saw Ocellated Antbirds, Bare-crowned Antbirds, and Immaculate Antbirds, and took photographs of three other "professionals"—the ubiquitous Bicolored Antbird (no. 37), the Spotted Antbird (no.

38), and the Chestnut-backed Antbird (no. 39). In addition, there were nunbirds, woodpeckers, and woodcreepers following the swarm as well as the compelling Rufous Motmot, one of the most handsome of its own family. Vera and I were also impressed with the wide variety of butterflies we observed in their own role as camp followers, attracted to the antswarm for the chemicals accruing from the droppings of the birds following the ants, which were after the beetles feeding under the leaves. A food chain in action, a "moveable feast."

But just when we thought we had identified all the players, a real star appeared—one of the storied prizes of the Neotropics—the Black-crowned Antpitta (no.

40). It seemed to materialize out of thin air and began energetically hopping around the forward column of ants. Over the next half hour we watched this magnificent bird at leisure, prowling the swarm and looking for prey. This is a big antpitta, one that is sought by all who chase antswarms, and on two occasions, it moved just close enough to where Vera was crouched so that she managed a good photograph. It was a splendid success.

We all declared victory, did high fives, and returned to camp for lunch, exhausted but feeling pretty good about ourselves. Everyone, that is, except "the Germans." They had brought their own lunch and stayed quietly behind on the off chance that something else of importance might show up. We would learn several hours later when they returned to camp that an even grander celebrity had decided to make an appearance—a Rufous-vented Ground-Cuckoo, one of the absolute rarest and most coveted of all the birds in Central and South America.

This impressive and secretive ground-cuckoo is like some immensely handsome roadrunner, shaded in a combination of muted greens and bronze and rufous, with touches of light lavender and highlighted by a bright blue streak flaring back of its eye. The bird can be secretly and ghostly still, not making any sound or movement at all, as it blends in perfectly with its surroundings, or else it can engage in noisy and aggressive snappings of its large bill as it rushes in among its prey. It is a bird seldom seen and almost never photographed. Perhaps aside from the monkey-eating Harpy Eagle, it represents the most sought-

Black-crowned Antpitta (40), Southern Darien Province, Panama, 1992

Rufous-vented Ground-Cuckoo (41), Southern Darien Province, Panama, 1992

Rufous-vented Ground-Cuckoo, Southern Darien Province, Panama, 1992

after bird in Panama. Serious birders go limp with the thought of seeing one, but few ever do.

So when "the Germans" came to tell us that they had seen the big cuckoo not one hour after we had broken for lunch, our spirits plummeted. A rare opportunity had been missed, and we sweated the night to be over so that we might possibly have another shot at it the next day. If it was still there. At dawn, we rushed back out on the Boca de Cupe Trail to look for the swarm where it had last been seen, hoping the big bird would be with it. Nothing. We waited another hour. Still nothing. Then the others who had joined us got bored with waiting and headed on down the trail, leaving just Vera and me and the German man to go it alone. About nine o'clock we spotted our first small item of interest—it was the Bicolored Antbird, up on a limb thirty feet high, nonchalantly preening and grooming itself. This was a good sign, suggesting that there was an army ant bivouac nearby and that this sentinel antbird was simply biding its time, waiting for the ants—which had presumably been sleeping in—to swarm up and get going.

Just about then, the German urgently motioned to me and pointed downslope to an old log. As we put our glasses on the log, we could see the big cuckoo, planted still as a statue, right next to it. The cuckoo must have been standing there motionless, as best we could tell and as unlikely as it may seem, for over an hour. No sooner had we figured out that the army ant bivouac was under the log than we heard the snapping of the cuckoo's bill, and began to actually see the ants stream out from underneath it. The Bicolored Antbird began to chirr, two Spotted Antbirds flew in, there was a woodcreeper or two—it was now official: the antswarm was on the move! Over the next forty-five minutes, as we stood motionless and partially hidden from the action, the

cuckoo moved aggressively back and forth through the swarm, snapping his bill and jumping a variety of frightened victims, including a small lizard, while running off any other bird that got in his way. He even seemed to strut at times; he was king of the swarm.

We managed several anemic shots of the cuckoo at fifty feet but were not close enough to adequately capture his delicate shadings, since the bird was moving in mottled light and shadows and our flash was at its limit. So I decided to take a gamble—and after first clearing my tactics with the sidekick and the German, I made my move. The next time the cuckoo disappeared from view behind a large tree, I took off on a cunning sprint to get closer to him and in range. I raised the camera, braced myself against a tree, and waited. It didn't take long. As the cuckoo reappeared through some brush near where I was poised, he hopped up on a low horizontal vine, thus providing a clear shot. I fired once and got him. I moved closer, fired again, and got a head shot. The big bird then hopped down and began to move on off to a more inaccessible part of the woods, and we were through for the day. But we had posted a huge win, one of our biggest: the extraordinarily secretive Rufous-vented Ground-Cuckoo (no. 41). The German, with his video camera, said he had enough footage to last him all winter and rushed off to find his own sidekick and tell her the good news.

Also around the swarm toward late morning we ran across another unusual creature, a Tayra, a large and interesting weasel, which can be extremely ferocious if cornered and is aggressively reactive toward those that threaten it or any of its family. If one Tayra is attacked or is in trouble, the rest of the family will converge on the aggressor with deadly effectiveness. Our experience, however, was benign as we simply observed it climbing a tree in an area where the swarm was particularly active. In addition to this weasel and our little house bats, we saw a number of additional mammals, including four different species of monkeys. But there was one mammal experience of the Darien that we wouldn't forget, and it involved the White-lipped Peccary.

This peccary is in many ways similar to the Collared Peccary, or Javelina, that we know well from the brush country of South Texas back home. The two more or less look the same, although the White-lipped Peccary is larger. And even though they both have a strong and distinct odor, the smells differ radically from one another. Where the Collared Peccaries are shy, usually found in small numbers, and are often first recognized by their odor, the White-lipped Peccaries can be extremely aggressive, are found occasionally in herds of over a hundred, and are often detected first by the sound of some huge foraging machine eating and working its way toward you. There have been those who have been killed by these creatures—usually when they attack the peccary first—and others who have had their hindquarters eaten away when they could not climb a tree fast enough or high enough to escape.

Vera and I had encountered at least one large herd each day we had been in the Darien, one in particular following a troop of foraging Spider Monkeys that were knocking fruit to the ground from the trees. Some of the nuts are so hard that only peccaries, with their powerful jaws, are strong enough to crack the shell. The Spider Monkey also serves as a useful sentinel to warn the peccary of any lurking Jaguar, which considers the peccary an important part of its diet. Some of these peccary herds we had seen numbered seventy-five or more animals, but Vera and I had been able to comfortably skirt them each time.

On the afternoon of our last day, having returned from trying to locate a manakin lek, we crossed a stream, rounded a bend at a fast-paced walk, and literally walked right into the middle of a herd. We were surrounded!

Two older males with the white-haired snouts that signaled their seniority, and foraging out on the perimeter of the herd, sniffed the air and caught our scent. The black hair on their backs bristled straight up, they both began to make menacing "clacking" sounds with their teeth, and then they charged. Vera and I took off and sprinted to the base of the nearest cecropia tree some thirty yards away. We turned around and looked as the two boars fortunately braked to a stop, sniffed the air once more, and then slowly trotted back to the herd. Fortunately Vera and I didn't have to climb that tree, for the cecropia is itself the home to a particular family of *azteca* ants that protect it from all intruders by attacking them with enthusiasm. It would have been a bad deal either way. We were lucky.

But our run-in with the White-lipped Peccary was the last bit of adventure and excitement to be drained from the Darien, and the next morning we flew on to Panama City for a day and a half of just winding down. We managed some light hiking along the Pipeline Road, which had been a productive birding spot in Panama for many years, made an obligatory pass at the Panama Canal just to say that we had done it, and finished our stay at an intimate restaurant in an old dungeon across from the French Embassy. But to Vera and me, Panama had been about antswarms and the special birds magnetically attracted to them; and although we would come across other swarms in the years to come, from Belize to Costa Rica to Venezuela, they would all be babies compared with the monsters of the Darien.

Among the Maya

I T HAD BEEN SEVERAL YEARS since Vera and I had patronized the watering holes of the Yucatan Peninsula, but in 1995 we set sail for Belize—formerly the colony of British Honduras—a country about the size and shape of New Jersey. It is tucked into the backside of the Yucatan Peninsula and has been home to the Maya for over 3,000 years. Most Americans visiting Belize today spend time snorkeling the reefs, fishing the flats, and knocking back margaritas with fresh lime; but Vera and I had come to explore the country's inland tracts of subtropical forest in search of its wildlife.

Belize's wilderness habitat is principally broadleaf jungle with towering mahogany, ceiba, and fig trees, but since most of the country has been heavily logged over the last three hundred years, what remains is principally secondary growth. There is, however, a relatively unspoiled tract of some 250,000 acres in the Orange Walk District of the north that supports a quaint little lodge known to birders worldwide as Chan Chich (L), the Mayan term for "little bird."

Chan Chich is a thirty-minute ride from Gallon Jug, which is, in turn, a thirty-minute prop flight from Belize City. It is owned by Barry Bowen, the Belkin Beer distributor for Belize, and was cheerfully and competently managed at the time by two American expatriates, Tom and Josie Harding. The little Chan Chich complex is comprised of twelve thatched cabanas on the site of a cluster of grass-covered Mayan burial temples, which had come under siege through the years by looters trying to burrow tunnels in to the treasures they hoped were buried there. Consequently, Chan Chich has evolved as a focal point for both cultural as well as habitat preservation.

Agami Heron (42), Chan Chich, Belize, 1994

The trails at Chan Chich wind for miles through a forest of rich microhabitats studded with unexcavated Mayan ruins and providing visitors with the opportunity to see as many as three hundred different species of birds. The flowering fruit trees in the Mayan plaza of the compound itself support a wide variety of birds, and from the porch of our own cabana we observed an assortment of creatures ranging from brocket deer to monkeys, toucans to trogons, gaudy parrots to parakeets. Also, in the heart of what is one of the largest tracts of tropical forest outside of the Amazon Basin, there is even a legitimate opportunity to jump a Jaguar. Vera and I didn't, but there had been some sixty sightings of the big cat in the Chan Chich area over the calendar year prior to our arrival. And that's a lot. The lodge naturalists have even erected trip-flash cameras in key spots along the trails to document the region's solid reputation for supporting one of the most impressive concentrations of Jaguar surviving in the Neotropics today.

On the first morning we were there, Vera and I were impressed with a variety of birds ranging from an Ornate Hawk-Eagle soaring overhead to a brace of Squirrel Cuckoos hopping through the branches of a nearby sapling to a lone Pale-billed Woodpecker hanging from the side of a giant mahogany tree. We saw Black-throated Shrike-Tanagers and Montezuma Oropendolas, and even photographed the rare Agami Heron (no. 42) in a shadowed glade where Little Chan Chich Creek crosses the main trail headed west.

The Agami is arguably the handsomest of the Neotropical herons, in waves of powder blue, maroon, and bronze-green, and with an impressive harpoonlike beak that is the longest of all the herons'. Extraordinarily secretive and solitary, it prefers to hang back in the shadows of trees that overhang the streams and ponds of the interior forests it calls home. The birds are very difficult to see and almost impossible to photograph well, and we were lucky to have gotten this one.

Later that same afternoon, we were also fortunate enough to startle several Ocellated Turkeys (no. 43) roosting in a breadnut tree, and as they dropped to the ground not far from where we were standing, we had no trouble in nailing one at point-blank range. Ocellated Turkeys have been almost eradicated from

the narrow range they formerly occupied, and here in Chan Chich and in neighboring Guatemala down near Tikal are two of their remaining strongholds. They are majestically large and handsome birds, every bit as imposing as our wild American gobblers back home.

But our most remarkable encounter at Chan Chich had nothing to do with wildlife, but with a visiting birder we first met on a path running through the forest behind the compound. She was hiking on foot—and she was totally blind. She was carefully working her way through the woods with the help of her cane and her husband, and they had been traveling the tropics together in much the same way for many years. They were Catherine and Robert Randall from Jack-

Ocellated Turkey (43), Chan Chich, Belize, 1994

Tody Motmot (44), Chan Chich, Belize, 1994

sonville, Illinois. He was a superb birder and enthusiastic fan of the rainforests, and she liked the woods every bit as much as he. Though she was unable to see anything in it, she could hear and touch and smell—and she was blessed with that certain luminosity of spirit that enabled her to absorb all the little subtleties of her surroundings. It was if she could taste the air and sense when forest creatures were about. And one of the poignant memories Vera and I took away with us from Belize was the image of the two of them standing side by side in the woods—he straining to spot some new bird, her head cocked to hear it—welded spiritually together out on a dark forest trail.

The next morning, and for every morning after that, we worked a piece of habitat that might seem eccentric to nonbirders but was known throughout the tropics as a special honey hole for local birds—

the garbage dump a quarter mile from camp. The garbage dump at Chan Chich is famous; it's a magnet for birds and other assorted wildlife that drift in for their daily feed. We encountered hummingbirds, toucanets, and aracaris, and we were also able to sneak fairly close to a few woodcreepers and puffbirds. We even became chummy with a little Gray Fox we could practically reach out and touch. The mixture of birds would change by the hour, but one little guy always seemed to be present—the Rufous-tailed Jacamar, alertly poised to sally forth after insect prey. And each day Vera would make it her special little challenge to see how close she could work to this bird, by circling it ever so slowly, talking to it in a manner ever so gently, and avoiding any direct eye contact with it as she did so. By the last day she was practically on top of the bird; had she been

White-necked Jacobin (45), Chan Chich, Belize, 1994

one foot taller and carrying a fishing net, she could have scooped it up and taken it home.

On the morning of our third day, not far from the King's Tomb off the Back Plaza Trail, Vera captured one of the very special and elusive birds of the Neotropics—the diminutive, stubbed-tailed Tody Motmot (no. 44), the smallest of its species at just over six inches in length. And several minutes later, not far off Norman's Temple Trail, we netted the common but handsome White-necked Jacobin (no. 45).

The last day, after taking time to explore some of the Mayan ruins at Chan Chich by climbing down a couple of the temples with our flashlight, we flew on to Flores, Guatemala, and then took a van ride to the Hotel Camino Real preparatory to our exploration of Tikal (M). We would, however, always remember our time in Belize; and the next year, Vera would go back by herself to try to locate wintering wood warblers and would in fact capture the Northern Waterthrush while wading in Little Chan Chich Creek and "pishing" it onto a partially submerged sapling nearby. The photograph of that little Chan Chich migrant would be the very one we would use in *Chasing Warblers*. Additionally, whenever our friends expressed interest in sampling the Neotropics, and we knew they did not want to rough it to do so, Vera and I would inevitably suggest Chan Chich—for the charm and comfort of the overall experience as well as the marvelous birds it would consistently deliver.

Tikal itself is a mystically unique venue for viewing rainforest birds, for few spots in the world support so many species among such impressive archaeological ruins. At Tikal Vera and I worked well-worn trails along ancient causeways at what was once one of the largest Mayan ceremonial and urban centers. Here on the flat Petén region of western Guatemala, this complex was reclaimed by the jungle for over a thousand years until rediscovered by mahogany

hunters in the mid-1950s and subsequently excavated and restored by the Guatemalan government.

There was clearly an otherworldly feel to our experience here as we quietly chased more Ocellated Turkeys and Crested Guans among the temples and altars, overgrown with epiphyte-laden trees and serving today as silent memorials to a civilization past. We were at times spooked by a sudden burst of movement from a band of coatis rounding a pyramid or harassed by a troop of spider monkeys throwing sticks and branches at us from the trees above. We would observe White Hawks and King Vultures circling above the unbroken forest in our field of vision, and once we spotted the rare Orange-breasted Falcon dive-bombing the ruins not far from where we were positioned.

Although we missed badly on a Slaty-breasted Tinamou, we nevertheless managed photographs of two special birds that, due to their outrageously boat-shaped bills and their easily recognized silhouettes, have come to symbolize the Neotropics to many: the Keel-billed Toucan (no. 46) and the related Collared Aracari (no. 47).

The toucan's enormous boat-shaped bill is actually not as heavy as it looks since it is comprised of a light, porous, honeycomb material. The bird uses it to good advantage to reach out and pluck what might otherwise be unreachable fruit, or effectively maneuvers it to ravage other birds' nests for eggs and babies. These stunning birds are also known as "gulpers" since they toss their food back when feeding and also tip their heads back while drinking to let the water run down their throats.

But it's the outrageously colorful bill of the Keel-billed Toucan, in particular, that makes it so striking and memorable. Creationists intent on challenging the core principles of evolutionary theory and natural selection need look no further than the Keel-billed Toucan for a persuasive Exhibit A, since it's hard to imag-

Keel-billed Toucan (46), Tikal, Guatemala, 1994

Collared Aracari (47), Tikal, Guatemala, 1994

ine that this rainbow-beaked stunner simply marched to its present form in ponderous, Darwinian fashion. It was most surely crafted in some mad moment of whimsy in the workshop of the Great Maker.

Vera and I were forced to work a little for both birds as we climbed first to the top of a pyramid mound, swung out onto a low branch of a quamwood tree, and then scaled it higher to get closer to the birds that were feeding in a fruiting tree nearby. When they worked in reasonably close to where we were perched, we captured them both and came away pleased with the results.

However, what we had no way of knowing then was that these particular birds would actually be the last rainforest birds we would photograph in this land of the Maya for nearly a decade, as Vera and I would

devote several years finishing up our warbler project and several more exploring other productive forests of Central and South America. As a finishing touch to our Neotropical adventures, however, Vera and I did return in 2003 to make two other stops in this part of the world, the first to an upscale fishing lodge in southern Belize call El Pescador Punta Gorda, the second to a new ecotourism lodge in northern Honduras named Pico Bonito.

We had not intended to go back, but we received a call from an excited Victor Emanuel in early March 2003. He had just visited the newly opened lodge in southern Belize and had heard credible reports of a colony of Agami Herons nesting in the mangrove swamps an hour by boat from the lodge. He wanted us to check it out. We felt we needed a photo upgrade of this grand bird, and to have access to a colony of them would represent an unbelievable opportunity. So we decided to do it.

We found the lodge at El Pescador Punta Gorda (N) to be one of the best we had been to in the Neotropics. It was located in Bahía de Amatique in the Gulf of Honduras, an hour south by prop plane from Belize City. The structure was three stories of mahogany and cedar, appointed with stylish plantation furniture and nestled four hundred feet high on a forested slope called "Big Hill." There were fifteen spacious cabanas arrayed around the crown overlooking twenty miles of carpeted rainforest that ran to the Maya Mountains due west. There was also a tram that took passengers and gear five minutes downslope to the boats docked on the Río Grande. From there, it was just twenty minutes downriver to the bay, and then out into the flats and cayes known for some of the best saltwater fishing in the world.

El Pescador Punta Gorda is all about fishing, and expert anglers have begun to pick up the scent: while the waters here are certainly productive when it comes to Tarpon and Bonefish and Snook, it may be, more importantly, the best place in the world to try for Permit. Permit is why they come here; it's supposed to be the most coveted of all the saltwater game fish since it's hard to seduce, difficult to hook, and fights like hell once you get one on. But in the flats of Punta Negra, Wild Cane Caye, and Snake Caye they can be found in large numbers; if you are a good fly fisherman and can cast accurately into the wind, you have a good chance of nailing one.

You're not going to put one on your wall, though, because the rules here demand "catch and release," and

Slaty-tailed Trogon (48), El Pescador Punta Gorda Lodge, Belize, 2003

Gray-throated Chat (49), El Pescador Punta Gorda Lodge, Belize, 2003

those inclined to treble hooks and Velveeta cheese need not apply. Manager Jim Scott has even established a celebratory ritual: if you catch your Permit, a flag is hoisted, there's a Permit pin for your hat, and you're even allowed a glass of special Louis XIII cognac at a dinner ceremony to acknowledge your achievement. Catching a Permit here is a big deal.

But there were no pins pinned or flags flown to celebrate the Agami Heron; the birds simply weren't there. The year before, as many as eighty nests had been observed in the mouth of the Río Mojo south of the lodge, but the colony must have moved somewhere farther down the coast for the new season. There were no birds to be found at all. It was a big disappointment.

There were nevertheless plenty of other birds to see and photograph at this marvelous location, and we came away with keeper shots of the Slaty-tailed Trogon (no. 48) and the fetching Gray-throated Chat (no. 49). El Pescador Punta Gorda will likely become a popular birding destination when more of the rich, surrounding habitat is made accessible. The facilities and food here are first class.

Our last "Mayan" destination was Honduras, and we gave it a shot in December 2003 simply as a long-weekend experiment as opposed to some first leg of a new, exotic adventure. We wanted to sample Honduras for two reasons. First, we had never been there; we had skipped over this lush country many times to cover the more celebrated habitats of Costa Rica,

Keel-billed Motmot (50), The Lodge at Pico Bonito, Honduras, 2003

Golden-hooded Tanager (51), The Lodge at Pico Bonito, Honduras, 2003

Panama, Guatemala, and Belize. We were curious. Second, we had recently heard of a new ecotourism facility, the Lodge at Pico Bonito (O), which had opened three years earlier near La Ceiba in the northern part of the country. It was supposed to be nice.

Honduras is a country about the size of Tennessee and twice the size of Costa Rica, but whereas the landscape of Costa Rica has been substantially decimated for agriculture, with only about 15 percent of its acreage still green and protected, Honduras is 65 percent mountainous and 40 percent forested, and it has over 700 varieties of birds. But perhaps because it has only one endemic, the Honduran Emerald, the big birding companies have yet to include it in their Neotropical programs. Perhaps they should. The lodge's two hun-

dred acres of property include a lush ridge that thrusts partway up to the 8,000-foot Pico Bonito, the jewel of the Nombre de Dios mountains and carries over 250 species of birds. The ridge itself actually divides the watersheds of the Corinto and Coloradito rivers on their separate runs down the mountain to the sea.

Even on the grounds by the pool we saw aracaris and toucans, orioles and tityras. Our cabana, no. 18, also had its mascots: oropendolas continually squawking in the cashew trees above the room; a nifty, wintering Hooded Warbler energetically feeding throughout the day in the low shrubs near the steps; and a pair of Blue-crowned Motmots that romantically hooted to one another not ten feet from our veranda in the early morning and late afternoon.

Vermiculated Screech-Owl (52), The Lodge at Pico Bonito, Honduras, 2003

But the property at the Lodge at Pico Bonito also boasts several stunners, and Vera and I had lined up the best birding guide in Honduras to help us sort them out. His name was Robert Gallardo, and he was raised and educated in southern California before moving to Honduras with the Peace Corps eleven years ago to set up a butterfly breeding program on the "Mosquito Coast." Since then he has become a renowned birding guide as well as an expert in orchids and butterflies. We wanted him to find for us the Yellow-eared Toucanet, which was known to work occasionally down low in the forests during the winter; the Lovely Cotinga, which dazzles regularly from some high trees near the river; and, finally, the elusive and much-coveted Keel-billed Motmot (no. 50), which was presumably found here with relative ease.

Although we missed on the cotinga and the toucanet, we successfully photographed the motmot up on the high ridge both mornings we went after him. This area of Honduras may well be the best spot in Mesoamerica to try for this bird since it is spotty throughout much of its limited range. Our short trip was also highlighted with photographs of the Golden-hooded Tanager (no. 51) feeding in a mountain apple tree at the base of the ridge as well as a Vermiculated Screech-Owl (no. 52) day-roosting in a cut-over cocoa plot down the road near the front gate.

But the Lodge at Pico Bonito isn't just about the birds. The beauty of the setting is breathtaking, the facilities first-rate. The grounds are stuffed with flowering and fruiting trees, the white plumes of three different waterfalls cascading down the lush, green mountain can be savored from cane-backed deck chairs on an elegant veranda of polished Honduran pine. There is even a butterfly farm and serpentarium just a five-minute walk from the pool. On the grounds themselves, Vera and I continually remarked that we had never encountered so many different species of butterflies—they seemed to be all over the place, many of which we had never seen before. The big Owl Butterfly was the most impressive.

Our cabana was nestled privately in a wooded grove and was well appointed and spacious, with dueling ceiling fans and yet a third above the hammock on our private veranda outside. Fully deserving of its designation as one of the Small Luxury Hotels of the World, and with excellent food and excellent service, it was clearly the best place in which Vera and I had stayed in all the Neotropics. When it came to accommodations, we ranked it number one. And it turned out to be a comfortable and upscale way to wind up our adventure in this marvelous part of the world. A little icing on the cake.

Venezuela Revisited

AFTER AN ABSENCE of almost five years from the Neotropics since that first Belize/Tikal run in 1994, Vera and I returned in January 1999 to rekindle a rainforest romance that had been allowed to grow dormant. We also wanted to figure out whether our fascination with Neotropical birds was deep enough to sustain what we estimated to be another four years or so of exploration and photography to complete another book. Admittedly we wouldn't be starting from scratch, as we had accumulated enough product from 1987 to 1994 to provide us with a reasonable base of experiences and photographs from which to build.

But at the time, having just completed one project in the form of *Chasing Warblers,* we weren't all that sure we wanted to commit our holidays and our pocketbook to another. This trip was to be a test case to determine if this rainforest adventure was still stimulating, a second honeymoon, if you will, to see if the relationship still had heat. We decided to begin slow and easy—no camp-outs, no deep Amazon treks—and settled on revisiting Venezuela and the marvelous Henri Pittier National Park (I), where we had harvested such success back in 1990. In addition we planned to explore for the first time some tropical forests of the Venezuelan Andes in the western part of the country.

To do this, we hired a young field ornithologist from Caracas named David Ascanio to guide us, as he had been recommended by Victor Emanuel for his knowledge of Venezuelan birds in particular. And so it was that in early 1999 the three of us took off from Caracas heading west to spend a week recharging our Neotropical batteries.

Blue-winged Mountain-Tanager (53), Henri Pittier National Park, Venezuela, 1999

We found Henri Pittier much as we had remembered it, and spent most of the first couple of days simply hanging out on the balcony of the Rancho Grande Biological Research Station. It was here on our last visit where we had been covered up with foraging mixed-species flocks and had come away with some of our most exciting product. It was good again. The same birds were back, the sparkle undiminished. Of the tanagers, we ran across all of the usual suspects from Golden Tanager, to Speckled Tanager, to Bay-headed Tanager, to Beryl-spangled Tanager, plus one of the most magnificent of them all and our runaway favorite of this lustrous family—the glorious Blue-winged Mountain-Tanager (no. 53). And after many attempts at this stunning bird over several days, as they blew up the mountainside on foraging runs in

packs of threes and fours and lit in the trees off the balcony, Vera finally captured for us this exceptional prize. This mountain-tanager is an absolutely gorgeous bird, and the colored plates of most field guides simply don't do it justice.

During the late morning of that first day, we jumped a family of White-tipped Quetzals, feeding in the trees behind the station, and moments later were pleased to find and photograph the Handsome Fruiteater (no. 54), an attractive cotinga endemic to this particular forest. Soon thereafter, there was a delightful Orange-bellied Euphonia (no. 55), a Russet-backed Oropendola (no. 56), and a Red-crowned Woodpecker (no. 57), all netted in trees off the top balcony. And, finally, a nifty Cinnamon Flycatcher (no. 58), taken in the early afternoon on an exposed

Handsome Fruiteater (54), Henri Pittier National Park, Venezuela, 1999

Orange-bellied Euphonia (55), Henri Pittier National Park, Venezuela, 1999

Russet-backed Oropendola (56), Henri Pittier National Park, Venezuela, 1999

Red-crowned Woodpecker (57), Henri Pittier National Park, Venezuela, 1999

Cinnamon Flycatcher (58), Henri Pittier National Park, Venezuela, 1999

Long-tailed Sylph (59), Henri Pittier National Park, Venezuela, 1999

pipe running off the back wall. It was one of the most productive days we had ever had, and once again the Río Grande balcony proved to be exceptional.

Our second day got off to an unusual start with the tentative approach of three young Venezuelan boys carrying in their cupped hands the motionless form of the Long-tailed Sylph (no. 59), a brilliant cloud-forest hummingbird with a gloriously long and colorful tail. They held it out to Vera in the form of an offering, a prize they had come upon but considered too precious to keep, or else as a gesture to assure that they would not in some way be blamed for the damaged body they now surrendered. The bird must have hit a window pane of the station and was lying stunned and still when they came upon it. Vera gently took the sylph and inserted its beak in a nearby hummingbird feeder to coax it to take nourishment in order to counterattack its likely dehydration. The bird's eyes remained closed, but its heart was beating faintly, and occasionally its tail feathers would give a slight twitch. By and by it began to drink, and then with purpose. Soon it fluttered up from Vera's hand to a thin branch near the balcony, permitting one rushed but manageable shot—then this elegant creature was away and gone. It was one of those moments!

In the afternoon of that same day we took the Choroni Road out of Maracay to the sea, a beautifully winding stretch that climbs to 5,000 feet, then slithers all the way to the coast. It has rich primary forest on both sides running up and down the mountain at the higher elevations as well as impressive bamboo stands that form shading canopies as the road crosses the Tamaire River near the sea. The Choroni Road is officially double-laned but is aggressively dominated by the municipal buses out of Maracay. Piloted by young macho males running high on adrenaline and testosterone, the buses barrel full throttle down the mountain with horns blasting away to warn all others to get out of their way. They want the whole road for themselves; not surprisingly, that's usually what they get.

We ended up mid-morning at the foot of the mountain at the Museo Cadafe, a somewhat modest tribute to a failed effort in the 1920s to dam the Tamaire River. Behind the museum, however, a hand-rail bridge crosses the river to a path that winds for a mile and a half through an impressive stretch of successional forest dominated by small cocoa plots and large stands of cashew trees.

We had worked about three-quarters of the trail, looking forward to breaking along the river for our customary lunch of cheese sandwiches and asparagus—sometimes sprinkled with Trinidad pepper—when we spotted several Gray-headed Tanagers bouncing back and forth across the trail some twenty

Wire-tailed Manakin (60), Henri Pittier National Park, Venezuela, 1999

feet ahead of us. Highly unusual! An army antswarm was likely on the move. It was indeed a small swarm, no more than fifteen yards wide, but it was driving the insects—mostly crickets, it seemed—onto the path right in front of us. We saw jacamars and woodcreepers and antshrikes. But what made the event memorable was the startling number of Gray-headed Tanagers in attendance—we counted twelve. We would never again see that many birds of the same species at an antswarm.

Though we were not successful with any of the birds at the swarm, on our way back to the Museo Cadafe we struck gold! Vera and I spotted the prized male Wire-tailed Manakin (no. 60) fifty yards away down a wooded ravine, sliding back and forth on a bare, horizontal branch, hopping a bit as he did so. This is a glorious and much-coveted little bird of the dry Venezuelan forests, in striking color combinations of red and yellow and black, punctuated by a stark, white eye that often makes the bird look artificial, like a small wind-up toy.

We cautiously circled the area where the bird was performing and crawled up the ravine slope and down the other side for a closer view. When he flew off to feed, we moved in closer to the display area to await his return. He flew back into the branch only once fifteen minutes later, wiggled a bit, then turned to face us. We fired and got the picture. Then he flew off for good and we had no second chance.

Later that day we headed for the Venezuelan Andes and spent the night in the town of Barquisimeto on the edge of a large expanse of dry scrub and desert lowlands several hours away from the foothills of the Andes themselves. Barquisimeto is the home of the *cuatro,* or four-string guitar, and many young males here spend their youth taking music lessons, as well as practicing football (soccer), as a stepping-stone to adulthood.

The next morning at dawn we drifted west of town to explore the scrub thickets and cactus forests of the area. One peculiarity of this scruffy country-side was that the occupants of the little shanties dotting the foothills here had developed a conspicuous preference for pink toilet paper—unintentionally contributing nesting materials for the birds that had also made this habitat their home. The landscape here was oddly pocked with splotches of pink, like small outcroppings of mimosa blossoms unevenly dispersed among the cactus and thorn trees, giving this modest patch of terrain a festive touch.

Late that morning we took off for a five-hour ride to the town of Bocono and then climbed up to the Guaramacal National Park, one of the most important of all the Andean parks. The road up and down the mountain was rock-rough and suited only for vehicles that could withstand the constant pounding on brakes and transmissions and suspensions. Interestingly enough, of the twenty-four different vehicles we saw over the two days we were on this mountain, all but two were Toyota Land Cruisers, some thirty years old and still going strong. We were told that most American models here usually become lame within eighteen months and have to be put down.

Our entire visit on the mountain was exhilarating as we awoke energized to crisp blue mornings of forty degrees and worked the trails all day looking for colorful birds to photograph. We saw a variety of stunners here, including the Green-and-black Fruiteater, the Andean Guan, and another Chestnut-crowned Antpitta—but our experiences were all marked by exceptional opportunities and numerous near misses. Though we were able to maneuver amazingly close to a number of our targeted birds, things for whatever reason just didn't seem to click, and we came away scoreless time and again.

We then moved on through Barinas to climb to

Spectacled Owl (61), near Bocono, Venezuela, 1999

9,000 feet for a much-needed action break at the Hotel Los Frailes, a charming former monastery up high in the *páramo* where we feasted on rainbow trout and relaxed for a day preparatory to a final push before returning home. The nights were especially memorable—crystal clear and flawless, and loaded with a sky full of stars, which would have been fully wasted over the bright lights of Caracas but were now reaching their full potential on this dark Andean slope.

A day later we came down from the *páramo* through elfin forests to the San Isidro Tunnel road one hour south of the hotel. After a forty-five minute walk down its main trail, we came to a steep-descending path through almost impenetrable foliage to the edge of a slope—and the display lek of the Andean Cock-of-the-rock, one of the most famous of Neotro-

pical birds. This was our target, the main reason we were here in the Andes.

The show they stage is fascinating. For starters, these grouse-size birds are a bright orange, and there were four of them scattered high up. They squawked and groaned, preened and fluttered, jumped up and down while stretching their necks in a downward thrusting and swaying motion that was a regular and oft-repeated element of their routine. However, it immediately started to rain, and we were forced to leave before making any attempt at photography. Yet we weren't overly discouraged since we had allocated all of the next day to go after these colorful birds.

The following morning as we hiked into the lek site, fast-moving dark clouds began to cover us up, lightening ripped the sky apart, and once again it started to shower. We stood stoically for three straight hours waiting for it to quit. But no sooner had the rain let up than a giant tidal wave of dark clouds billowed up through the valley with blinding speed and enveloped us in a wet fog for another four hours—we were finally forced to throw in the towel. We hadn't fired a shot in five days. This was a major disappointment, another promising opportunity foreclosed, because we were to leave for Caracas the next morning, and we knew it was unlikely that we would ever get back this way again.

Our latest failure punctuated the ongoing challenges and frustrations of Neotropical photography—of equipment failures, rained-out mornings, and brush-blocked shots. Put into perspective, however, these setbacks and misses are no different in scope than obstacles faced by others with demanding pursuits of their own—with disaster eager to strike at the bat of an eye. Like competitive golfers plagued by crooked key putts on the finishing holes. Or big-

game hunters shut out when their quarry spooks at the very last moment. Or sports fishermen with snapped lines and thrown hooks and nightmares laced with memories of record big fish lost. It's all part of the game, whatever game it happens to be.

We had no way of knowing at the time that only a year later we would meet the brilliant and far more elusive Guianan Cock-of-the-rock in some lush, humid forest on the opposite side of the country, and a year after that, the Andean Cock-of-the-rock itself in an astonishing lek in a cloud forest in southern Peru. But although we were impressed with the Venezuelan Andes and the delightful birds we encountered there, we were disappointed over our failure to post any wins. And we were only partially consoled when, the next morning early, we photographed a Spectacled Owl (no. 61) in a wooded stream bed near Bocono (P) shortly before our flight back to Caracas, then on to Dallas and home.

The Lipstick Bird

$\mathcal{V}$ERA AND I HAD KNOWN for some time that if we had any pretensions of producing a representative sampler of important Neotropical birdlife, we had to get to Brazil. And although we were fired up for the adventure, the country was so large and daunting, with so many diverse habitats to choose from, that it was hard to figure out just where to begin. In size alone, Brazil blankets half of the continent of South America and equals the combined area of all the lower forty-eight states in the U.S.

We initially considered the lush Amazon Basin of the north, which drains the largest river in the world, as well as the seasonal wetlands of the Pantanal in the southwest, which rivals Africa's Okavango Delta—both habitats renowned for the variety and importance of their birdlife. But we finally settled on what was the oldest piece of preserved forest in Brazil: a fog-shrouded, montane cloud forest at an elevation of 3,000 feet called the Itatiaia National Park (Q). It was only two and a half hours from Rio de Janeiro and was supposed to be both Ted Parker's and Phoebe Snetsinger's favorite forest in the Neotropics—for us, that carried weight.

Vera and I checked into a charming, family-owned inn, the Hotel Do Ype, with individual chalets and good food in preparation for combing the mountainside for those glamorous birds endemic to southeastern Brazil. This particular mountain ecosystem is also known for its ancient boulders and rock formations, which bulge oddly and impressively from the green forest floor. Many tourists visit this region simply to check out this geological curiosity.

Our room was romantically positioned on the lee side of the mountain with a beautiful view of the valley below, but it was a steep climb up from the main dining area, itself a steep climb up from the road below that connected to all the forest trails. This meant that each time we hiked out of the forest to return to the hotel for meals or a rest, we ended our little outing—no matter how long or exhausting it might have been—with a fifteen-minute, thirty-degree climb carrying heavy camera gear. That was our finishing lap, and we dreaded it every single time. And though it was the only negative in a week of exceptional positives, it was a nagging one, and one that didn't seem to get any better as the week wore along. We even wished for reserve transportation of some sort for no other reason than to take us up to our room at the end of a hard day. And one afternoon late, we even paid three U.S. dollars to a local farmer for a hitched ride on his tractor up the hill. It was a delightful transaction, a triumph of the easy way over the hard way, and another sneaky little win for self-indulgence over grit.

Another unusual feature of the Hotel Do Ype was that no employee or family member or anyone else on the grounds spoke one word of English. Portuguese was of course the official language, with Spanish a faded second, and the only English words we heard during most of the week we were there came ironically from the hotel radio, where the local station of choice banged out exclusively American songs.

Unfortunately, my broken, border-town Spanish represented a pathetically inadequate bridge to Portuguese, and this rendered simple directions, explanations, and permissions confused and incomplete at times. It all started at 7:15 the first morning when, after specific arrangements had been secured at the hotel, we took written authorization with us to the guardhouse of a government park at the entrance to a wonderful stretch of mountain habitat called the "Jeep Trail." Why this trail needed a guard in the first place was itself a mystery since the only things of apparent value were the celebrated birds of the surrounding forest.

But the guardhouse had a guard, and one with that peculiar, official smirk we found not uncommon to uniformed personnel in Neotropical countries. After a series of discussions with his superior by phone, and with the gloating self-satisfaction of petty power, he puffed up and denied our written permission for entry. No explanation was attempted, not even in Portuguese, nor did there appear any opening to charm him with a "favor" to look the other way. So we had to turn back, at least for the time being. But rather than try to clear up the "misunderstanding" later in the day, the sidekick and I simply returned the next morning at 6:45, well before the guard had arrived for duty, and proceeded briskly up the trail, where we enjoyed a full morning of birding. While on the mountain, we were able to run down a variety of species new to us, but unfortunately not the rare Black-and-gold Cotinga, for which the "Jeep Trail" is particularly well known, though we did hear its mournful whistle once high up in the canopy.

Coming off the trail several hours later, we smiled and waved at the guard, who smiled and waved back. It seemed we had somehow cracked the code of Brazilian park-system bureaucracy, and it went more or less like this: avoid asking entry permission of anyone uniformed—it only gives some official the opportunity to exert his influence and deny it. Just get to the gate early when the coast is clear, and go on in. When leaving, smile your most winning smile and wave. Minor officials here seem perfectly comfortable with this arrangement, since their job description deals exclusively with denying entry, but is presumably silent on what to do with friendly gate-crashers waving on the way out.

Rufous-capped Spinetail (62), Itatiaia National Park, Brazil, 1999

Later that first morning we negotiated an easy but productive trail through some secondary forest that connected our hotel with the much larger and more commercial Hotel Simon, located a mile down the mountain. Along the way we used a recorder to tape the songs of several birds and would then play them back to coax the birds out of the thick brush for a closer look. In this manner we were able to capture some photographs of the Rufous-capped Spinetail (no. 62), an attractive member of the ovenbird family, as well an aggressively curious Ferruginous Antbird.

On the grounds of the Hotel Simon itself is a caretaker's house with a small yard overrun with hummingbird feeders, and it was here over several days, and among the numerous flower beds that dominated the property, that we were able to capture records of some of the stunning and endemic hummingbirds of southeastern Brazil. Our favorite was the Black Jacobin (no. 63). And even though we also had several opportunities at the staggering Frilled Coquette, exclusively working the stands of some small purple flowers that dotted the grounds, we simply weren't pleased with the softly focused product. We remembered, however, that the equally stunning Tufted Coquette of Trinidad had likewise been partial to small purple flowers.

We spent most mornings of the following days hiking up and down Tres Picos trail, which begins its ascent not five minutes from the grounds of the Hotel Simon. The trail climbs steeply through a mixed forest of primary and secondary growth, rich in bromeliads and bamboo and crisscrossed by clear streams along the way. The Tres Picos trail also boasted attractive arrays of purple and pink flowers lining the sides of its early stretches and was smothered by crowds of ancient trees running up to the "three peaks" at the top, making its whole package particularly compelling. Plus, in a week of working this trail from top to bottom, we saw few other hikers, but lots of colorful new birds—always a winning combination.

We met Surucua Trogons and Spot-billed Toucanets, Red-breasted Toucans and a pair of Rufous-capped Motmots, making their nest in a hole in

Black Jacobin (63), Itatiaia National Park, Brazil, 1999

Dusty-legged Guan (64), Itatiaia National Park, Brazil, 1999

the red clay bank that lined the road below our hotel. For photographs, we continued to pick up a bird here and there, including the Dusky-legged Guan (no. 64), a striking Ferruginous Pygmy-Owl (no. 65) in the trees up a hill not far from our room, and a female Blue Dacnis (no. 66) in some fruiting shrubs off one of the main trails running down from the lodge.

But our biggest success of the trip involved a bird we had admired from afar several times earlier on the Tres Picos trail—the Saffron Toucanet (no. 67). It's a uniquely mustard-colored member of the toucan family, endemic to the forests of southeastern Brazil,

with bright red markings running down the upper part of its beak and through the eye like smartly applied lipstick.

We first saw it in the trees running down the steep path from the hotel, though it was far too high up for us to even consider a shot. But just when we were about to say good-bye and move on, the bird suddenly dropped to the ground in pursuit of some prey we couldn't see, behind a small bush not thirty feet from where we were standing. The good news here was that it couldn't see us, either, thus permitting the sidekick to quickly tiptoe closer to it for a point-

Ferruginous Pygmy-Owl (65), Itatiaia National Park, Brazil, 1999

Blue Dacnis (66), Itatiaia National Park, Brazil, 1999

blank shot when the bird next showed itself. She got set, and then seconds later the colorful toucanet jumped to an angular branch not five feet off the ground and just fifteen feet away. It was perfect, and she nailed it—and then she named it. It would be "The Lipstick Bird." It was a great shot—so good, in fact, that we consider it one of our best.

But I also had a win, and it came on the last morning of our stay. I had returned alone to the Tres Picos trail to climb high in pursuit of the endemic and wonderful Blue Manakin (known previously as the Swallow-tailed Manakin), which Vera and I had heard before calling at a lek thirty yards or so off the trail. It is a stunning bird with a black face, red cap, and powder-blue body; and its call is one of the characteristic sounds of the local woods. I quietly maneuvered back into the forest where the birds were sporadically mewing and churring, and sat frozen on the

ground until the birds settled down. Several males were moving about, but I stayed still and waited.

After about twenty minutes, the situation changed radically as a female suddenly darted to a branch only a few feet above my head and sat. And then here came the males, four of them, and they positioned themselves on a branch several feet off the ground and an astonishing three feet away from where I was sitting. There they aggressively ignited their "cartwheel" routine—point blank, right in my face—making growling, mechanical sounds in unison. It was a group display designed to impress and win over the female, although the dominant alpha male would be the only one rewarded for his team's success. Only he would get the girl. Those fortunate enough to witness a Blue Manakin display come away dazzled by the routine, as well as amused by the bizarre implications of feverish team courtship, yet unrequited love for all but one.

Saffron Toucanet (67), Itatiaia National Park, Brazil, 1999

Blue Manakin (68), Itatiaia National Park, Brazil, 1999

The males were so thoroughly riveted to their own performance that they were oblivious to my presence, and though the show went on for no more than a minute, its image would last a lifetime. At twenty feet, the whole thing would merely have been incredible; at three feet, it became otherworldly. The birds then flew off to a more private part of the woods, and though I couldn't manage any shot of the group action, I did snap a solo male Blue Manakin (no. 68) some five minutes later to memorialize this bizarre encounter.

On the last day Vera and I were in Brazil, we hooked up with two of V.E.N.T.'s key tour leaders, Kevin Zimmer and Andrew Whittaker, who had been working southeastern Brazil over the previous week and were now winding up their own birding tour at Itatiaia. These two know more about Brazilian birds than anyone in the world and have recently agreed to collaborate on a new field guide on the birds of Brazil. It was fun to compare notes with two such experienced professionals, and both these guys seemed sufficiently impressed with our Saffron Toucanet and Blue Manakin wins to pump us up a little; Vera and I certainly motored on about them enough. However, it's possible they were being too polite to indicate otherwise. I thought I saw Kevin roll his eyes once, but then again, I couldn't be sure.

Canopy Queen

IN EARLY 2000, Vera and I took stock as to where we were headed with our Neotropical bird project and what would be required to take it to term. So we made a list of those birds that we considered "essential" to capture and those "core" countries that we still wanted to explore. We were admittedly defining our own terms.

The birds we earmarked as remaining priorities—a few a bit wistfully, I admit—looked essentially like this: the Harpy Eagle, the Resplendent Quetzal, the Hyacinth Macaw, the Capuchinbird, both the Guianan and Andean Cocks-of-the-rock, either the Toucan Barbet or the Versicolored Barbet, the Bare-necked Umbrellabird, the Three-wattled Bellbird, the White-plumed Antbird, and finally either the Spangled or Blue Cotinga. Translated, this meant finding and photographing the largest and fiercest eagle in the world, the grandest of all the trogons, one of the most splendid New World barbets, the planet's largest macaw, its niftiest antbird, and six of the most remarkable cotingas. A tall order, but that about covered it. If we were able to photograph these targeted birds, adding them to what we had already accumulated, we felt we would have a respectable sampler of the special birds of the Neotropical forests. Others, of course, would have their own compulsories and favorites, but for Vera and me, this would have to do.

As far as mandatory habitats and countries left to visit, the Manu National Park of southern Peru, the Mindo and Tandayapa valleys of the western Andes of Ecuador, and the Pantanal of southwestern Brazil rounded out our top priorities. Perhaps even the wild and woolly jungles of Bolivia and Suriname, but we weren't sure. All four represented extremely important areas, with stunning and unique birdlife. We had even flirted from time to time with a trip to Colombia, which holds 10 percent of the planet's biodiversity and hosts more species of birds, amphibians, and orchids than any other country in the world. But it also hosts more kidnappings than any other country, and we knew we weren't ever going to get comfortable with that kind of risk. Even Steve Hilty, who co-authored the much-acclaimed *A Guide to the Birds of Colombia*, told us he hadn't been back since 1986. But while Colombia can claim 1,800 resident birds, it doesn't have so many charismatic, endemic ones— stunners that can be found only in Colombia. Of course, the Multicolored Tanager and the Saffron-headed Parrot are found there, but we concluded we could, as they say, learn to live without them. As for our targeted birds, Vera and I were going to be able to run them down in those countries contiguous to Colombia (Panama, Ecuador, Venezuela, Peru, or Brazil) and consequently didn't need to go to Colombia at all. So we didn't.

But Vera and I also knew we had to radically change our photographic style and approach to this business if we were ever going to succeed. We now had to focus exclusively on our "hit list." We could no longer squander our time nonchalantly patrolling forest trails, snap-shooting whatever flew across. We determined that our first order of business required a return to eastern Venezuela to take a run at three big ones: the Harpy Eagle, the Guianan Cock-of-the-rock, and the Capuchinbird, which is that bizarre cotinga locally named the "Calfbird" because, among its other peculiar habits, it moos like a cow.

And to get this done, we had determined that David Ascanio was our man. David is arguably the best field ornithologist living in Venezuela today, and Vera and I had been pleased with our experience with

him the year before in the Coastal Cordillera and the western Andes. In addition to his birding knowledge, we were particularly impressed with David's sense of organization and his emphasis on safety, which was going to become increasingly more important with some of the fresh and dicey challenges we had up our sleeve.

We met in Puerto Ordaz, a medium-size town in eastern Venezuela where the black-water Caroni River collides with the white waters of the mighty Orinoco as it slices its own way across Venezuela on a 1,600-mile run to the Atlantic. This big and important river drains the ancient Guianan Shield on its flow eastward, and we were headed to its delta in the Río Grande Forest Reserve (G) to try to find the most majestic and sought-after bird of the Neotropics—the celebrated Harpy Eagle. This area was known to have one of the highest densities of nesting Harpy Eagles in the Neotropics, and David's scouts had reported seeing one at work rebuilding a nest there a few weeks before. So in mid-March 2000, we drove to the small community of El Palmar, only a couple of hours away from the nest site.

Our local guide that next morning, Vicente, was to be our constant companion for the following three days, and he proved of value right away. On our first hike into where a local farmer had presumably sighted the big bird, we had our first mini-thrill of the trip, as we jumped back from a four-foot Fer-de-lance right on the path itself, poised to strike. Vicente, in the lead, fortunately saw the viper first and quickly cautioned us back from it. Rather than kill it, we decided to coax the snake back into the woods, but the unappreciative reptile got confused, charged, and made lunging strikes at us several times until it finally got itself reoriented and slithered away into the brush. David declared that in his fifteen years of guiding, he had seen only one other Fer-de-lance before, which substanti-

Black-collared Hawk (69), Río Grande Forest Reserve, Venezuela, 2000

Long-tailed Hermit (70), Río Grande Forest Reserve, Venezuela, 2000

ated what we had always heard—that these snakes are not easy to locate in the field.

As for the Harpy, we were encouraged by reports that there had been fresh activity at the nest site, and as we got closer to the nest tree, we had a confirming thrill as we heard the Harpy's "unmistakable" cries. We took off on a dead run to at least get some glimpse of this great eagle before it flew off. And we did see the bird—but it wasn't a Harpy. What we had heard were the similar whistling cries of a Black-faced Hawk, which is an impressive bird in its own right, but a Harpy Eagle it's not.

And the Harpy was not to be. In three days we struck out. It simply didn't come. Of the three birds we had targeted for the chase, we were now zero for one. We did, however, back into a keeper shot of a Black-collared Hawk (no. 69) fishing in a nearby ox-bow as well as a Long-tailed Hermit (no. 70), a fiercely territorial forest hummingbird prone to challenge all intruders—whatever their size. After we fired a shot as it rested nearby, it fluttered in front of each of us, one at a time, until finally it gave a little squeak and zipped off for good.

After we had reconciled ourselves to the fact that the Harpy had eluded us, we took off on the second leg of our adventure, heading south in pursuit of the Guianan Cock-of-the-rock and the Capuchinbird. Several hours out of El Palmar we hit the town of El Dorado, crossing the Río Cayune and the marvelous old iron bridge built by France at the time of the Eiffel Tower and then sold with much flourish to Venezuela. Although it has long since been abandoned to traffic, the bridge still serves today as a minor tourist attraction and a continuing source of national pride. However, it seems that Venezuela never paid France for the bridge, and now after all these years, France has decided that if it can't get paid, it wants its bridge back. Venezuela has agreed to make a "gift" of the bridge if France will bear the cost of dismantling and transport, and although serious delegations have been formed to discuss the matter, we're told that progress is slow.

South of the Cayune, the landscape quickly changes from dry forest to humid forest to wet forest, and at times the foliage becomes so aggressively pervasive that it actually leaks out onto the road, attacking it from both sides. Without the steady traffic to beat back the invading brush, the encroaching forest would have overtaken the highway in no time at all. From the El Dorado Bridge to La Escalera (R), the gateway to the Gran Sabana, is sixty miles of some of the most productive forests in Venezuela, and we were headed to a point fifty miles south of the bridge to the dysfunctional little town of Las Claritas, where we had stopped for water and sausage ten years earlier on our desperate dash across the Gran Sabana with "The Beekeeper" and "Hatchet Tongue."

This time around we were here to rendezvous with "The Ice Cream Man." His real name is Henry Cleve, and he owns and manages—along with his wife, Magaly, and his daughter, Selva—what was then the only decent place to stay within a hundred miles of Las Claritas. His establishment is called Barquilla de Fresa (Spanish for "strawberry ice cream cone") and was the name of a counterculture arts and crafts shop Henry owned in Caracas before he moved to Las Claritas to look for gold.

Henry failed as a gold miner, and then he went into the aquarium business, supplying the trade with exotic fish he would take from the local rivers. That is, until the mining activity polluted the waters, and another business went down the tubes. It was about

that time that Ted Parker, who was exploring the area looking for new birds and new habitat, talked Henry into putting him up for the night. Since then, a real ecotourism business has come to life, and Henry's home has become ground zero for all birders who migrate through this region. There are manicured lawns and fruiting trees, and the little home is bathed in family charm. Henry even raises poodles on the side for sale. The Cayenne Jays nest in the trees by the bedroom windows, the brilliant Crimson Topaz can be seen on many spring mornings at the feeders, and Channel-billed Toucans blow into the tall trees bordering the yard each night to roost. "The Ice Cream Man" said he even saw a Harpy Eagle from his kitchen window the year before.

Barquilla de Fresa was to be our home for five nights, and what made our stay all the more remarkable was its proximity to the played-out little mining community of Las Claritas, a shantytown of defeated expectations pocked with cur dogs and slatterns, knife fighters and drunks, and representing a raw slice of humanity at its least inspiring. Some of the local sports here even carried pistols, we're told, reminiscent of the old Wild West days. But they didn't bother us since we were nightly cocooned behind high fences and locked gates, not far from the productive forests and home of the stunning Guianan Cock-of-the-rock.

David knew exactly where to find the bird, and the next morning we clawed our way up a thickly wooded hill in a remote tract of forest to the backside of a large bare-faced escarpment split with narrow rock crevices where the females were nesting. Since it had rained heavily the night before and was even misting slightly that morning, the climb was slippery and treacherous, and we used a rope most of the way to inch up the steep hillside, tree by tree, until we were high above the lek area itself. There were dangerous holes in between the rocks and tree roots, covered over and camouflaged by fallen leaves, and serving as hidden and troublesome traps for careless steps. We had several close calls, and once I fell through with one leg up to my thigh, but fortunately avoided spraining a knee in the process, although it did ache angrily for a couple of days.

We must have waited for over an hour for some action to unfold, sitting quietly under our umbrellas in the soft rain, shielded from the swarms of mosquitoes that hovered around us by the netting we had draped over our heads and the camouflaged cotton gloves we had wisely thought to bring along. I was positioned at the bottom of one steep hill and my sidekick was stationed on the other side, higher up on a separate rock formation where she was able to see one of the females on her ledge nest. Yet the little brown bird was so perfectly blended into the surroundings that Vera didn't even notice her until she actually moved once.

But we were after the colorful males and finally heard a couple moving into the immediate vicinity with a series of cawing squawks that sounded like an awkward cross between a mad crow and a large, loud cat. These birds were absolutely gorgeous, a light sherbet-orange with a striking fan-shaped crest, outlined in black, that splits to cover each side of its beak. Although both of the cocks-of-the-rock are about the size of a small chicken, the Guianan Cock-of-the-rock of the eastern regions is a bit smaller and a far lighter shade of orange than the Andean Cock-of-the-rock of the west. It also has a more tightly compressed and flattened crest as well as silky barbed fringes sprouting from its lower back.

After motionlessly watching several of the males drift in and out of the trees over the next hour, a handsome male finally came to perch on a vertical sapling about fifty feet from where I was crouched. This was obviously the bird's preening perch, because

that's where he stayed for as long as we were together. And though I managed a couple of shots of him before he finally flew off for the day, they were only marginal and didn't make the cut. It was nevertheless a satisfying wildlife experience—here in a cathedral of lush vegetation, face to face with one of its high priests, who was staring back at us with some curiosity perhaps, but mostly, I suspect, in brooding resentment over our impertinent penetration of his lair. It then started to rain hard, the reflective moment passed, and we urgently roped our way back down the hill and out onto the trail. It would rain hard through the night, and off and on for twelve hours after that, and there would be no more opportunities with this splendid cotinga. We were zero for two.

We awoke at five o'clock the next morning to a driving rain, but rallied anyway, and when the rain briefly stopped, we took our car out on the road to look for new habitat to work later in the day. The three of us were the first ones out that morning, climbing La Escalera aimlessly as we explored the landscape, sipping our coffee as we rode. We had been driving for no more than twenty minutes when we spotted it lying motionless in the middle of the road. We glided to a halt and got out. It was a giant snake—the largest viper in the world. It was a Bushmaster!

It was alive, but it seemed perfectly content to lie there motionless and absorb the heat from the asphalt after so many hours of cold rain. It was about seven feet long and as thick as a grown man's biceps. It had a large viper head with a black line through the eye and a rich caramel body with inverted black triangles spanning its length. It also had a primeval-looking black ridge running along the length of its back. We tried to coax the snake off the road before someone came along and tried to run over it, but big Bushmasters are at the top of their own food chain and aren't easily motivated to do what they don't want to do.

Ruddy Tody-Flycatcher (71), La Escalera, Eastern Venezuela, 2000

They are also so deadly that they are obsessively feared by the natives of the Neotropics, and yet so rarely encountered—since they are limited in number and don't move around much—that even many locals have never seen one. But if one of these snakes tags you, it can be bad. A couple of years earlier, a Belgian birder in Peru had lost his leg, and nearly his life, when a big one took him high and hard above the knee. It was speculated by some who were there that the big snake was most likely protecting her nest, as the Bushmaster is the only viper in the world that lays eggs as opposed to giving live birth.

After throwing some sticks, and even some water,

on the snake to get its attention and move it on off to safety, the large serpent finally began to crawl ever so slowly across the road—just as a truckload of uni-formed government personnel pulled to a stop to see what was going on. On spotting the giant reptile, they immediately became hysterical, jumping up and down and threatening to kill the snake but far too scared to get close enough to do anything about it. This resulted in a lot of hand waving and cursing and spitting, re-quiring David to calm them down—much as one would overstimulated small children with night-mares—while at the same time affording Vera and me the opportunity to drive the big guy into the bush.

And when it finally reached the safety of the tangle at forest's edge, the snake's demeanor changed in a flash as it wheeled to face us in a strike position so swift and menacing that it froze us in our tracks. The government guys broke and ran. Then the big viper dropped down, uncoiled, and silently slipped from sight into the undergrowth. It had made its point.

To many, a snake of such proportions would quite naturally provoke a large measure of abhorrence and fear. Vera and I were certainly brought up that way in Texas, where rattlesnakes were a permanent part of our landscape, and we were inoculated early on against charity toward creatures that were venomous and crawled. This despite the fact that documented bites were not all that common and were disproportionally weighted toward young rural males ("good old boys" in training) pumped up on alcohol, flush with bravado, and intent on screwing around with them. Much in the manner of the drunken redneck's classical last words: "watch this."

But to the three of us that particular morning, there radiated a sinister majesty from the giant serpent—by its remarkable coloring and sheer size alone—that awed rather than repelled. It was the King of the Vipers, and it sent chills racing through each of us as if being spellbound by a wickedly black tornado that was passing ever so slightly out of harm's way.

And of course it was the luckiest snake in Venezuela in that the three of us happened to be the ones to find it out there on the road that morning, and not our government friends or any one else traveling along who would have surely tried to run it over. And also that our leader happened to be a unique Venezuelan male who felt an almost religious passion that all natural creatures should be protected, one who was not compelled by some macho duty to kill it and then proudly nail its skin to the wall.

After our little snake episode, and somewhat anti-climactically, we stopped in a small clearing for lunch, and Vera brought home a nice photograph of the diminutive, four-inch Ruddy Tody-Flycatcher (no. 71)—a cinnamon-colored beauty endemic to the tepui area of eastern Venezuela. And no sooner had we succeeded with the Tody than, not fifty feet away a bit deeper in the forest, we heard a long, eerie, single-note whistle. Vera and I had never heard it before, which meant absolutely nothing. David hadn't either, which had significance. We taped its song and played it back, and after five minutes, the bird came creeping tentatively into view and began circling us cautiously through the brush. It was a Tepui Tinamou, a bird so rare that fewer than twenty people in the world had ever seen one, and its voice—we would learn later—had never before been recorded until now. David was ecstatic with this rare find, a shiny and florid feather in his professional cap, and we were only disappointed that the light conditions on the dark forest floor negated any photographic support to enhance his accomplishment. It was nevertheless a great win for David, and Vera and I were excited for him.

That same night we met Marco Cayuso from Caracas, a professional mountain climber who described himself simply as "The Vertical Man." His career was climbing, his office high up. He performed rescue operations in the Himalayas, directed high-scaffolding repair work on tall buildings, and even lifted TV crews into the rainforest canopy to film White-faced Monkeys for the Discovery Channel. And he was here in Las Claritas, as absurdly eccentric as it was now beginning to feel, to hoist Vera and me eighty feet up in a giant laurel tree so that we could photograph a strange bird that mooed like a cow. It was the Capuchinbird, an exotic cotinga that stays high in the trees of the Guianan Shield forests, and the only way to get a decent shot of the bird—which has seldom been accomplished—is simply to get up there topside where it hangs out.

Months earlier, we had directed David—who had some impressive climbing experience of his own—to interview several candidates for this canopy assignment on our behalf, and now Marco was our man. It was now time to go over the ground rules and gear so that there would be no fumbling or anxious hesitation the next morning. We examined harnesses and ropes, pulleys and snaps, and came away reasonably comfortable that we had the best equipment and the best man for the job. We had been clear with David about our guide requirements from the start. We were not interested in some self-absorbed macho type, but rather a climber who was focused on technique, process, and safety. And we also wanted someone who could operate well under pressure if things, for whatever reason, didn't go so well.

Vera and I were not in this for the adrenaline rush, or for the therapy of a cheap thrill, though some of our friends back home remained vaguely unsettled by our behavior, since their own risk tolerances stayed sensibly confined to the intermediate slopes at Vail or marginally unbalanced investment portfolios or both. There were those who thought we were crazy to attempt such a thing, many more who politely yawned with their mouth closed, and finally a few who said—with varying degrees of insincerity—that they wished they could come along, too. But for Vera and me this was simply a means to an end—to try to capture photographs of the illusive Capuchinbird.

The day before we had sought out the best archer in a small Pemón Indian village nearby to shoot a monofilament line over a top limb of a strategically located tree—rope to follow—so that Marco could climb it and set up the equipment before Vera and I attempted our own ascent. As we approached the lek that first morning, it sounded like a West Texas feedlot: the Capuchinbird males high up in the lek tree were all "mooing" to attract the attention of the females that had flown in early to judge their performances. The tree we were to climb was about thirty yards from the lek tree itself, and it was our strategy to catch the males coming and going to it, or perhaps perching in the area immediately around it. That was, at least, the plan, but there was no play book to guide us and we had no idea whether it would work. The birds might simply be put off by our presence and stay away.

Marco was already high up in the tree when we arrived, ready to begin, his support straps securely fastened. We attached our own waist harnesses and gave Marco the signal to use his foot pulleys to hoist us by rope to the top. The limbs from which we were to operate were as high as an eight-story building, but on that first morning they looked to be several times taller than that. We were seriously questioning just what in the hell we had gotten ourselves into, as it was becoming increasingly apparent that we were on the verge of doing a decidedly foolish thing. Both Vera and I had butterflies, and my own courage was thinning by the minute, unnerved by that unique brand of anxiety that often seems to accompany poor personal judgment. But we both sucked it up and made it to the top without incident—or, as it turned out, all that much difficulty.

It would later be acknowledged around the kitchen table that my sidekick's first ascent to the top had been purposeful and confident, suggesting a seasoned climber, which she is not. She would be christened "The Canopy Queen," and that's how everyone would refer to her for the balance of our stay in Venezuela. My climb, on the other hand, was judged to be comparatively graceless—resembling, some said, a swaying sack of wheat being lifted aboard a cargo ship. I wouldn't be christened anything at all.

However, once Vera and I reached the top limbs of our tree, we then had to get comfortable with the play of our harnesses and the awkward straddling of limbs no thicker than telephone poles. Then there was the tricky business of trying to secure our camera equipment so we wouldn't lose key pieces in a death spiral to the ground. What should have been a routine operation of replacing film, securing flashes, and changing out lenses became a tense and anxious effort, and we were constantly fearful of dropping something important at a critical moment. Why we didn't is still a wonder. And just when we were becoming gradually at ease with all this—and as if to somehow warn us against undue optimism—it started to rain, forcing Vera and me to desperately unleash our umbrellas in an effort to keep our equipment dry. This while sky-high at eighty feet, riding small limbs. None of it was fun.

But by and by we began to get a handle on the equipment issue while at the same time gaining some modicum of confidence in the integrity of our support systems. And, of course, Marco was right there. He was our safety net, and Vera and I would come to develop a keen respect for his temperament and his skills. In many respects Marco was an unlikely-looking hero. He had fawn eyes and a ponytail, a Venezuelan of Spanish descent with the soft, comfortable manner of a young priest. But he was weasel quick and wiry strong, and he stayed focused on each of his movements and each piece of his equipment—all of the time. Two years later, Marco would be a member of the first Venezuelan mountain-climbing team to successfully scale Mount Everest.

"The Vertical Man" was important to us not only for our safety, but also for our peace of mind. Our adventure would not be productive at all if we felt compelled to maintain a constant death grip on our support ropes, fearful of maneuvering around for good shooting advantage. But after we had gotten over our early-stage jitters and had managed to work through some of the difficulties of organizing ourselves, Vera and I took time to marvel at the fact that we were literally where no one had ever been before—in the canopy of this giant laurel tree in an eastern Venezuelan rainforest, surrounded by bizarre birds that were all mooing like cows. It was surreal.

We would come to discover over the next several days that the Calfbird males spent their time on various lookout perches mooing and preening within sight of each other, scattered around a lek perimeter from seventy-five to hundred feet away from where we were straddling our own limbs. This was much too far away for our flashes to be effective, and the only chance we had to photograph one of these birds was when a female would fly into the area, provoking the males to chase her. And of course she wanted to be chased, for she had come to the lek area specifically to select the best male for mating. It was her choice to make. All the males could do was moo loudly, look good, and hope—since only one or two would be chosen for breeding, the others consigned to bachelorhood, isolated and anxiously randy out on some lonely limb.

The most action we experienced, however, by several orders of magnitude, came at dawn when all the males seemed to congregate at the lek site in response to several females who regularly cruised the neighborhood at that time. The mooing then was of trail-herd proportions. Although it was too dark then for suitable photography, we did have a few birds actually fly in and land within several yards of where we were sit-

Capuchinbird (72), La Escalera, Eastern Venezuela, 2000

ting. We suspect few people have ever been that close to a Capuchinbird in the wild before, but then again, the list is probably not long of those who ever wanted to be. During the heat of the day there was little going on, but toward late afternoon things would pick up. That's when a few females would tend to return, there would be a short flurry, and then it would be over. We spent several days operating within this pattern of activity.

The object of our affection, the Capuchinbird, is one of the strangest birds of the forest. It has a bare, blue-gray face shaped like that of a vulture, with bulging black eyes, and a body with shades of brown and cinnamon feathering that gives it the appearance of some small forest mammal. It is by all measures an ugly bird. But it's a fascinating one. Two orange-

colored tail coverts pop up and flash like orange tail-lights every time a male leans over in one of his frozen-stare poses directed at a rival. And when he does his moo-call (actually a three-part *grrr-aaa-oooo*), he sits perfectly erect, a cowl of feathers hooding the back of his head like the Capuchin monks for which he is named. The bird will then lean backward, slightly beyond the vertical, expand his transparent diaphragm, and let loose. It's quite a bird.

All told, Vera and I spent about twenty hours in the tree over three days straddling our respective limbs, with little product to show for our efforts, though we did encounter several other canopy birds ranging from a Purple-throated Fruitcrow, to a distant Spangled Cotinga, to a covey of Paradise Tanagers. On the last afternoon we were there, we coaxed

David to climb up in the canopy with us for one last attempt at this bizarre cotinga. And as it has happened to Vera and me so many times before, we got lucky just as time was running out. For as we were losing the last bit of good light on this very last day, and as an ugly black storm was moving rapidly our way from the east, a female blew into the area—and chaos erupted. There was mooing and screaming, and males were bouncing through the trees like startled grasshoppers. And one stopped just long enough at thirty feet away to stare down a rival, so Vera was able to squeeze off a do-or-die shot to memorialize our rendezvous with the Capuchinbird (no. 72). Then he flew off, the sun disappeared, and it started to rain.

But we all did high fives, for it was a special kind of experience that none of us would ever forget. And later that evening, after a hot shower and full meal, we all sat around the kitchen table and savored each detail of our extraordinary day—"The Ice Cream Man," David, "The Canopy Queen," "The Vertical Man," and I—and celebrated well into the night, some sipping cokes, others becoming marginally damaged on Polar Bear beer and White Cat wine.

Bellbirds

*F*OR AS LONG AS VERA AND I had been exploring the Neotropics, one of the birds that had intrigued us most was the engagingly strange Three-wattled Bellbird, a resident of the cloud forests of Monteverde in Costa Rica. In fact, the first sound we heard that first afternoon we drove up the mountain back in 1987 was its loud "bonk" call that can carry half a mile. This bird is an immensely handsome cotinga, about the size of a small pigeon, with a rich chestnut body offset by a pure white neck and head. But its most distinguishing feature, the one for which it is named, is a set of three black wattles, each about three inches long, growing from the base of the upper mandible and each side of its gape. Although we would, over the years, encounter several other species of bellbirds, like the Bare-throated Bellbird in Brazil and the Bearded Bellbird of Venezuela, our allegiance always ran back to the one in Costa Rica that flaunted the three black worms.

I had cavalierly dismissed the bird as being photographically improbable, perhaps not even necessary for our project, but Vera saw it differently: she was adamant that we have it, and it was my job to figure out how. Although we knew that we could locate the birds without much difficulty, these cotingas call from high up in the canopy and are extremely difficult to get near. We had no strategy at all for determining how to get close enough to one for a photograph. That is, until one day in early January 2000, when we came across an article about a research project in Costa Rica. Spearheaded by a local biologist named Debra Derrosier Hamilton, the project focused on the vertical migration habits of these bellbirds.

After a few phone calls we located Hamilton in Monteverde, where she lived, and without hesitation, she directed us to the Pacific coast of Costa Rica and the small resort of La Ensenada on the Gulf of Nicoya. Here, she said, the bellbirds wintered in January and February of each year and tended at that time to feed at lower levels on mistletoe and other fruiting trees. So two weeks later we took off for La Ensenada to rendezvous with Debra and her two research associates and friends, Pedro Bosque and Victorino Molina, as well as Debra's four-month-old son, whom she carried with her in a backpack wherever she went and whom everyone affectionately called "Baby Bonk."

Hamilton, a short, energetic blonde in her mid-thirties, raised in New England and educated at Duke University, was co-leading this British Embassy–funded bellbird project along with the renowned Monteverde biologist George Powell. Their research was shedding harsh light on the bellbirds' annual migration patterns, which did not—as had long been assumed—revolve exclusively around a change in seasons. Instead, migration was driven by the ripening of wild avocados in various altitudinal zones over their range. These wild avocados are not the hand-grenade-size, domestic issue that made guacamole famous, but rather a local variety no larger than a small pecan. Since the wild avocado represents up to 80 percent of the bird's diet, the dependable availability of this fruit is critical to its health.

When the birds finish nesting in Monteverde in July, they come down the Pacific side of the mountain several hundred feet where they will feed until the fruit is gone in October. It's in this mid-elevation zone, with its better soil, where the greatest danger now lies, because the land has been significantly cut over for coffee and other agricultural priorities like cattle and bananas. This has meant eliminating the wild avocado trees to make room for such crops, and only a few suitable patches now remain here on the Pacific slope to service the entire mountain population of some 700 bellbirds. In July one might find up to ten bellbirds feeding in one fruiting tree at the same time. This is quite extraordinary—and disturbing. It clearly punctuates the bird's vulnerability, for if something should happen to these remaining trees, the birds might not be able to survive.

They are already in trouble. Their populations have been greatly reduced over the last twenty years, with estimates of decline in the 70 percent range. Michael Fogden told Vera and me that when he arrived in Monteverde in 1978, he recorded up to sixty-five "bonks" a minute from the resident bellbirds calling during the breeding season. Today, he said, he would be lucky to hear ten "bonks" a minute. With time running out for this exceptional cotinga, Hamilton, Powell, the Fogdens, and others are scurrying to find workable solutions. They are building brake corridors to connect viable habitat tracts, they are promoting initiatives to plant new orchards of the wild avocado, and they are trying to raise funds to preserve the few remaining mid-elevation plots. No less than the survival of the mountain bellbirds is at stake.

After spending July–October at these middle elevations on the Pacific slope, these birds will fly all the way over the mountain spine of the country to the Caribbean coast in Nicaragua near the Costa Rican border. After the wild avocado season ends there, they will reverse course and cross back over the same mountain range to the Pacific coast, arriving close to New Year's Eve, where they will hunker down until the second week in February. So it was here on the Pacific coast of Costa Rica at La Ensenada, with its gentle gulf-side charm, that Vera and I made plans to ambush the Three-wattled Bellbird.

La Ensenada Lodge (S) is a twenty-room resort on the Gulf of Nicoya, founded and now run by the Tretti family, who emigrated here from Italy in 1977. Vera and I had a room perfectly positioned for the gulf breezes in the shadow of a giant ebony tree, dined on pasta most evenings, and remarked more than once that this was a convincingly comfortable way to chase cotingas. Rarely had we gone after a bird so imposing in a setting quite so nice.

And we saw one immediately, although we heard it first, as we drove into the small resort. It was perched and calling on a broken branch high in a tall, stand-alone tree off the road. That's one great thing about this bird: it's not some shy skulker darting secretly among the shadows. If it's around, you know it. When not foraging, it may sing on one of its several perches all day long. It will first open its beak so wide that the bottom mandible seems to touch its breast, revealing a cavernous black gape. With a fully open mouth, the male will then begin his three-part call: the first, an extraordinarily piercing, thin whistle, followed by a soft swishing sound, and then decisively capped by the loud "bonk" that washes over the entire area. It's one of the loudest calls of the Neotropical woods.

This particular male was joined by an olive-colored adolescent that looked remarkably like the female except that he had a large knot on his forehead, representing a first-growth wattle. He had come to the adult's perch to begin his training, and it would take him some seven years to reach full mating maturity and legitimately compete with some adult for his throne. He needed the practice. As "the kid" attempted, with awkward inefficiency, to inch up the limb toward the adult, the old bull would leap back over him toward the trunk, cutting him off. Then the bull would edge the youngster way out on the tip of

the broken limb and finally blast him away with one loud "bonk." This was all part of the training.

The male treats the female much the same way, but with predictably different results. After she flies to his visiting perch, having been attracted there by both his song and his overall "studliness," he begins to romance her with his not-so-subtle routine. He first leaps back and forth over her several times to get her full attention, then he fiercely shakes his wattles in her face to make sure she's impressed with his equipment, and finally he screams in her ear. That's the way she seems to like it, and they will proceed to mate. Behavior like this is what makes bellbirds exceptional and endears them to serious birders worldwide.

There were bellbirds at La Ensenada, and we must have seen five different ones over the three days we were there. But we couldn't get close enough to any one of them for a score. They were simply too high up. The shorter fruiting trees near the house wouldn't begin to produce ripe fruit for a couple of weeks, and the bellbirds we did encounter were foraging on mistletoe in an inaccessibly wooded ravine a mile from the compound. They were also continually harassed by bands of White-throated Magpie-Jays, which aggressively patrolled the grounds and bullied the bellbirds away from the compound area whenever they dared enter it.

But this lowland habitat was loaded with other impressive birds. We knocked down photographs of the Black-headed Trogon (no. 73), the Orange-fronted Parakeet (no. 74), and the Spot-breasted Oriole (no. 75); we also chased families of Rufous-naped Wrens as they vigorously worked the shrubs around the cottages. In addition to the land birds of this dry coastal forest, we also jumped waterbirds in a high-saline lagoon on the back side of the property. The lagoon hosted the usual egret and heron

Black-headed Trogon (73), La Ensenada Lodge, Costa Rica, 2001

Spot-breasted Oriole (75), La Ensenada Lodge, Costa Rica, 2001

Orange-fronted Parakeet (74), La Ensenada Lodge, Costa Rica, 2001

Three-wattled Bellbird (76), La Ensenada Lodge, Costa Rica, 2001

suspects, to be sure, but it was also replete with an al-most unbelievable congregation of wintering Blue-winged Teal. Late one afternoon we counted roughly 2,000 of them clustered together, cheek to jowl.

But we struck out with our bellbird, and it took us a full year to organize ourselves to make another run at him. When we did return in February 2001, we found just one lone bellbird and just one ripening olive tree in the entire area. But, as it turned out, that was all we needed. The bellbird was a handsome male that carried the middle of his three wattles draped back over his beak, as the fully mature birds often do, and the olive tree of choice had reached that quintessential stage of ripeness that attracted

him to it every two or three hours throughout the day. And on several of those occasions he would drop down just low enough—to about forty feet, and ad-ditionally clear of blocking foliage—so that we were able to squeeze off a few acceptable shots. Thus, after twice tracking this bird up on the mountain at Monteverde, and twice more down on the coast at La Ensenada, we were finally able to capture the Three-wattled Bellbird (no. 76). The sidekick was pleased, and I was off the hook.

As it turned out, though, our little adventure had an amusing and unsettling side effect on the service staff at La Ensenada, who stayed confused by our be-havior and unsure as to our purpose. This because the one splendid olive tree, so appealing to our star bellbird, just happened to be nestled in the bare-dirt yard of the staff quarters not fifteen feet from the communal washroom. Since Vera and I were obvious friends of the Trettis, and paying guests of the lodge as well, the staff fully expected us to be elegantly sunning ourselves poolside, with cool rum drinks, enjoying the tranquil, blue views of Nicoya Bay. But here we were with floppy hats and camouflaged clothing squatting on stools with camera gear, which to them must have looked industrial in strength. They brought us iced tea from time to time, but were obviously embarrassed by the process and always seemed anxious to scurry back to the normalcy of their kitchen routines.

The yard itself had its obligatory menagerie of dogs and small children and young girls putting out laundry to dry, along with a gaggle of short grandmother types

Three-wattled Bellbird, Monteverde Cloud Forest, Costa Rica, 2001

peeling potatoes in the shadows. They, in turn, were monitored by a three-member troop of Black Howler Monkeys that lolled in the canopy shade throughout the day and made periodic passes at the olive tree themselves. Background music in the form of Spanish melodies, wafting from a small radio inside, gave the entire scene its defining texture. Hardly a typical wildlife experience, especially considering the importance of the quarry, a bird regarded by many to be one of the grandest of the Neotropics.

Although we had finally captured our bellbird down here on the Pacific coast, we had always expected to take him high up on his nesting grounds in the Monteverde Cloud Forest (B). That's where we headed next, several months later in May, to try for another photograph while up on the mountain in pursuit of other targeted birds. This time around, things broke our way from the start. Deep inside the forest, we connected with a handsome male, "bonking" with his mouth fully agape and his three wattles fully extended.

Though the magical woods of Monteverde host creatures that can dazzle you with their beauty, they also ring with sounds and songs that are provocative with their own assault on the senses. In addition to the "bonking" of our bellbird and the ethereal melodies of the Black-faced Solitaire, there is another signature sound from the understory here that weaves its own kind of magic—the "Toledo" call of the Long-tailed Manakin.

This manakin is from that glamorous family that includes the Blue-backed Manakin of Ecuador, the Lance-tailed Manakin of Venezuela, and the Blue Manakin that I had recently photographed in southeastern Brazil. Jet black and sparrow-size, with two long tails that sometimes cross at the end like ice tongs, it also has a powder-blue back and a flat scarlet

cap that make it stunning. But you often hear this bird before you see it, its "Toledo" call first alerting you to its presence. The three-part call, " *To-le-do,*" is actually performed by not one manakin but two— the dominant alpha male and his subordinate beta understudy. The two birds sit high in the tree as they jointly synchronize their call to signal any female in the area that they are available. If she is interested enough to fly in and check them out, they drop to their lek limb with a flash of exuberant spontaneity and perform for her. They would most likely be joined by another understudy male or two to round out the team.

Vera and I found a lek of these birds near the Ecological Farm, a small family preserve uniquely rich with its own wildlife since it sits on the Pacific slope in a fertile transition zone where dry forest morphs into wet. On our first day at the lek we were rained out. On the second day the sidekick went at it alone, and I took off in search of an Emerald Toucanet. No sooner had I left than the action accelerated dramatically as three males dropped down on the horizontal display limb close to the ground and began performing a series of yo-yo leaps, up and down, resembling mechanical toys in high gear. The female darted in to join them and began an excited and enthusiastic wiggle dance of her own.

It was a good show, but there were vines and brush blocking the view into the lek limb. The birds were also extremely skittish, and any movement at all would startle them to flight. Vera concluded that the only way she was going to capture the alpha male was to pre-focus on his favorite landing spot just before he made his final flutter into the lek limb. And as tiring as this approach can be, steadily aiming the camera at one point for long periods of time, she did just that. After an hour of waiting, the little alpha male

Long-tailed Manakin (77), Monteverde Cloud Forest, Costa Rica, 2001

blew into that precise spot, and Vera tagged him. Then forty-five minutes after that, he flew in once more and she had an "insurance shot." It was that second shot that became the "win" with the colorful Long-tailed Manakin (no. 77). It became one of our favorite Neotropical photographs.

We spent the next two days working the Ecological Farm, where we photographed both a Blue-crowned Motmot (no. 78) and a serviceable Emerald Toucanet (no. 79) while also spotting an Eyelash Viper. Colored dark purple with some cinnamon splotches, the snake was curled up like a thin doughnut on a branch hanging out over the trail. If one of the resident guides had not pointed it out to us, we wouldn't have noticed it at all. It had been hanging out at that particular branch for three days or so, leaving each night to hunt and returning each morning. It was the only Eyelash Viper we had ever encountered, though it was far less glamorous than the bright yellow and lime-green ones that we had admired so often in various zoos.

We left early the next morning on a special expedi-

Blue-crowned Motmot (78), Monteverde Cloud Forest, Costa Rica, 2001

tion to the back side of the mountain to look for another of our targeted birds of the forests here: the
Bare-necked Umbrellabird. We met Victorino at four
o'clock about twenty minutes downslope from town,
and strapped ourselves and our gear to the four-
wheeler he had borrowed from his wife. The three of
us then took off to negotiate the steep trail for another thirty minutes to the forest's edge. It had rained
most of the previous day, the trail was a sea of mud,
and traction was a scarce commodity as we slipped
and sledded down the mountainside, holding on for
dear life.

But we had a marvelous dawn view of the big

Arenal Volcano in the distance, surrounded by clus-
ters of low-hanging clouds. We then entered what is
the largest tract of remaining transitional forest left
on the Atlantic slope of Costa Rica, a brooding and
thickly clotted section of woods in which we hoped
to find the Bare-necked Umbrellabird, one of the
largest cotingas in the world.

These umbrellabirds of Costa Rica and western
Panama are imposing—crow-size, jet black, and re-
gal—their big heads covered with a crest that curls
out over the beak like an umbrella, hence the name.
The birds have long, broad wings and a short tail, but
the signature feature of this cotinga—the one that

Emerald Toucanet (79), Monteverde Cloud Forest, Costa Rica, 2001

renders his whole appearance astonishing—is the bare-skinned throat patch resembling a vermilion red apron when relaxed, but which can be inflated to the size of a large tomato when making his booming call to woo the ladies, or in an effort to intimidate competitor males. Hanging from this throat patch like an umbilical cord is a thin, wattled appendage with a little tuft of black feathers at the tip. There is no other bird in the world quite like it.

We knew this to be a promising stretch of forest to find the bird since, in years past, as many as three different males have been reported scattered throughout these woods in what is characterized as an "ex-

ploded lek." However, they are hard to locate, and the only decent picture we had ever seen of one was taken by Michael Fogden nearly fifteen years before. His was outstanding.

As we came down the path that first morning, we heard the bird's low, booming call, which sounded like someone vigorously blowing—in one sustained breath—on a half-empty bottle. Then the call stopped. It became eerily still, and there were no other sounds coming from the forest at all. The reason for this expansive quietness, we would come to learn later, is that this umbrellabird is fiercely territorial and doesn't permit other creatures to share his

Bare-necked Umbrellabird (80), Monteverde Cloud Forest, Costa Rica, 2001

neighborhood. He runs them all off—be they guans, parrots, toucans, or even monkeys. Hence the absence of other wildlife songs or sounds. Thirty seconds later, the big black bird flew over Vera to check her out, but then we saw or heard nothing more for over an hour.

Finally, having grown impatient with the waiting, I simply took off through the tangle of the forest in the general direction where we had first heard the cotinga calling. I was hoping for some sign of a bird some have come to name the "ghost of the forest." I had penetrated the woods for no more than ten minutes when I actually saw him. There he was, sitting on a limb in a tree one hundred and fifty feet away—proudly erect, seemingly aloof, basking in the satisfaction of his own splendor. I went back to get Vera and Victorino, and when we returned, he was still there. Except for short foraging runs every hour or so, the large cotinga would stay on that same perch all morning long. This presented a terrific opportunity for a photograph—except that a fog proceeded to roll in and covered us up for several hours. Then it started to rain steadily, and the rain would continue all through the next morning. We ultimately had to leave empty-handed, and although we were thrilled to have at least been able to observe this great bird, we were nevertheless dispirited over our failure to take advantage of the opportunity.

But the big guy is too special to quit on, so Vera and I returned a year later, in May 2001, to take another shot at him. This time we arranged to make camp at the San Gerardo Field Station, an education and research center for tropical birding administered by the Monteverde Conservation League. The station sits on the Atlantic slope 4,000 feet above sea level and several miles east of the divide from Monteverde. It's a thirty-minute walk from there to where we had located the Bare-necked Umbrellabird the year before. We brought with us a guide, Chico, and a cook, Roberto, to round out our team. We were set.

Although this was another of those situations with no electricity and no hot water, the station itself had charm. Late each afternoon after a full day in the field, we would sit on the second-story porch overlooking a lush green canopy running downslope to the blue Arenal Reservoir, and to the Arenal Volcano, which anchors the reservoir on its south shore. The volcano was usually ringed with clouds, and although we didn't witness any form of eruption, it nevertheless rumbled often and occasionally belched polite plumes of smoke. So with Swallow-tailed Kites strafing the air space in front of us and the sounds of howler monkeys, bellbirds, and antthrushes providing a background chorus, we sipped our drinks and watched the day end. Then the rising moon would crest the volcano top, the fireflies would begin to swarm in large numbers, and night would be upon us. It was in this manner that we spent several pleasant days at San Gerardo, and we had the place entirely to ourselves.

As for the big bird, we finally got him. But it wasn't as easy as we had hoped—his favorite perch was bathed in dark shadows at sixty feet, and he also used it far more infrequently than he had the year before. We were forced to position ourselves strategically in different areas around his perch in order to try to ambush him coming and going on one of his foraging runs.

But what a creature he was! And Vera and I conclude that he ranked right at the top of our short list, along with the Three-wattled Bellbird, in representing the very best that the Neotropics had to offer. He boasted the deep, low whistle that hauntingly resonated through the forest to establish his dominance, he flaunted the black crest covering his beak like an open umbrella, and he flashed the stunning red apron that serves to distinguish him so impressively. And just once, when a competitor male flew into his territory to whistle aggressively back at him, this big cotinga inflated his throat patch to the shape of a hot water bottle, and we came away with a keeper shot of the Bare-necked Umbrellabird (no. 80).

The Blue Cotinga

VERA AND I had not intended to return to Panama. Even though our last trip to the Darien in search of antswarms and antbirds had been a huge success, we had yet to target any other special bird to lure us back. But in June 2000, while making a presentation on warblers at the Academy of Natural Sciences in Philadelphia, Vera and I had a conversation over dinner with Bob Ridgely that changed our mind.

We had been discussing some Neotropical birding trips that we might take together and were particularly intrigued with joining this great ornithologist in southern Ecuador to run down a certain new species of antpitta he had discovered for science there a couple of years before. But at some point our conversation turned to a family of turquoise-blue cotingas and the near impossibility of being able to photograph them. They hang out so high in the canopy that you can never be sure where to find them and thus work close enough to one for a photograph. Then Bob mentioned that he had actually seen one of these exceptional birds, the stunningly iridescent Blue Cotinga, feeding in some cecropia trees close to a new lodge outside of Panama City called the Canopy Tower (T). Several days later we called its owner, Raúl Arias de Para, and made arrangements to visit the lodge at the end of the year, thus reengaging with this marvelous country and its impressive birdlife.

The Canopy Tower is arguably the most unusual facility of its kind in the world. It is located in 50,000 acres of the bird-rich Soberanía National Park, and it's only forty-five minutes by car from the Panama City airport. It was opened in December 1999 to coincide with the implementation of the Carter-Torrijos treaties, which ceded the ownership and operation of the Panama Canal back to Panama. The Canopy Tower is a twelve-room boutique hotel, improbably fashioned from a 40-foot secret radar tower used by the U.S. to monitor Noriega's drug flights out of Colombia prior to Operation Just Cause in 1989. The structure is a four-story hulk of galvanized steel rising through the forest canopy and topped by a fiberglass dome that housed the radar antennae. To spruce it up for the ecotourism trade, the structure was painted a faded aquamarine, with the dome a saffron-mustard color. From the air it looks like a giant yellow golf ball perched on a fat, teal tee.

When we first heard of the Canopy Tower, it all sounded far too contrived to be appealing, and our expectations were not all that high before our first visit. It was hard to imagine how one could inject suitable warmth and comfort into a structure that had at its core all the aesthetic appeal of an aircraft hangar. Vera and I were also skeptical of the wildlife integrity of a rainforest so near a major population center. Would there, in fact, be any interesting bird activity at all?

However, we found the Canopy Tower to be extraordinary and predicted that it would become a hot ecotourism destination in short order. The facility was comfortable and stylish, the food legitimately good. But Vera and I liked it primarily due to the charm of the whole experience. We stayed each night in the Blue Cotinga Suite and awakened each morning to the roar of howler monkeys in the trees just outside our window. We photographed canopy-perching birds from the dining area one floor above and took our nightcaps on the dome topside under a sky full of reverent stars. A sea of green canopy stretched deep to the north, the distant lights of downtown Panama City glistened to the south, and the movement of boats sliding through the canal

could easily be observed due west. We had never stayed in any place remotely like it.

But at the end of the day we tend to measure success by the diversity of the wildlife and the quality of the photographic opportunities. And here it all seemed to work. The habitat of the Soberanía Forest, though principally secondary growth, has been preserved through the years because the canal depends on forests for proper functioning. These humid tropical forests keep the air filled with moisture through the process of transpiration and thereby generate the rainfall that replenishes the Chagres River as it continually feeds the canal about fifty million gallons of fresh water a day to lift each ship about 85 feet above sea level. Since the forests have been preserved, the wildlife here is abundant.

In fact, though many birders visiting Panama still gravitate by habit to the renowned Pipeline Road, Vera and I found the one-mile slice of private path running down Semaphore Hill from the Canopy Tower to the highway below to be even better. It was, in military terms, a "target-rich environment," and one of the most productive stretches of birding habitat we had encountered. Vera and I actually photographed over 35 species of birds, and observed at least three times that many on this path during the few days we were there. Over the years, we're told, nearly 290 different species of birds have been recorded in the area. We were covered up with tanagers and trogons, aracaris and toucans, and benefited from numerous drop-dead views of three different species of motmots: the Broad-billed Motmot, the giant Rufous Motmot, and the ubiquitous Blue-crowned Motmot. By all measures, an extremely good birding experience.

The three signature birds of the Canopy Tower are the Blue Cotinga, the dove-shaped bird of turquoise blue that was the focus of our trip to Panama; the

Chestnut-mandibled Toucan (81), Canopy Tower, Panama, 2001

Great Jacamar (82), Canopy Tower, Panama, 2001

Western Slaty-Antshrike (83), Canopy Tower, Panama, 2001

Masked Tityra; and the Green Shrike-Vireo. But we didn't do well with any of them. We captured only one pathetic photograph of the illusive cotinga feeding a hundred feet away; we saw the tityra well, but the photograph was inadequate; and we had only a few shadowed glimpses of the shrike-vireo, though we heard its persistent three-note song throughout the day, deep beneath a top layer of canopy foliage.

Scoreless with the marquee birds, we were nonetheless successful in photographing others like the Chestnut-mandibled Toucan (no. 81), the Great Jacamar (no. 82), and the Western Slaty-Antshrike (no. 83) on Semaphore Hill, as well as the Violet-bellied Hummingbird (no. 84) at the feeders at the base of the tower. But our biggest success came with the White-whiskered Puffbird (no. 85), a particularly im-

portant win for us since it was the first book-quality picture of one we had taken. Over the four days we were at the Canopy Tower, we saw and photographed three different White-whiskered Puffbirds, the first two being females, but the last, a handsome, cinnamon male with his tell-tale white whiskers impressively on display.

We nearly didn't see him. We were both absorbed with a pair of raucous Collared Aracaris working the midlevels of the canopy when Vera spotted some twitch of movement downslope in a ravine off to our left. And there he was, sitting quietly in a small sapling about ten feet off the ground. Although it was a beautiful, sunny day and the light was reasonably good, the bird was buried in shadows forty feet down the incline.

After taking a few marginal shots for the record, we decided to take on some risk to try for something better. We needed to get closer. But we also knew that attempting to climb down the steep and tangled slope to get nearer the puffbird without startling him would likely fail. So I squatted on the incline and began to scoot on my rear ever so slowly down the slick and muddy slope, sliding and inching my way toward the bird while purposely avoiding any eye contact that might alarm him. And the tactic worked far better than it had any right to as I was able to edge within fifteen feet of him. The puffbird just sat there, slowly and nonchalantly surveying the area for insects, while I began to take my shots. But the sidekick was not to be left out, though she expressed little appetite for sliding through the mud like "some farm animal," as she delicately put it. So she conveniently discovered a back way into the same area, using vines and fallen logs for support, and cleanly worked her way into strike range. In this manner we both netted the White-whiskered Puffbird and came away pleased with the results.

In addition to the birdlife of these forests, Vera and I saw an impressive array of mammals. We jumped red squirrels, howler monkeys, a female sloth and her baby, tamarins, capuchin monkeys, a large tribe of coatis, agoutis, and the odd kinkajou that hung from its prehensile tail each night outside our balcony to eat the banana with which we had bribed him. A Lesser Anteater (*Tamandua*) was even seen close by, though not by us—and they are fun to run across anytime.

The man who made all of this happen at the Canopy Tower is Raúl Arias, an ex-banker and politician-turned-entrepreneur who, despite his twinkling

Violet-bellied Hummingbird (84), Canopy Tower, Panama, 2001

White-whiskered Puffbird (85), Canopy Tower, Panama, 2001

sense of humor, is clearly a man of fierce determination to have wrestled to the ground all of the obstacles he faced in bringing this important project to life. He sees the lodge as the focal point of a nature boom for Panama, and he's on to something here—for while Costa Rica has left every other country in the region biting dust in terms of ecotourism, with its effective marketing, splendid park system, and user-friendly government, the good spots there are still hard to get to (it takes four hours to reach Monteverde from San José). And Costa Rica is becoming so increasingly crowded with tourists during the high season that the wildlife experience has become significantly compromised. For example, in 1987, when Vera and I first went to Monteverde, there were just three hotels and four guides for maybe 10,000 visitors a year. By 2000 there were fifteen hotels, twenty guides, and 50,000 visitors a year. Everything rather neatly times five. Plus a pizza parlor, a butterfly farm, and a discotheque. One wonders if Starbucks and the Gap can be that far behind. Panama, on the other hand, has all of its ecotourism successes ahead of it, and what with more accessible rainforest and more resident species of birds than Costa Rica, Raúl is leading what could well be a competitively successful charge. Plus all the infrastructure in this country is "first-world," compliments of the U.S. government and the U.S. taxpayer.

But the Canopy Tower was only the first. Right on its heels came the recently completed $35 million Gamboa Rainforest Resort along the Chagres River, sponsored by the Smithsonian Tropical Research Institute. Its mission is to combine low-impact adventure tourism with conservation and relevant research. It has aviaries and tropical guides, orchid and butterfly exhibits. But its feel is "commercial," and the facilities seemed specifically designed to court convention business as well as cruise-ship stopovers.

At the lodge Vera and I spent part of each day with Raúl and his wife, Denise, who operates a successful jewelry design business of her own. We hiked the famous Pipeline Road together, visited the Neotropical Raptor Center at Clayton to be briefed on the Harpy Eagle release program there, and began to make plans to visit Smithsonian's research station at Isla Barro Colorado to perhaps find and photograph a Harpy of our own. As a special dividend of our stay, we were joined on New Year's Eve for a morning of birding by former president Jimmy Carter and his wife, Rosalyn, from Plains, Georgia. In addition to being heroes to the Panamanian people for his leadership in returning the canal to Panama, they themselves are enthusiastic birders, both with life lists begun in 1988 that now top 700. They were attracted to the lodge, much as we were, to experience its wonderful birdlife.

Although our trip to the Canopy Tower in early 2001 had been a success, Vera and I knew we had left the big one behind—the gorgeous Blue Cotinga—and we knew we had to return for another try. So in January 2002 we went back to take specific aim at a remote and beautiful bird that at the time had rarely been successfully photographed. We also knew that our only real shot to get one would come during some fruiting-tree situation when the bird would drop from the canopy to feed. And the forest surrounding the Canopy Tower included two female cecropias, which predictably fruit during early January of each year and regularly attract the Blue Cotingas to them when they do. This was our chance, most likely the only one we would ever have.

The year before, one of these trees had been ready and ripe, its seedpods full, but it was also the one farthest from the lodge—over a hundred feet away. Our photograph of the single bird that had come to feed looked like a small blue dot on a large green blanket because our 300m lens, even with a 2x extender, was

Blue Cotinga (86), Canopy Tower, Panama, 2002

woefully inadequate to flatter a 7-inch bird perched that far away. But this year the tree nearest the lodge was also fruiting and, at only sixty feet away, was marginally within our strike zone.

The cotinga usually arrived right after dawn, stayed for about five minutes to feed, then flew off for the day. At least that's what we were told. But on the first two days Vera and I were there, he didn't come at all. On the third day he skipped the morning but drifted in to feed in the afternoon while Vera and I were away in the woods chasing other birds. So it came down to our last day in Panama—Vera and I decided to invest the entire afternoon in a stakeout.

Around five o'clock the big guy fluttered into the back cecropia; the Blue Cotinga had arrived. We were ready. But almost immediately, even before we could square away for our first shot, a Slaty-tailed Trogon blew into the same cecropia and spooked the cotinga away. Then a half a minute after that, a Chestnut-mandibled Toucan slammed into the same tree, spooked the trogon away, and stayed to display and call over the top of the canopy for over five minutes. Then he too left.

But it was now getting late, time was running out, and we would soon be losing critical light. We were once again on the verge of being shut out when suddenly, out of nowhere, here they came—not one but two glorious males, and they began dancing in the nearest cecropia, preparing to feed on the seeds encased in the soft, green tubular pods.

The two birds continued feeding in the tree for fifteen minutes—a lifetime in the wildlife photography business, as this sport more often than not is one of flash opportunities and no second chances. But Vera and I jumped on the one we had and bracketed with as many variations as we could manage. And it worked, for we succeeded with a bird many have admired from afar but few have ever photographed—a bird of such a luminous turquoise blue that, when contrasted with the muted green backdrop of the cecropia's foliage, it exploded on our senses like a firecracker going off in a small church. It simply took our breath away! While there are admittedly other birds in the forest of the Neotropics, like the hummingbirds and tanagers, which are perhaps technically more colorful, there are few whose beauty ever dazzled us more than did this spectacular Blue Cotinga (no. 86) on that fading, soft green afternoon in the steamy lowlands near the Panama Canal.

Blue Cotinga, Canopy Tower, Panama, 2002

Manu

IN LATE AUGUST 2001, Vera and I flew to Cuzco, Peru, preparatory to exploring Manu National Park in the southeastern part of a country shaped much like California but three times its size. We had targeted Peru for some time, for it's a land flush with nearly 1,800 species of birds, second only to Colombia.

High up in the Andes at 11,000 feet, we were charmed by the Incan city of Cuzco with its terra cotta quality, reminiscent of Tuscany, and its narrow streets laced with ancient stone. It was initially inhabited by the powerful Incas toward the end of the tenth century and then conquered and occupied by Francisco Pizarro and the Spaniards in 1543. Vera and I were especially intrigued by the indigenous Andeans, called Quechuas, especially the brightly clothed women who shepherded their llamas and alpacas on the hillsides near popular tourist sites, tactically positioning themselves for photo-for-pay opportunities, and often cradling a baby lamb in their arms for a fetching artistic effect.

The most remarkable of these ancient sites was Sacsayhuaman (pronounced similar to "sexy woman"), a pre-Incan fortification of imposing scale built with massive stones weighing several tons and fitted precisely together like perfectly aligned pieces of a giant jigsaw puzzle. It was difficult to comprehend how even today, with our sophisticated stone-cutting and diesel-driven equipment, modern man could improve much on such an accomplishment.

The next morning early, Vera and I took off in an open-bed truck with our Indian driver, Guillermo, and a field ornithologist and guide from Cuzco, Doris Valencia. While most tourists in Cuzco were migrating north on pilgrimages to Machu Picchu, Vera and I were pointed south down the mountain toward the steamy Amazon Basin. During the high season, as many as 8,000 visitors a week swarm out of Cuzco by train or helicopter or the Inca Trail to Machu Picchu, but fewer than half that number work their way down to Manu over an entire year. We were part of the smaller group, the one seduced by the fantasies of the lowland forests below.

The Andean road we took that first morning from Cuzco descends from 11,000 feet for over 160 miles of switchback, spanning two mountain ranges and several discrete ecological zones, to the Amazonian flats at 600 feet above sea level. It's a stretch that Victor Emanuel regarded as, he once told Vera and me, the "birdiest" road in the world. He also lamented at the time that there was no good way to exploit it since there were no places to stay anywhere along the way. That was in 1993. Today there are several lodges between top and bottom, and we were heading toward the most exceptional of them all, the Cock-of-the-Rocks Lodge, eight hours away down the mountain in a cloud forest zone at 4,500 feet.

To get there, however, you have to "do the road"—which until just recently was so narrow and dangerous that only alternate-day travel was permitted in any one direction. On three days of the week all vehicles went down the mountain, on the other three days they all came up. On Sundays, two-way traffic was permitted, thus creating a free-for-all that made it predictably dangerous to be on the mountain at all. The road from Cuzco today has been modestly widened, thus permitting two-way travel daily, but it's nevertheless advisable to line up an experienced driver to help negotiate it. Although Guillermo had twenty years of working this road under his belt, we were not so comforted to learn that a small van from Cuzco, traveling in our same direction, had slid off the road two days earlier, killing two. The upper stretches of

the road seemed especially tricky and were lined with crops of crosses, painted a baby-blue, memorializing those in times past who had gone off the mountain.

However, it was a beautiful day to travel, the sky was clean and blue. We found the mountain faces to be a patchwork of delicately terraced potato plots worked by the men—it was the local crop of choice in a subsistence economy based on agriculture and cooperative labor—and we were once again dazzled by the brightly clothed women herding their animals, dressed in skirts of hot pink and turquoise and yellow, with layers of equally colorful petticoats. While some wore high-crowned hats peculiar to the region, others wore bonnets that looked like thin lamp shades with little fringes around the rim. These Andean women sparkled against their muted backdrops like spring flowers that had broken through the dark soil of thaw to make their first colorful statements of the season. They dotted the fawn-colored landscape with starbursts of color and made our descent through these upper layers of the mountain especially memorable.

We crossed the large and swift Río Urubamba, which flows north beneath the walls of Machu Picchu, and an hour later, then the Río Paucartambo at a quaint bridged city of the same name that had once been an old and important Incan fortress. We would cross twenty-six streams and rivers before we reached the end of the line at Shintuya.

Six hours out of Cuzco we climbed to the top of a ridge on the Eastern Cordillera of the Andes, and in a stretch of elfin forest bathed in mist, we unceremoniously crossed the entry point to Manu National Park (U), marked simply by a wooden sign with a painted map of the region on it. There were no gates, no guards taking tickets. Then again, this was no ordinary park. When most of us think of parks these days, we imagine swing sets and softball fields and summertime concerts. Or else those broad expanses of the American West choked with convoys of tourist buses and over-populated with New Age gift shops and interpretation centers. Parque Manu was not like this.

To begin with, it is no less than a 4.5-million-acre chunk of unspoiled habitat, about the size of Massachusetts, that buffers the western edge of the Amazon Basin. It embraces an entire ecosystem—from the golden grasslands of the upper Andes down through layers of montane cloud forest at the middle elevations to the flat green carpets of the Amazon Basin below. The area was originally preserved by the Peruvian government in 1968, was designated by UNESCO as the Manu Biosphere Reserve in 1977, and shortly thereafter was honored as a World Heritage Site. The park encompasses the entire watershed of the Río Manu, from its headwaters and the many streams that flow to it down to its confluence with the Río Alto Madre de Dios.

The wildlife it contains is astounding. Manu supports over two hundred species of mammals, more species of birds than North America, and three times as many butterflies as all of Europe. The park is home to Harpy Eagles, Jaguars, and thirteen species of monkey, including both the Emperor Tamarin as well as the smallest on the planet, the Pygmy Marmoset. There are giant anacondas and caiman and otters living in the streams and *cochas* of the Manu lowlands; there are Andean Cocks-of-the-rock and Spectacled Bears in the cloud forests above. All this not in just one country, but one park within one country—in an area so wild that it has never been fully explored. Quite remarkably, even today several Indian tribes of hunter-gatherers live along the headwaters of the Río Manu where they continue to use stone axes and bow and arrows to hunt. They have had little or no expo-sure to civilization, and some are even hostile to outsiders.

When the president of Peru, as part of a publicity tour, helicoptered into the upper Manu one January morning in the mid-1980s, they peppered his "big bird" with six-foot arrows. All the government guys quickly fled, and no one has been back since. Also as recently as the year 2000, a boatload of birders was motoring slowly up the Río Manu when an Indian brave—some say a member of the Yora tribe—shot one of his six-foot arrows, feathered with the primaries of a Cuvier's Toucan, over the bow of the boat as a warning. This was in the park we had just entered.

After a couple of hours, we worked our way down the mountain to a special piece of cloud forest at 4,500 feet—the Cock-of-the-Rocks Lodge. It had been a good trip, with the most memorable bird encountered along the way being the brilliant Scarlet-bellied Mountain-Tanager. But Vera and I had now arrived at what was one of our principal destination points of southern Peru. It was the home to one of the largest known Andean Cock-of-the-rock leks in the world, and it was only a five-minute walk from our lodge. This was the reason we had come to this piece of forest, to photograph this bird.

We had first met the Andean Cock-of-the-rock a couple of years earlier at a four-bird lek in the Andes of Venezuela. But we were rained out the two days we were there and had come away with zero product to show for our efforts. We now had a fresh opportunity because the lek here was only several yards from the road itself and the birds were always on display during breeding season. We also knew we could photograph them, because they had become so recently habituated to people there that we would be able to work suitably close to where they were performing to secure a decent shot. What we didn't know was that the whole experience with this glamorous bird over the next three days would turn out to be quite so stunning and productive.

Early the next morning while it was still dark, Vera and I entered the gated entrance to the lek area where generations of these birds had engaged in their courtship rituals under the protection of the lodge's private ownership. A thin strip of deck was positioned just inside the locked entrance, which was upslope from the main activity. Since we were the only guests at the lodge, the sidekick had received special permission to station herself closer to the action, farther downslope in a one-person blind. She was thus required to work her way down the hill in the dark so that she would be quietly seated before the birds began to drift into the area at first light.

She was able to organize herself without dropping any equipment, or stepping on things that bite, and as the approaching dawn began to permit fractional visibility, she realized she was positioned at absolute eye level to where the action would soon unfold. The alpha male blew in first and began a solo display on a bare horizontal branch about twenty feet away, directly in front of her. Then he gave his signal squawk to kickstart the action. As the morning began to gradually break, more and more birds began to drift into the lek area. Finally, about six thirty, all of the key actors and support players seemed to be in place. There was a total of eight male birds and two female birds in attendance, but Vera's principal focus was riveted on the two males directly in front of her: the alpha male, which seemed to be the loudest and most athletically active of the two, as he repeatedly bowed and dipped his body aggressively forward, and his understudy and main rival, bird B, which was positioned not ten feet away from him. The rest of the males were scattered in pairs around a general area some sixty feet in diameter.

The two brown females stationed themselves close to the alpha male, or else spent their time shuffling back and forth directly on his display limb.

The entire spectacle was loud, colorful, and action-packed. For starters, these birds make a lot of noise, similar to what one would expect from a yard full of screaming, squawking chickens. Secondly, the panorama of color was simply breathtaking—the male cock-of-the-rock is a brilliant red-orange about the size of a bantam hen with a large, fan-shaped crown that all but covers his beak. The bright orange is offset by jet-black wings and an elegant pearl-gray back. There are arguably few big birds in the forests of the world today more handsome than a male cock-of-the-rock, and the two lead birds were right in her face. And though it was still too early to manage acceptable photographs, it became sufficiently lighter by seven o'clock so that the glow from the morning sun, shining upslope through the dark green foliage, created an ambient background of a soft aquamarine to artistically offset these colorful orange cotingas.

All the birds strutted and dipped and jockeyed for position, but the alpha male dominated his key perch and wouldn't be budged from it. When bird B once tried to challenge him on the subject, they went to battle, locking their claws and screaming at each other as they tumbled through the air to the ground. Seconds later they were back in their assigned seats as if nothing had happened, their respective roles once again validated. As for the females, they both wanted the alpha male, and on several occasions one of them would edge up close and peck him several times on the back of the neck, signaling her willingness to mate. But in each instance the male would ignore her invitation, so fully absorbed did he seem to be in his own seduction routine, and presumably indifferent to the result it was designed to achieve. No mating took place while we were there, perhaps because it was too early in the season for him to be sufficiently motivated to commit. Who knows, but it seemed odd.

About a quarter past seven, the birds began to drift away from the lek until finally only the alpha male was left. Then he too gave a final squawk and flew down the mountain to feed. Several of the male birds returned later in the afternoon for a while, but the activity then was anemic compared with that of the morning, and only once did we see a female enter the area. Vera and I would return to this special arena each morning and afternoon for three days, addicted to the colorful wildlife spectacle that unfolded each time before us, shooting roll after roll of film, until we finally decided to call it quits and declare victory. We had finally been successful with this glorious cotinga and

came away with a splendid photograph of the Andean Cock-of-the-rock (no. 87). It filled the frame.

But this cloud forest was not exclusively about the cock-of-the-rock, although admittedly he was the hottest ticket in the neighborhood. There were other birds and creatures here that gave this habitat interest and weight. There were monkeys all over the place, highlighted by a troop of about twenty Brown Capuchins that would swing in to the lodge site every morning about eight o'clock, each lining up to receive its daily allotment of two bananas, generously dispensed by the friendly cook who had been patronizing them for years. Amusingly, however, one young capuchin male was continually bullied away by the alpha male from participating with the others, and the cook had to secretly slip the juvenile his two ba-

Andean Cock-of-the-rock (87), Manu National Park, Peru: Cock-of-the-Rocks Lodge, 2001

Bay-headed Tanager (88), Manu National Park, Peru: Cock-of-the-Rocks Lodge, 2001

nanas when the big male was otherwise preoccupied.

There were also other glamour birds around the lodge and off the road running alongside it. Each morning we jumped such specialties as the Crested Quetzal and the Highland Motmot on the deeply wooded hillsides, and took photographs of the Bay-headed Tanager (no. 88) and the Saffron-crowned Tanager (no. 89) in some stunted trees around the fruit trays at the lodge itself. But the other "star" that we were chasing—second only to the cock-of-the-rock—was the brilliant Versicolored Barbet (no. 90).

We had seen many barbets through the years, all the way from the Amazon to Africa, but to Vera and me, this was our favorite. It was the most striking of them all. And, of course, we desperately wanted to try to photograph it. We went vigorously after this

bird for several days and finally, after many near misses and on our last day in the area, Vera was successful in taking both the male and female together in one frame—quite an impressive feat in its own right since she was shooting a wide-open aperture in low light.

The next morning early, we saddled up and headed down the mountain for a rendezvous with a boat and a captain and the Mother of God River. Driving down to the big river that morning, we passed an unusually beautiful stretch of forest with its trees dripping epiphytes, many forming a bromeliad-laden arch over the clean-moving San Pedro River, to which we were running parallel. We were told that this section of woods was locally recognized for its verdant beauty and misty green hillsides and was called, for reasons never made clear, "the place where you take off your underwear."

The morning was misty and cool and the four of us crawled down the mountain at five miles an hour with all the windows opened wide to absorb the sounds and smells of this marvelous countryside. Background music, in the form of birdsong from the outside and melodic Bolivian folk songs from the car radio inside, gave the morning drive its romantic spin. We saw Scaled Fruiteaters, and Bluish-fronted Jacamars, and Masked Trogons, but all too soon it seemed we had broken through the cloud forest zone and were swiftly descending through the waves of foothills with giant bamboo and fern trees and morning glories smothering both sides of the road.

We reached the lowlands and a string of cocoa plantations before moving through the small community of Atalaya, where during the rainy season we would have ordinarily picked up our boat. But since the river was too shallow at this time of year to permit it, we moved on farther to Shintuya where the road—which had begun back up the mountain at Cuzco—finally peters out on the banks of the upper Mother of God River. After spending the night at the small and rustic Pantiacolla Lodge, we stepped into our boat the next morning and headed for the Manu Wildlife Center—six and a half hours and another seventy miles downstream.

Our boat was a sleek, long-nosed, 35-foot vessel of cedar that was canopied and painted in alternate colors of red and gray. Our bowman was a teenage Machiguenga from the upper Manu, our captain was of Piro stock from Cuzco, and our power, at 55 horses, was provided by Evinrude out of Waukegan, Illinois. And it took all three working together to effectively manage the river. The captain, with fifteen

Saffron-crowned Tanager (89), Manu National Park, Peru: Cock-of-the-Rocks Lodge, 2001

Versicolored Barbet (90), Manu National Park, Peru: Cock-of-the-Rocks Lodge, 2001

years of experience, was continually challenged to negotiate the shoals, sandbars, shallows, and tree falls
on a stretch of water that always seemed to be creating new islands and carving out new channels. The
bowman's job was to steer around and pole us
through impediments and trouble, and on several occasions double U-turns were the order of the day just
to maneuver around the knots of obstacles barring
our route.

Although the river is a bit tricky during the dry
season and threateningly shallow in many spots, it
becomes even more challenging during the rainy season because of imposing tree falls mining the river
and the heavy volume of water rushing its course.
When the river was first discovered by the Spaniards
in the mid-1500s, it was during the height of the
rainy season when the river was on a violent ram-
page. The first Spaniard who saw it then issued an
oath of such awe and alarm, "Madre de Dios," or
"Mother of God," that the oath itself became the
name of the river. The sidekick and I mused that if
today one of our earthy Texan friends discovered that
same raging river, his own exclamation of astonishment would render its future name something decidedly colorful—but nonetheless partly scatological.

But the Mother of God River is impressive. It is
copious and cool, a swift-moving flow of aqua blue
and olive, rocky-shored and high-banked, with a
wooded backdrop of cane and balsa that is occasionally sprinkled with bright coral trees. We also saw an
abundance of wildlife on the river, and although we
looked hard for the ever-elusive Jaguar, which is spotted occasionally on its banks, we were not successful.
We did observe a few pairs of Blue-and-yellow Macaws, wheeling flocks of Sand-colored Nighthawks,
and several species of herons fishing gracefully in the
shallows. But what impressed Vera and me most

about this swift mountain river was its absence of any
visible scars inflicted by civilization. During the six
and a half hours we spent on this pristine waterway,
we saw less than half a dozen small craft, and the
only other evidence of people—the trash so abundant on all the rivers Vera and I had been on before—was one piece of blue plastic about the size of a
dinner plate and later another piece, slightly larger.
That was it—two spots of debris in nearly seven
hours on a public stretch of river. We found that
impressive.

Compared with other Andean rivers, the Alto
Madre de Dios is soft and tame, not only from the
force of its flow but by the circumstances of its history. Not so far away as the toucan flies, on the western side of Cuzco near the mountain village of San
Juan, and several miles before its confluence with the
Río Livitaca, the raging and uncivilized Río
Apurimac, with its ravenous velocity, has carved a
canyon gorge some 10,000 feet deep. It's one of the
deepest river gorges in the world. It was also in this
mysterious and inaccessible stretch of wild canyon
that the ferocious movement known as Sendero
Luminoso, or Shining Path, was born in the early
1980s. It became one of the most ruthless guerrilla
organizations in South America and reached its peak
in the early 1990s, then was snuffed out for the most
part by the middle of the decade.

After about four hours on the Alto Madre de Dios,
our swift, clean river merged with the slow-moving,
milk-coffee-colored Río Manu. This stretch of the
Madre de Dios—having dropped the "Alto"—eventually embraces the Río Tambopata at the southern tip
of Peru to then slice through the upper part of Bolivia
on its journey across Brazil to mate with the Amazon a
little bit east of Manaus. After absorbing the Río
Manu, the Río Madre de Dios changes character to

become visibly more turgid while its banks become consistently sandier and less studded with rocks.

We stopped to take our lunch at the small trading post of Boca Manu, and then motored on for another couple of hours to our final destination, the Manu Wildlife Center, a relatively new lodge managed by the influential conservation group Selva Sur. The accommodations consisted of twelve private, thatched bungalows, no electricity, but all the amenities and services to accommodate the eccentric habits of serious naturalists: breakfast at four thirty in the morning as well as coffee, tea, and crackers around the clock for those who either rise early or do their exploring at night to look for owls, snakes, tapirs, and such. Despite the absence of electricity, there was good food and hot showers. Quite frankly, these amenities—along with dry wool socks—are all one really needs at the end of a tough day in the field to resume feeling marginally civilized.

Vera and I found the surrounding forest to be especially rich. It was primary forest, with its concomitant open understory, sliced with a grid system of seven miles of wide, clean trails. But what made this habitat special was the enormous diversity of its wildlife and the sheer volume of creatures it seemed to contain. The prime indicators of an unhunted primary forest were all present, and there are not many accessible places in the Neotropics today where that is still the case. There were thirteen species of monkey in residence as well as all of the big birds—the first creatures that usually fall to the hands of hunters—like the curassows and screamers, the trumpeters and guans. And there were also three different species of colorful macaws continually strafing us from above.

As has been acknowledged, a Neotropical forest can be uncannily silent for hours at a time and tends to give up its treasures reluctantly and infrequently.

But not here. There was nonstop action; there was an incessant chirring. Vera and I couldn't patrol a trail for more than ten minutes without encountering something of interest—an army antswarm here, some monkeys swinging through the trees over there. A nunbird is spotted to the left, a motmot flushes to the right. There goes a male curassow; here comes a mixed-species flock. We were constantly covered up with wildlife even though we weren't working all that hard to find it. We were out to photograph a few targeted birds and, in the process, were stumbling across all of this wonderful stuff.

In addition to the productivity of the extensive trail system here, we found other exceptional venues for observing the wildlife. There was a salt lick deep in the forest that nightly drew the Lowland Tapir, attracted to the lick for certain minerals that help its digestion. A blind had been constructed to permit discreet viewing. Similarly, thirty minutes downriver was a clay lick, or *ccolpa,* where macaws and parrots would congregate during the dry season for mineral nourishment, and a floating blind had also been strategically positioned there to permit comfortable and close observation. We visited bamboo islands with their endemic specialists, two different canopy towers in emergent ceibas to view creatures that inhabited the treetops, and finally several oxbow lakes with their herons and screamers and oversized otters.

The Manu Wildlife Center was quite a place. We were to stay a week; we could easily have stayed two or three. In an area encompassing the Manu airstrip two hours north on the river, down to the clay lick thirty minutes south of the lodge, over 650 different species of birds have been recorded—more varieties than are found in all but a handful of countries of the world. In 1986, up at Cocha Cashu in Manu National Park, Ted Parker and another expert birder,

Scott Robinson, established a one-day record of sighting 331 species of birds.

The first afternoon we arrived at the lodge, we hiked to a thick stand of bamboo near the river to look for some birds called "bamboo specialists"—namely, those birds which feed on insects that are partial to bamboo. We jumped six different species that afternoon, including the Manu Antbird and the rare Rufous-fronted Antthrush.

It was also here that Vera and I began to fully appreciate Doris's skills as a guide. Quite frankly, the guide situation had concerned us from the outset since we didn't know much about her, and we questioned how much legitimate field experience she could have possibly acquired over the few years she had actually been at it. A native of Cuzco, about twenty-five, with blue-black hair worn to her waist (sensibly knotted up under her hat for the field), she told us on the first day we met that she had been birding for only four years. Vera and I were afraid that we had been dealt a green and bright-eyed rookie, a Steve Hilty wannabe, desperate for some on-the-job training. But we needn't have worried. As the week wore on, it became clear that Doris could identify by both sight and sound absolutely every bird in the woods, and she navigated her surroundings with an intensity that allowed her to pick up on all the little things. During our time together, there was not one question we lobbed her way—on birds, or mammals, or flora, or even the natural history of the area—that she didn't field with ease and substance. And though she had never really been far out of southern Peru, she knew southern Peru cold. Steve Hilty told us later that he considered her one of the best birding guides in the entire country.

Doris was also sensitive to the fact that once Vera and I had zeroed in on a targeted bird, we needed some space to concentrate on the photography part and didn't want someone hanging on us every minute. And she didn't. She was there when we needed her, she went scouting for other opportunities when we didn't. She was feminine with a tomboy attitude, a woman excelling in a macho male's world.

The first night we were at the center, Vera and I were working by candlelight on our notes for the day when my hat—which was resting on the table—moved. Something was definitely underneath it, and in a rainforest setting that's not necessarily a good thing. We stepped back from the table and slowly lifted the hat with an extended coat hanger, only to find a small gray mouse chewing enthusiastically on the hat's lining—with a tail that seemed at least three times as long as its body. We eased the hat back down and, fifteen minutes later, looked again. It was still there, fearless, still chewing. The little gray visitor would make nightly appearances around the bungalow for the balance of our stay, although we began to set out some crackers as a substitute for the hat, which seemed to work fine.

Later that night we were awakened at three o'clock by the mournful calls of the Undulated Tinamou, at four by the roars of Red Howler Monkeys, and finally at five by the low hoots of the resident motmots. We were up by then, ready to venture downriver to one of the most storied wildlife spectacles of the Neotropics—the macaw *ccolpa*. This *ccolpa* is a large, red-clay bank that attracts parrots and macaws by the hundreds during the dry season to counteract some of the toxins that unripened fruit carry that time of year. We boarded a floating blind about 75 feet from the bank, well before the initial battalion of birds was expected to drift in at six thirty. The Blue-headed Parrots came first; we counted over 200. Then about 80 Mealy Amazons (no. 91) arrived, followed soon after by over

100 Red-and-green Macaws (no. 92). There are probably few other places on the planet where so many big, colorful birds are magnetized to one spot, and this clay lick at Manu is truly a world-class production.

The next day we again rose early to glide due west down the river just as the moon was setting directly in front of us in a manner that gave the appearance of being swallowed by the river itself. We were motoring downstream to a section of forest that hosted a canopy platform in a giant ceiba overlooking a floodplain with algae-choked sloughs and serpentine

creeks. The ceiba here was said to be several hundred years old, by some estimates the largest tree in the Manu. It had luxuriant, golden green leaves high at the top as well as massive horizontal limbs as thick as Volkswagens spreading out from the tree's trunk three-quarters of the way up.

This was a canopy experience markedly different from our one in eastern Venezuela a couple of years before when we were stalking the Capuchinbird. Vera and I had spent several days riding small limbs of a large tree while tethered to the trunk by harnesses.

Mealy Amazon (91), Manu National Park, Peru: Manu Wildlife Center, 2001

Red-and-green Macaw (92), Manu National Park, Peru: Manu Wildlife Center, 2001

This time around, though significantly higher up, we were able to gracefully patrol a wooden platform with the stability and comfort of a ship deck. And one that presented an exceptional viewing opportunity. We observed Plumbeous Kites nesting in our own tree, as well as Gilded Barbets and Spangled Cotingas perching in the trees nearby. There were also several pairs of macaws that occasionally flew beneath the platform, and that was an experience in its own right—to look straight down on these big, colorful birds as they wheeled beneath us. Like straddling rainbows.

Later that morning, Doris took us deep into the forest to seek out targeted birds, and it was clear she was becoming increasingly comfortable with the two of us and our style. She had begun to view Vera, in particular, as a kindred spirit of sorts who loved to observe all the little creatures of the woods, up close, and with the same keen interest as she. She began to slowly open up her little bag of tricks and share with us her special honey holes, which she would have likely kept to herself only a week before. One was the lek of the Band-tailed Manakin.

Doris knew exactly where to find it, and soon we had worked our way through the tangle to an area where two colorful males were performing on a bare horizontal limb in a tree twenty feet up. The birds would shimmy and shuffle laterally along the branch, periodically thrusting their folded wings forward in a sign of aggression. Often, at the same time, they would fan their tails so that their white "bands"—for which the birds are named—became markedly visible.

We cautiously slipped into the area to sit quietly for a while, hoping the manakins would get easy with our presence. We had brought stools to sit on and face netting as well as gloves to protect us from the mosquitoes. There were mosquitoes and sweat bees and flies hovering all around us, and once I counted five different butterflies on my shirt at the same time, drawn there by my perspiration. But we were too far away from the birds to be effective. Since these little guys are

Band-tailed Manakin (93), Manu National Park, Peru: Manu Wildlife Center, 2001

only about 3 ¹/₂ inches in size, we needed to close the gap to about ten to twelve feet to permit any kind of decent shot. And we couldn't. We were blocked by impenetrable vines and couldn't claw our way closer to the birds without spooking them. We were stymied.

So Doris led Vera around to the backside of another lek, not thirty yards away, but completely hidden from view, where two other males were also performing. She guided her through a small opening in the tangle so that she could get within striking range of the dancing birds. It was in this manner that the sidekick managed a keeper shot of the Band-tailed Manakin (no. 93), a bird that resembles in many ways its more famous cousin, the Wire-tailed Manakin, which we had collected in the dry forests of Venezuela.

The next day, we were again on the river early, heading full throttle downstream to an entry point of several oxbow lakes, those severed and sutured meanders of the river that the Indians call *cochas*. It was a gorgeous morning, with the mist rising seductively from the water like lavender smoke to a powder-blue sky. Then it happened! There was a loud thud as we hit the submerged log, and the boat was suddenly on its side, skimming along at a 45-degree angle, full tilt. But before we had any time to be alarmed, the boat was righted again and balanced. It had been close; we had nearly gone over. Our young Machiguenga "lookout" had obviously been asleep at the switch, seduced by the morning magic or, more likely, daydreaming about those opposite-gender kinds of things that afflict teenage boys of all tribes. And Vera and I had been negligent, too: there were our life jackets, stacked up like orange cordwood in the bottom of the boat. We had been lulled by a week of smooth, calm waters and had nearly paid the price for our carelessness.

After disembarking, we walked for twenty minutes through successional forest to reach the *cocha,* a thin strip of fresh water that at one time had been connected to the big river. There we boarded a two-paddle catamaran to slowly edge up the shoreline looking for creatures peculiar to this habitat. We saw many waterbirds here, including Rufescent Tiger-Herons and Hoatzins and Horned Screamers, and were especially impressed with the loud noise made by the screamers as they flew off when spooked by our approach. Their "scream" seemed to equal the decibel levels put forth by the high-volume macaws and howler monkeys that we heard frequently.

But our most impressive encounter involved a trio of Giant Otters swimming and diving like porpoises as they hunted up and down the river. These aren't the sprightly little river otters we know back home, but rather ferocious predators six feet in length and weighing up to 75 pounds. They hunt in packs and can take down and gut a five-foot caiman. They've even been known to hold off a Jaguar. Around these parts they are called "river wolves," and their long canine teeth render even their smiles menacing.

We also observed several caiman cruising the shoreline, the ancestral enemy of the Giant Otter and the reason many believe otters have formed social packs like lions and wolves—for family protection as well as hunting effectiveness. Although the caiman we sighted were only in the eight- to ten-foot range, they are known to grow to twenty feet. Doris told us of a young primatologist from a California university who, just the year before, foolishly went swimming near here—and was eaten by one. It was said to have been enormous.

The remaining days at Manu were spent revisiting some of the forest trails in an attempt to get photographs of the recently rediscovered Rufous-fronted Antthrush and the common and ubiquitous Black-faced Antthrush. And although we managed photos of them both, they weren't terribly good. The only time these little skulkers would move through an area clear enough for a shot was at a sprint, resulting in predictable images of their blurry backsides as they reentered the brush.

But the antthrushes were one of our few disappointments in what had been a stimulating and productive week in the richest wildlife environment to which Vera and I had ever been exposed. Not only had there been wildlife diversity on a grand scale at the Manu Wildlife Center, but the open primary forests and strategic venues such as canopy towers and clay licks had given us unparalleled opportunities for viewing and photography. And all this was in an area

wild enough to support several tribes of Indians still committed to using primitive weapons for both hunting and waging war.

These thoughts were very much on our mind as Vera and I took a prop flight from a dirt strip up near Boca Manu to Cuzco, and then the next day to Lima preparatory to our flight back to the states. The contrast between where we had just been and the civilization to which we were now returning was punctuated to a degree almost unimaginable as our flight from Lima touched down safely in Dallas five minutes before American Airline Flight 11 slammed into the World Trade Center in New York—and our world lurched into its new agenda.

The Harpy Eagle

OWARD THE END OF JANUARY 2002, David Ascanio e-mailed us from Caracas that one of his scouts in the Río Grande Forest Reserve (G) of eastern Venezuela had discovered a Harpy Eagle's nest with a three-month-old chick in it. The report carried weight because the scout, Javier, was respected for his ability to find these nests and interpret the particular stage of their development with some accuracy. He was known in the area as "el Hombre Harpía," or simply "the Harpy Man." The news was also encouraging in that a chick this young would still have its parents coming to feed it on a regular basis, thus permitting an opportunity to photograph one of the handsome adults.

In times past there have been productive Harpy Eagle areas along the Tambopata River in southern Peru, Darien National Park in Panama, and even the remote Kanuku Mountains of Guyana, but Vera and I felt our best chance for one of these great raptors lay in the Río Grande Forest Reserve. Over the last ten years this region of Venezuela has consistently reported more nest sightings than any other area of the Neotropics. No one seems to know whether that's because the habitat is a particularly fertile breeding ground for Harpies or because this timber-exploited reserve is overrun with lumbermen who regularly run across the birds and report them. Or both. But despite the extensive range of this great predator, which nests all the way from southern Mexico to Argentina, the Río Grande Forest Reserve is where most birders go these days to look for one. In addition, the Harpy Man and his brother have carved out a small niche in the food chain of the ecotourism business here, which prizes the monkey-eating Harpy Eagle above all other Neotropical birds, and they have their own scouts out in the woods looking also.

The year before, Vera and I thought we might have had a legitimate run at a Harpy on Barro Colorado Island in Panama, but the eagle left the island inexplicably and was subsequently shot by poachers in the forests nearby. But now in eastern Venezuela this fresh opportunity appeared, so we ran down Marco Cayuso ("the Vertical Man") in Caracas, hired a driver named Julio Mayer from Puerto Ordaz, and took off for the little community of El Palmar at the edge of the Río Grande Reserve. We checked into the Hotel Tarquipire, a rustic motel affair with cinderblock rooms, iron doors, and some of the aesthetic touches of a Caracas jail, to hunker down and make camp preparatory to our eagle hunt the next morning. Vera and I had allocated a full five days to find and photograph it. It would be now or never.

Our stay at Hotel Tarquipire coincided with a V.E.N.T. tour led by David and the much-respected Steve Hilty, the expert Neotropical ornithologist and author of the recently published *Birds of Venezuela.* These two know more about Venezuelan birds than anyone else in the world, and they were just winding up their eastern Venezuela tour in El Palmar with hopes of finding one of the Río Grande Harpy Eagles themselves.

Our own plan was to climb a tall tree next to the Harpy nest tree so that we could photograph the parent when it came flying in to feed the chick. That was how it was scripted. To make it work, we had hired "the Vertical Man" to get us up there, much as he had done with the Capuchinbird two years before.

While our own assault the next morning would require a drive of two hours and a subsequent three-hour hike to the nest site, Steve and David were going to take their own group to look for a two-year-old subadult Harpy that had been spotted much closer by.

Late that first night "the Vertical Man" joined us after an afternoon spent at our nest site—with some good news and some bad news. The good news was this: the nest was indeed active, it had a chick in it, and he had seen one of the parents fly in once to feed it. Perfect. The bad news: the nest was buried deep in the crotch of a 130-foot emergent ceiba in a patch of successional forest flush with the river; Marco had been unable to find a suitable tree nearby to provide us a clean sight line. Not perfect at all. But we had to check it out ourselves, so we got up at three o'clock the next morning and took off for the nest. The walk in was tricky and difficult, an old hunting trail slippery and tangled with roots, and we forded several streams in the rain, sometimes tight-roping logs that spanned them by using broken limbs as stilt poles for balance. When we finally got to the target area, we found that Marco had been right.

The giant ceiba was over 300 feet away across the river, surrounded by thick stands of saplings, which were inconveniently tall and leafy enough to block our view of the nest from the forest floor, but far too weak to permit the weight of our climbing any one of them in search of a better angle. The only alternative was to scale the nest tree itself, but that presented its own set of problems, not the least of which was the possibility of disturbing the birds and thus risking the parents' abandonment of the chick. We didn't think that was such a big risk—we knew of researchers who had spent time at active Harpy nests before without any difficulty—but we didn't feel qualified enough to make that call. There was also the issue of a possible attack by the powerful, angry adults, although we had been told—once again by experts—that Harpies are surprisingly docile up high, even at their own nests. We weren't automatically buying that one, either.

But even if we had wanted to try the big tree, we

would first have had to negotiate the Río Grande, which was pulsing spiritlessly, but menacingly, before us. The only solution seemed to be a distressed dugout canoe that had been abandoned at water's edge, but it looked far too unstable to use. "The Vertical Man," in fact, tested it when he crossed the river to retrieve his climbing gear, but the boat sank coming back. We fished him out of the water and called it quits for the day. We were now going to have to figure out some kind of Plan B. Plan A was in flames.

A reasonable Plan B began to take shape that night, as Steve and David had returned from the field to report seeing a handsome subadult Harpy in a tall tree that had once held the nest in which it had been born. Although the nest had long since been destroyed, the Harpy juvenile was known to return to this home tree from time to time. The large teenager, we were told, was nearly as impressive-looking as the adult, though it didn't yet have the dark band across its chest or the black striping on its legs. At this stage of development, it was mostly white and greatly resembled a mature Crested Eagle.

The experts conferred. In his opening brief, "the Harpy Man" declared he knew the bird to be about two years old and stated that he hadn't seen the mother come to feed it in over a year. Hilty demurred: he thought the bird was closer to eighteen months old and was most likely a male. David added that the juvenile bird was certainly mature enough to have become a competent hunter, but that the mother was still likely to bring him food from time to time if the weather had been bad and the hunting slow. David also thought it peculiar that this secretive bird was now showing himself back at his nest tree, and this might well indicate that junior was hungry. And looking for mother.

Early the next morning, in a light rain, Marco, Vera, "the Harpy Man," and I took off for the nest,

hoping we would find the bird where he had been seen the day before, and also hoping he would be perching free enough from any obstructing foliage so we might manage a clear shot. We also desperately needed the rain to stop to make it work.

We found the big eagle where he was supposed to be—in his old nest tree—and he was superb! We positioned our equipment on the side of a hill with a un-blocked sight line to the bird. We didn't need to risk spooking him by having Marco try to get us up in a tree closer by. We were going to take the clean shot offered and be grateful for it. And even though the lighting was terrible, with a killing white sky as a backdrop, we were able to squeeze off several bracketed shots before the bird flew off for the day. Seconds later we heard the panic screams of monkeys nearby and surmised that our young hunter had made a pass at a neighborhood troop on his way out of the area.

The next morning we returned, and so had he! We were now set to go for the winning shot if only we could manage some decent light as well as some traction to stabilize the tripod on what was becoming an increasingly slippery slope. It was still raining, so we clothes-pinned our ponchos to saplings—as makeshift lean-tos—to keep our equipment dry until the weather cleared. If the bird would only stay around until then.

A peculiar thing happened next—the Harpy teenager began to flex and flap his wings while at the same time making a loud and plaintive screech. Despite the immense size of the bird and his imposing visage, it was clear—he was calling for Mama. That a creature this large could beg for food like some baby bluebird was astonishing, and he kept it up off and on for over an hour. Then suddenly out of nowhere, but actually sweeping in from our left, a large Harpy flew in to touch down briefly on an exposed limb of the same tree. It was Mother! After a short pause, she flew up to

Harpy Eagle (94), Río Grande Forest Reserve, Venezuela, 2002

Harpy Eagle, Río Grande Forest Reserve, Venezuela, 2002

the top of the tree, and junior flew over to the exposed limb where she had first landed. Then Mother flew off. The airlift had lasted forty-five seconds.

We raised our binoculars and saw junior perched out on the bare limb, clutching a small mammal—already substantially eaten—that Mother had dropped in for him. The prey had a stout tail and small paw, but that's all of its anatomy we could recognize. "The Harpy Man" thought it might have been a White-faced Capuchin, a regular part of the Harpy's diet in this region, but we couldn't be sure. We could still see junior well enough, but unfortunately he was facing away from us. So "the Harpy Man" and I circled downslope to get out in front of him for a possibly better shot. Then we got lucky—the eagle whirled back around to face Vera, still positioned on the hill. Although the weather only cleared for a total of about

twenty minutes the entire day, with brief flashes of sunshine and bright blue skies, it was just enough time to manage several keeper shots of the coveted Harpy Eagle (no. 94).

Toward mid-afternoon a dark storm began to engulf us, lightning owned the sky, and horizontal sheets of wind began to try to cut us off at the knees. We knew we had to quickly flee before the rising creeks coursing through the lowlands here trapped us, and as it turned out, we scampered up and out with little time to spare.

Of all of the birds of the Neotropics the Harpy Eagle is the one that serious birders want most to see. And with good reason. It is the largest forest eagle and most powerful bird of prey in the world; it ranks in size with Steller's Sea-Eagle. It is three feet long, weighs eighteen pounds, and has a wing span of over seven feet. The female is a third again as big as the male and can weigh more than twice as much as our American Bald Eagle. The big bird, however, is rarely seen, since it doesn't soar in the sky like other raptors and prefers to secretly hunt in the thick rainforests, obscured by the giant trees of its habitat. This makes it almost impossible to find. The birds are also vulnerable to local extinction because of hunting pressures and habitat destruction, and their reproductive rate is so slow that they produce only once every three years or so.

In Panama at Smithsonian's Barro Colorado Island Research Facility, a couple of introduced birds subsequently left the island and were shot by poachers nearby. Now in conjunction with the Peregrine Foundation's Neotropical Raptor Center, a marketing program is underway to educate the people of Panama about the value and prominence of this big eagle as well as the need for its preservation as a national resource. The Harpy Eagle is the country's national bird.

The Harpy Eagle is not only ferocious, it even looks ferocious, with a wild elegance and deeply set eyes. It was originally named by Spaniards for the old woman of Greek mythology who was half-woman, half-bird. This raptor is also immensely strong and feeds on sloths, monkeys, anteaters, and even small deer, swooping skillfully through the forest at chase speeds up to 50 miles an hour. But the most impressive features of this great bird are the incredibly powerful legs and feet that enable it to snatch a ten-pound howler monkey or a fifteen-pound sloth off a limb to which it is desperately clinging. The feet themselves are the size of a grown man's hand, and its talons—at five inches—are equal to the claws of a Grizzly Bear, with a grip so strong it can easily crush the skull of a large monkey.

Alberto Palleroni of the Neotropical Raptor Center near Panama City told Vera and me that a couple of

years earlier, while working with a rehabilitated Harpy Eagle, he had an experience that forever impressed on him this predator's immense strength. He was holding a mature eagle on his outstretched arm, much as a falconer would a falcon, when a chained dog got loose and sprinted across the compound grounds. The Harpy reflexively shifted its weight to track him and, with a talon pressure greater than that of a Rottweiler's jaws, broke Alberto's arm. In two places.

The morning after our Harpy win, we decided to leave El Palmar and drive south to Las Claritas to visit "the Ice Cream Man," for we had heard that he now had the lustrous Crimson Topaz coming to his feeders at Barquilla de Fresa. Along the way we made a pit stop at El Dorado on the Cayuni River at a unique campground owned and managed by an area mini-celebrity named Bruno, who was raising an eleven-month-old Jaguar whose mother had recently been killed by poachers. Bruno had become the cub's de facto parent and was the only one who could safely go near the wild cat. We were told that the young Jaguar had grown up eating out of the same dish as his best friend, a Highland Tinamou, until one day the young Jaguar casually leaned over and ate the chunky little forest bird, thus ending the relationship.

Bruno, it seemed, also had a colorful history: he was a Swiss national who had once been a member of the French Foreign Legion and had recently married a torch singer from Caracas named Vanessa who was now managing the campground with him. He was also under contract as an advisor to the Venezuelan National Guard, with his most marketable skill set whispered to be in the field of "interrogation." There wasn't anyone, it seemed, who wanted to mess with Bruno—or with his pet Jaguar, either. We motored on.

Once we reached Las Claritas, we unfortunately found that "the Ice Cream Man" had a full house, so we defaulted to a surprisingly clean and air-conditioned new hotel in town called Chalet Raymond, where we took all our meals at a four-table outdoor café, Mi Rinconcito. It was also good. And even though we missed on the Crimson Topaz, I celebrated a birthday meal at this little restaurant; Vera, Julio, and Marco surprised me with a birthday cake shaped like the face of a big bird—with chocolate cupcakes for eyes—and with an inscription that cleverly read "Harpy Bird Day." It was a thoughtful gesture, a bit precious perhaps, but one that was not easy to properly execute on short notice in a town like Las Claritas.

This turned out to be our last trip to Venezuela, as Vera and I had finally succeeded with the last of our targeted birds in this bird-rich country. In photographing the Harpy Eagle, we had achieved a goal that had tantalized us from the very beginning. But it was one we were never that confident we could pull off because the Harpy is fully inconspicuous in the one hundred square miles of thick forest it patrols, and the few birders who have ever seen the eagle have simply jumped it by accident. That we had also been fortunate enough to manage a photograph of this great predator—with its prey—was a special dividend. We were very, very fortunate.

In Africa, the glorious wildlife of the continent is dominated by what is known as "the big five," which include the elephant, the rhino, the cape buffalo, the lion, and the leopard. To see or photograph or shoot "the big five"—whatever the particular persuasion—is everyone's first order of business. Vera and I speculated that if the birds of the Neotropics had a "big five," it might well include the Scarlet Macaw, the Resplendent Quetzal, the Keel-billed Toucan, perhaps the Andean Cock-of-the-rock, and, of course, the Harpy Eagle. And although our macho hunter friends might consider the accomplishment overwhelmingly delicate by comparison, Vera and I could nevertheless claim we had bagged a "big five" of our own.

Hyacinth Macaws
of the Pantanal

WHEN PEOPLE ROMANTICIZE Brazil's great ecosystems, they invariably highlight the immense rainforests of the Amazon Basin. Fair enough. But south of the Amazon River and east of the Andes lies what is the world's largest freshwater wetland, home to the greatest concentration of wildlife on the continent. It's the low-lying drainage of the upper Paraguay River known as the Pantanal (V) ("swamp" in Portuguese). During the rainy season, the grassy lowlands here are flooded to an area the size of Colorado and embrace the southwestern part of the state of Mato Grosso—itself about the size of Texas—as well as small parts of eastern Bolivia and eastern Paraguay. During the dry season, these lowlands are transformed into rich pasturelands for cattle, and their shrinking pools of water attract staggering concentrations of wildlife. It's one of the most pristine and biologically rich environments on the planet.

The Pantanal and Mato Grosso also boast a colorful history. In 1925 the great English explorer Percey Fawcett mysteriously disappeared while looking for his "Lost City" of gold somewhere in the drainage of the Rio Xingu. A few years before that, and in the northwestern part of the state, President Teddy Roosevelt mapped the then unexplored Rio Duvida ("River of Doubt"), later named for Roosevelt himself, in an adventure that injured him severely and from which he barely escaped. It is said his health was never the same after that.

In a less glamorous and more unseemly chapter, Mato Grosso became notorious during the latter half of the twentieth century when the land was aggressively cleared of Indians to make room for agricultural priorities like pastureland for cattle. The "cleansing" was, in part, done the old-fashioned way—many Indians were either driven from the area or simply shot. Other family units, however, were sprayed with poisons from crop dusters and were sent blankets and clothing laced with tuberculosis and smallpox.

This unconditional and relentless clearing of the land, however, was dealt a serious setback recently when the mammoth Hidrovia project, which was to create a 2,000-mile canal linking this area to the Atlantic Ocean, was defeated by the Brazilians themselves in order to protect the environmental integrity of the Pantanal. Had the canal project gone through, as many felt it would, this marvelous wetland would have been dramatically compromised, much as our own Everglades has been today, and eventually drained as development from agriculture and industry grew up around it. This was a significant conservation win for a country not known for having posted many of them.

Our own designs on the Pantanal were modest—we simply wanted to photograph a large blue bird that lived there: the majestic and endangered Hyacinth Macaw. In late May 2002, Vera and I went to the Pantanal to find it. We flew to São Paulo and then to Cuiaba, the capital of the state of Mato Grosso, which contains the headwaters of the important Paraguay River in addition to hundreds of other rivers and streams that vein it richly. To find the big macaw, we took along with us an experienced guide of the Mato Grosso area, Braulio Carlos, a thirty-five-year-old, academically trained economist who had opted early on for a career in wildlife and who had been leading birding tours in the Pantanal for fifteen years. Vera and I found him to be resourceful and competent, with an exceptionally good ear, and our adventure would not have been productive at all without him.

The three of us drove south out of Cuiaba to the small colonial town of Pocone, where we picked up

the entrance to a 90-mile, packed-dirt road called the Transpantaneira, which slices through the Pantanal all the way to the Rio Cuiaba and its terminus at Port Jofre. On each side of the road for its duration are the pasturelands of private cattle ranches, *fazendas,* and the road itself is crisscrossed by rickety planked bridges that traverse the streams and pools of water that have collected during the rainy season. A lot of our photography that first afternoon, as we inched our way south, was done from these bridges.

Vera and I saw enormous congregations of wildlife as kingfishers, caiman, chachalacas, and kites swarmed the roads and water holes like insects, in addition to large numbers of egrets, herons, storks, and guans. The highlight of our outing that first afternoon, however, was a pair of splendid Southern Screamers (no. 95), flattered by the glow of the late-afternoon sun, as well as a "herd" of over one hundred Jabirus feeding in a field not far from the road.

Toward sunset that first day, some forty miles south of Pocone, we drifted into Pousada Santa Tereza, a comfortable twelve-room country inn on the lovely Pixaim River. Pet parrots and toucans were working the trees of the compound, and *pantaneiro* cowboys were patrolling the pastures around it. The local birds around the cabins included finches and horneros, cardinals and ibises, but the most interesting member of the local menagerie was a docile and affectionate Collared Peccary that hung around outside our room making little whining sounds until we fed him some trail mix, or rubbed his stomach vigorously with our foot, which made him purr like a cat. Whenever we hiked into the gallery forest, our new friend would follow smartly at our heels—like some proud pointer—when in reality he was an unremarkable yet endearing little javelina from the Pantanal.

At five o'clock the first morning, I drifted through

Southern Screamer (95), The Pantanal, Brazil, 2002

the back door of the small kitchen to run down what turned out to be some excellent Brazilian coffee—poured, as was the custom, through a tired old sock. Another unusual feature of that first morning was finding the small dining area completely filled with the family who ran the *pousada,* along with all the hired help who worked there. There were grandparents and grown children and babies; there were cooks, boat skippers, and sweepers. All were huddled around the

TV watching the World Cup, live from South Korea. The national Brazilian team was in the process of beating Turkey in the first of a string of wins that would lead to its winning the world championship. Everyone was up early and engaged, 120 million Brazilians nationwide, as Brazil through the years has won the cup more than any other country in the world, and soccer around these parts has become more a religious experience than simply a national pastime.

Toco Toucan (96), The Pantanal, Brazil, 2002

One of our principal targets of the Pantanal was the glamorous Toco Toucan (no. 96), and it came to us on the first day we were there. Three wild toucans blew into the trees surrounding the house to scout for food around the compound, and we had marvelous opportunities for photographs then and each morning thereafter during our stay at Santa Tereza. This was the third toucan Vera and I had photographed in the Neotropics, the Keel-billed Toucan and the Chestnut-mandibled Toucan being the other two,

and we considered it our best shot.

About nine o'clock we struck out for the gallery forest that runs parallel to the river, and over the days we devoted to his capture, we jumped eight different male Helmeted Manakins. Although we had a number of good opportunities to get close to this bird, which—at nearly six inches—happens to be big for a manakin, we have always found it challenging to photograph any small, black bird that's constantly darting through thick brush in low-light conditions.

These particular manakins don't bunch up in a lek, as many of their species do, but are fiercely territorial and respond aggressively to playback of their three-note song and periodic "meow" calls. Consequently, we were able to prevail with this exotic bird, and the sidekick brought home a nice shot of the coveted Helmeted Manakin (no. 97).

After lunch each day, and as an afternoon diversion, we would walk down to the dock with some raw meat on a hook and a monofilament line to fish for the piranha that populate the rivers here. In no time at all we would have a mess of fish for a piranha soup, since the fish itself is too bony to eat outright. The piranha is a fish about the size of a large bream, or sunfish, with rows of razor-sharp teeth and a legendary ability to use them. In times past there were undoubtedly men who were attacked and stripped to the bone, but today most piranha bites come from careless fisherman trying to remove hooks from the fish's mouth. With this in mind, Vera and I were careful to remove the hooks in the safest possible way: we let Braulio do it—with long-nosed pliers.

Late each afternoon of our stay at Santa Tereza, we eased down the picturesque Pixaim River in a small skiff to photograph the wildlife among the trees lining its banks. The river is delicately beautiful, not blue and fast like a mountain stream, but green and slow—more like a serpentine oxbow lake than a river—clean and clear with hyacinths covering the shoreline, and the trees themselves, lashed with ivy and creepers, leaning out over the water to reflect a mosaic of verdant shades on the surface. There were egrets prancing

Helmeted Manakin (97), The Pantanal, Brazil, 2002

Red-billed Scythebill (98), The Pantanal, Brazil, 2002

Bare-faced Curassow (99), The Pantanal, Brazil, 2002

mincingly in the shallows, there were herons gliding through the foliage like relics of a lost age. We were reminded just how spiritually enriching it is to spend the last couple of hours of a day sliding languidly down a beautiful, quiet river observing its wildlife. It was one of the most enjoyable parts of our trip.

We jumped howler monkeys and capybara and even a lively family of five Giant Otters, which curiously circled our boat for over thirty minutes. The capybara itself was also a surprise as it jumped from the shore to the water in a big belly flop like some aquatic sheep diving in for a dip. But instead of swimming to the other side of the river, with its head held out of the water as a dog or a deer might do, it

simply disappeared from sight, never to be seen again, swimming away beneath the surface.

Another highlight of those afternoons was spotting over two hundred Snail Kites roosting in the trees along the shore as well as taking a keeper photograph of the striking Red-billed Scythebill (no. 98) working a tree close to the water's edge. And when we docked each night and disembarked from the boat, two eight-foot caiman always came hustling out of the water after us in hot pursuit. These creatures were obviously in the habit a being fed, and not surprisingly looked to us as a reliable source of handouts rather than as prey.

On the morning of our last day we squeezed off a rushed shot of a female Bare-faced Curassow (no. 99)

Hyacinth Macaw (100), The Pantanal, Brazil, 2002

Hyacinth Macaw, The Pantanal, Brazil, 2002

as she hurried across the trail in the gallery forest. It was the only keeper shot of a curassow we ever managed. Shortly thereafter, we packed up and headed south about twenty miles to a different stretch of habitat and a seven-room, rustic country inn named Pousada O Pantaneiro. We had come here to specifically locate and photograph the largest parrot on the planet, the exceptional Hyacinth Macaw.

This captivatingly blue bird has been endangered for some time, practically doomed to extinction by its own beauty, as the illegal pet trade had driven its numbers to a low of 2,500 birds as recently as ten years ago. Although a Hyacinth might well bring as much as $12,000 on the black market, rigorous enforcement of antitrapping laws has gradually permitted regeneration of population levels in the wild to about 5,000 birds. These particular macaws are restricted to the woodlands of Para, Brazil, the rocky valleys of northeastern Brazil, and the mother lode here in the Pantanal wetlands.

And it was here in the Pantanal where we intended to concentrate our efforts, specifically in the large acuri palm plantations common to the western part of the state. The Hyacinth Macaw, with its massive head and bill—the largest of its kind in the world—is able to crack nuts and digest fruit that is inaccessible to all other birds, and these oil-palm groves were a logical place to look for it. As it turned out, we had no trouble finding the birds at all. Sometimes it works that way.

On a private ranch forty-five minutes from the *pousada* we found the macaws feeding in large numbers among wavy green grasses studded with 20-foot acuri palms under cloudless blue skies. We were also lucky on the weather; it could have been different—there could have been rain, or even cloudy skies, which would have rendered the color of these attractive blue birds an unappetizing slate-gray. Our chal-

lenge now was simply to sneak close enough to one of them for a photograph.

As we crept through the grasslands where the birds were feeding, some of them became attracted to our movements and began strafing the meadows, flying low in pairs and looking back over their shoulder at us, "*kaaing*" loudly as they flew past. These birds are, by nature, both fearless and intensely social, and the flyovers seemed more a form of curious reconnaissance—just checking us out—than an alarmed, mobbing behavior directed toward suspected predators. But it was hard to say; maybe it was a combination of both. Over the following twenty minutes, more and more macaws began to converge from all directions

Jabiru (101), The Pantanal, Brazil, 2002

White-eared Puffbird (102), Chapada National Forest, Brazil, 2002

to land in a lone 75-foot tree that stood far taller than the sprinkled plantation palms surrounding it. The tree was obviously the lookout roost.

We headed slowly that way where—improbably— we also discovered two Jabirus making their nest in this same tree. We stood silently by as the macaws continued to spiral into the top branches, some producing scolding and growling sounds like a small dog. The Jabirus remained unfazed. And when it seemed that every single one of the macaws had been drained from the surrounding landscape, we counted an astounding fifty-two Hyacinth Macaws (no. 100) and two Jabirus (no. 101)—all in this one tree. It was one of those extraordinary field experiences that was impossible to ex-

plain, and Vera and I were rewarded with excellent shots of the imposing bird. One picture stuffed the frame with macaws, and another showcased the two storks, with attendant macaws showboating in the background. We couldn't have asked for more.

Over the week we were in the Pantanal, we found the days blue and cloudless, the nights crystal clear. And under the Southern Cross and a Milky Way conspicuously thick and creamy, we slowly prowled the back roads in an open-bed truck looking for night things. Our target was the big cat, the Jaguar, which Vera and I had yet to encounter but which is seen here with some regularity. One was actually spotted during the morning of our first day in the

Rufous-winged Antshrike (103), Chapada National Forest, Brazil, 2002

Coal-crested Finch (104), Chapada National Forest, Brazil, 2002

area. So each night of our visit we would periodically stop the truck, turn off all the lights, and play a tape of the urgent and desperate calls of a female Jaguar in heat to attract the male. It was supposed to work, but it never did—the great cat never showed.

On our way out of the Pantanal several days later, heading for the last leg of our trip up in the Chapada National Forest, we jumped a Yellow Anaconda swiftly crossing the road. Before we could get to it, however, the snake reached a lagoon on the other side, and we could observe only the top one-third of its body above the surface of the water. We had never seen an anaconda, but this one was only seven feet long. That's a big snake, to be sure, but it's a wee anaconda. They grow much larger, some having been reported to be well over thirty feet. It also seems that every cattle rancher throughout the Pantanal has a photograph of a giant anaconda framed on his wall, bloated from having just dined on a member of the local herd.

Four hours later, we entered the Chapada National Forest (W) on the western rim of Brazil's Planalto Central, a markedly different piece of terrain that contrasted sharply with the flooded savannas where we

had just been. It was like migrating from the Florida Everglades to Arizona. This new terrain, about an hour northwest of Cuiaba, is characterized by red sandstone mesas and impressive outcroppings amidst a *cerrado* brush habitat of both chaparral and dry, gallery forests. While most people decry the destruction of the Brazilian rainforests, it is, in fact, the *cerrado* habitat of the central plateau that is disappearing the fastest because of its aggressive conversion to agricultural monocultures like pastureland for cattle.

We stayed on top of the mesa in an upscale inn called Pousada Penhasco, with tennis courts and a swimming pool, flourishing buffets, and a marvelous view of the basin 2,500 feet below. And in the scrub thickets down the road, we picked up three birds indigenous to this unique habitat: the White-eared Puffbird (no. 102), the Rufous-winged Antshrike (no. 103), and the handsome Coal-crested Finch (no. 104). But it all seemed a bit sterile compared with the charm of the family inns we had found in the Pantanal, with their simple boardinghouse fare, their laid-back styles, and their oil-palm plantations swarming with Hyacinth Macaws.

Tandayapa Valley, Ecuador

 F YOU WERE TO CARVE a sweet spot out of the Neotropics, a little slice of its heaven, you would want to drill into a small core on the Western Slope of the Ecuadorian Andes (X) in a subtropical zone 6,000 feet high, flush on the Equator. Here the temperature stays between 55 and 75 degrees year round, the humidity ranges between 40 and 60 percent, and the prevailing weather seems to produce days that are a unique combination of glorious spring mornings welded to refreshingly cool fall afternoons. We are talking about the forested ridges of the Tandayapa Valley, known to contain some of the richest montane avifauna anywhere on the planet. It's only a ninety-minute drive west of Quito.

Birdlife International has labeled the western Andean slopes of Ecuador and Colombia as the "Choco Endemic Area," and its forty-six endemic species represent the most of any other endemic area in the world. The Tandayapa Valley has twenty-one of these, and it's here that Vera and I went next to look for some of its charismatic birds, specifically two of our final targets: the celebrated Plate-billed Mountain-Toucan and the implausibly costumed Toucan Barbet. In addition to these two "stars," this thin, six-mile-long valley supports two different quetzals, two fruiteaters, a couple of nifty manakins, the most glamorous of the tapaculos, a giant Andean Cock-of-the-rock lek, a gazillion tanagers, seven different antpittas, and perhaps the richest variety of hummingbirds in the world. For truly exceptional birds, the Tandayapa Valley ranks at the very top for Neotropical birding and exceeds even the "sizzle" production of hot spots like Monteverde in Costa Rica or even eastern Venezuela. At least, in our opinion.

Before Tandayapa, however, we spent several days in a small country inn called Séptimo Paraíso in the equally lovely and bird-rich Mindo Valley, the next valley over on the backside of the volcano Pichincha near the little town of Mindo. Our guide was Tony Nunnery, an American expat who lived upridge in the Tandayapa Valley itself, and our driver was Fausto Valencia, an Ecuadorian trout farmer who lived fifteen minutes down the road from Tony.

Séptimo Paraíso was a twenty-room inn, about two years old at the time, with serviceable charm, well-appointed rooms, and B+ food. The inn was located in a beautiful valley of lush vegetation at an elevation of about 4,000 feet and accented by its own swimming pool. Despite roomy accommodations, the walls were noticeably thin, and one morning early we were awakened, not to the usual songs of antthrushes and motmots but rather to our Ecuadorian neighbor next door. He was robustly singing operatic arias at five in the morning, which was simply his cheerful way of starting a new day—not, as one might expect, because he was three sheets to the wind from having been aggressively overserved the night before.

But no matter the eccentric distractions, Vera and I found the birdlife at Séptimo Paraíso to be impressive. We spent four days navigating the trails that traversed the hills and the valley around the hotel property and working the two-mile path that ran up to the main road. We even encountered what we estimated to be five different families of Toucan Barbets, the largest and one of the most colorful of its species and endemic to this sliver of slope here in the Andes. The birds had staked their territories throughout the valley, but they stayed well out of our range. We also came up empty-handed with two wary and secretive Rufous-breasted Antthrushes, an elusive Scaled Fruiteater working downslope, and, high up the hill, a Crimson-rumped Toucanet that continually gave us

the slip. Our losses continued to mount with failed efforts pursuing the Golden-headed Quetzal as well as a raucous pair of Choco Toucans, despite having repeatedly wonderful views of both.

We were ambushing all these marvelous birds, quite effortlessly it seemed, but couldn't seem to work suitably close to any of them for a picture. Our timing was off. We were here in Ecuador during what is the driest month of the year, which is splendid for those who prefer sunny skies and splashing about the pool, but not so terrific for optimum bird activity. The fruit-eating birds like the quetzals, barbets, and toucans had just finished nesting and weren't responsive to tape. And the rainy season, which would have ignited the breeding activity for insect eaters like the antthrushes and antpittas, had not yet begun.

Then suddenly our luck changed! As we returned one morning down the main path leading to the inn, we were startled to hear a peculiar one-note, metallic *bing,* which Tony recognized immediately as one of the song notes of the Club-winged Manakin. He was close by, feeding in a short melastome tree just off the road, a food source he seemed fearlessly interested in defending, thus enabling us to squeeze off several winning shots when we were able to inch close enough to do so.

This manakin is less than four inches in size, and though he's not as colorful as some of the hotshots of his family, like the Wire-tailed Manakin and the Red-capped Manakin, or even as acrobatic as those of the blue-backed tribes, we liked him every bit as much. He may have become our favorite—although, quite frankly, we tend to confer this status a little too easily when we have just observed a stunning new bird. The romance inevitably wanes over time, the distinction fades, and a fresh "favorite" is ultimately born. So it goes.

Club-winged Manakin (105), Western Slope Andes, Ecuador: Mindo Valley, 2002

But this Club-winged Manakin (no. 105) might have staying power since the little guy is legitimately handsome, if not gaudily ornamental, and Vera and I have found ourselves becoming more attracted to birds uniquely patterned than those which simply blow you away with their dazzle. We have also come to prefer cotingas to tanagers, antbirds to humming-birds, and—more times than not—interesting behavior to that of striking beauty.

This particular manakin is interestingly and uniquely patterned—with a rufous-chestnut body,

scarlet cap, and remarkably designed wings: they are black and bluntly squared, with wavy, cream-colored flight feathers that seem thickened, even twisted a bit. When making its display move, the bird will lean over and raise his wings back over his back while making a whiny little "meow" call. It's a terrific little bird.

The grounds of Séptimo Paraíso, nestled here in this little pocket of the Mindo Valley, seemed to have everything. In addition to those birds previously encountered, we jumped the Red-headed Barbet, a Swallow Tanager—which sallied forth to nail insects more like a flycatcher than a tanager—and even a lone, male Golden-winged Manakin not fifty feet from our room.

On our last afternoon, we drifted down the mountain several miles toward Mindo and stopped over at a small residence, Mindo Lindo, owned by two local conservationists, where we photographed the Velvet-purple Coronet and the Violet-tailed Sylph (no. 106), two of the most glamorous and famous of the Ecuadorian hummingbirds. Then it was back over the mountain, passing the home of the famous naturalist Niels Krabbe, coauthor of *Birds of the High Andes,* and finally down into the Tandayapa Valley, where we were scheduled to hunker down for four days.

We stayed in the guest room of the weekend home of our driver, Fausto Valencia, and his wife, Amparo, which they had styled the Clearwater Lodge, and we enjoyed excellent ethnic fare for the length of our stay. It was, hands down, the best food we were to have in the Neotropics. The lodge, interestingly, is situated precisely on the Equator—we had cocktails on the living room couch in the Northern Hemisphere, and then moved to the dining room in the Southern Hemisphere to take our meals.

The lodge overlooks Tandayapa, a small community of one-story buildings that had been painted a variety of gay, Jell-O colors by a group of British schoolgirls a couple of years earlier as an international goodwill project of sorts. Fausto's property also claimed color from the wide variety of birds attracted to its rich habitat, highlighted by several male Andean Cocks-of-the-rock that blazed past the outside deck of his home, coming and going from their lek site down by the river twice a day—in the morning and late afternoon. There were also Golden-headed Quetzals that fed in the avocado trees along the stream and regularly nested in the guava trees upridge in the open pastures.

The cock-of-the-rock lek itself was remarkable and had been discovered by Tony only a year before. We

were told no more than ten to twelve people had ever been privileged to see it. Working our way down the mountain on an undeveloped trail to reach the lek took us twenty minutes one early morning, just at first light. The alpha male arrived first and called to the others, which began to drift into the area in large numbers. By six-thirty that morning, we estimated there were twelve different males calling from the trees along the slope. We were told that this particular lek might well be the largest accessible Andean Cock-of-the-rock lek in the Neotropics. It was also measurably different from the large lek we visited the year before in southern Peru: the Peruvian birds were reddish orange, these Ecuadorian guys a blood-red. And the noise generated by this Ecuadorian lek was substantially greater in volume—like a yard full of squawking chickens *and* the combined sounds one might expect from a small pen of feeding pigs or an angry troop of chimpanzees. The colorful and noisy birds put on a good show.

Over the next several days we also climbed high to look for Plate-billed Mountain-Toucans, which are consistently found foraging on the ridgetops throughout this valley. Although we consistently struck out with this bird, we did observe several mixed-species flocks of colorful Blue-winged Mountain-Tanagers and Grass-green Tanagers, as well as several Green-and-black Fruiteaters. Our biggest failure, however, involved the Ocellated Tapaculo, a large and colorful bird of red-rufous and black, covered with white spots. At least that's what the field guides show. Vera and I have never seen one, despite having called in several birds outrageously close to where we were waiting to pounce, so skulky and tentative are they in their habits and so determined to remain hidden from view.

The most interesting wildlife specimen we encountered during these high-ridge mornings, however, had nothing to do with the birds—but rather with two

Violet-tailed Sylph (106), Western Slope Andes, Ecuador: Mindo Valley 2002

Toucan Barbet (107), Western Slope Andes, Ecuador: Tandayapa Valley, 2002

enormous earthworms, of all things, which we observed moving ever so slowly across our path. One was tan, the other a rusty red. They were both two feet long, and thick as German sausages! They are known to grow to three feet and are clearly the elephants of the worm world. Giant Antpittas, we're told, love to eat them by picking away small chunks, or even slurping them down whole like spaghetti. The worms also come outlandishly colored in purple and blue, though we didn't run across any of those. The two giant worms we did capture we pitched in Tony's compost pile.

As for Tony, our guide, he was a forty-two-year-old vegetarian from the hills of Mississippi and East Texas—an All-American high school diver, ex-school-

teacher, composer-pianist, and Costa Rican lodge manager who wound up owning seventy-five acres of a north-south-running ridge in some of the lushest habitat in the Tandayapa Valley. From the front deck of his house he has seen some 280 species of birds, more varieties than regularly nest in all of Great Britain.

But Tony has never had a car, a credit card, or a bank account, and he currently lives by choice without electricity in a house he built himself. In the trendy world of Patagonia and the North Face, but with the sartorial preferences of the hippie he always thought himself to be, he proudly remains an army-navy-surplus kind of guy. With braided hair to his waist, he first might seem just another moonbeam dropout from the '70s who, having gone meditative

Plate-billed Mountain-Toucan (108), Western Slope Andes, Ecuador: Tandayapa Valley, 2002

and mystic, is usually found tending bar in some small desert town, all the while claiming to those who will listen that he prefers to live that way because he likes the sunsets—rudderless and without purpose. But not this guy. Tony has never been one to confuse independence with inertia, and has become a focused and accomplished bird guide in no time at all, with a keen eye and a "musician's" ear and that penetrating curiosity that all the good ones have. Also, he and his kindred spirit and companion of five years, Barbara Bolz, a tall and adventuresome blonde from Germany, oversee a world-class hummingbird operation in their front yard, which is without equal—thirty-one different feeders requiring six gallons of sugar water a day, and refills every two hours.

These "Hummingbirders" have attracted a steady group of about twenty different species of hummingbirds that feed daily at their home and another confirmed eighteen varieties that make periodic visits. To put this in perspective, the total of thirty-eight species compares with about twelve that feed at the Hummingbird Gallery in Monteverde, Costa Rica, and perhaps fifteen or so at the Asa Wright Nature Centre in Trinidad. It's a world record for one spot by a mile, thus proving the point that if you "build it, they will come." That is, if you just happen to be living in an equatorial subtropical zone on the western slopes of the Andes and are passionately motivated to spend 80 percent of your time feeding sugar water to hummingbirds.

Plate-billed Mountain-Toucan, Western Slope Andes, Ecuador: Tandayapa Valley, 2002

Tony and Barbara, not surprisingly, call their home "Pacha Quindi," meaning "Hummingbird Place," and it draws birders from all over the world to their front yard for the show. It also draws a large number of winged predators attracted to this honey hole for such concentrated prey, and in addition to daily raids by marauding Bat Falcons and Tiny Hawks, Barbara was surprised the first morning we arrived to witness a Squirrel Cuckoo ambushing a Buff-tailed Coronet for breakfast. None of us had ever heard of that.

But hummingbirds aren't this couple's only focus, as Tony and Barbara are taking the revenue from visiting fees and plowing it back into an imaginative reforestation program on their property as they continue to plant trees and shrubs that can support a wide variety of indigenous birds. They are quite a couple! They wear their own kind of hats!

Hummingbirds weren't our only focus, either. Vera and I were here in this lush valley to run down a special toucan and an endemic barbet, and we were a long way from pay dirt with two days to go. Then we got lucky. On our next-to-last morning, a pair of Toucan Barbets drifted into a fruiting tree and began their sonorous "honking" duet routine, swaying back and forth as they did so, even "clacking" a bit off and on. One dropped down just low enough while feeding to permit a winning shot, and we were able to score with one of the most sought-after signature birds of this part of the world—the Toucan Barbet (no. 107).

As for the special blue toucan, we got him too, but only after finding an active tree hole off a narrow trail that was carved around the back side of Tony's property. A pair of the birds had been nesting here earlier in the season. And to our good fortune, we found the toucans nesting again, a second clutch. It was the break we were looking for. So Vera and I set up a stakeout to try for a shot as the male and female alternately flew in to relieve each other in their nest duties. This occurred every hour or so. Vera worked her way up the side of a slope, which positioned her at eye level to the nest hole, and that's where she stationed herself for several hours the last day we were there, patiently awaiting the right shot.

On one occasion a toucan peeked out of the hole and then exited sooner than usual, apparently attracted to the noise of a foraging flock of small birds moving through the canopy above it. The toucan flew up and quietly stationed itself among them. And then, as we watched in wide-eyed wonder, it leaned over ever so slowly and snatched a small feeding tyrannulet from a branch nearby. The toucan proceeded to shake it twice and then gulp it down. We were stunned. This wasn't a case of a raptor dive-bombing on silent death wings to take its prey, but simply a gorgeous yet ferocious bird, hungry for protein, nonchalantly plucking the small flycatcher from the nearby foliage as if it were nothing more challenging than a ripe, red berry. Then the toucan flew back to the nest hole, pausing momentarily at the entrance, and the sidekick nailed it. We had captured one of the bluest of all the toucans, the exceptional Plate-billed Mountain-Toucan (no. 108).

Suriname

MANY PEOPLE have never even heard of Suriname (Y), mainly because it was, for most of its recognized history, a small colony of Holland called Dutch Guyana. It didn't have its independence or its new name until 1975.

Suriname, a country about the size of the U.S. state of Georgia, is also nestled in an obscure part of the northern shoulder of South America, sandwiched between Guyana on its west (made infamous by Jonestown and the 1978 "Kool-Aid" massacre) and French Guiana on its east (an administered department of France once most noted for its vicious penal colonies like Devil's Island and its incarcerated celebrities, Alfred Dreyfus and "Papillon"). That is, until 1968 when the European Space Agency began to launch satellites from French Guiana due to its favorable geography along the equator.

Suriname is nevertheless a fascinating enclave of blended cultures and mixed metaphors with a history and rhythm uniquely its own. It doesn't seem to belong in South America at all but rather to either the west coast of Africa or Indonesia. Almost no one speaks Spanish in the entire country, not even as a secondary language. Not one word. The official language has been Dutch— all the schools, newspapers, radio programs are in that language—from that time in the seventeenth century when Holland received Suriname in a trade with England for New Amsterdam, the small colony that would later become New York. But the common language of the interior is a pidgin creole called Sranan Tongo, which is to Suriname what Swahili is to Africa.

This bizarre mosaic of indigenous cultures is a result of a history dominated by British and Dutch colonization, Portuguese

Jews who were some of the original plantation owners, descendants of escaped African slaves called "maroons" who had fled to the jungled interiors to establish discrete communities and cultures all their own, and indentured workers imported to an agriculture economy from Java, India, and China. All this diversity works far better than one might expect, and there is a remarkable degree of tolerance among the various cultures living side by side in the capital of Paramaribo. It's probably the only place in the world, for example, where there's a mosque right next door to a synagogue, and a large, wooden Catholic church right down the street from a Hindu temple.

But the country as a whole is bifurcated, because 90 percent of its small population of only 460,000 Surinamese is concentrated either along the coast of the country or in the port capital of Paramaribo, where nearly 250,000 of them live. The remnant population is scattered throughout the interior, including six tribes of some 40,000 maroons, isolated and unmixed through the years, with their own languages and animist/voodoo-based religions. The interior is also inhabited by five principal tribes of the original Amerindians, living along the rivers. The two unpaved roads running out of Paramaribo from the north dribble only part way south into the heart of the country before terminating completely. The rivers serve as the only roads after that. The bottom line is this: there are city/coast people and there are "bush" people, two separate cultures and two ways of life, and if you understand that, you are well on your way to getting a handle on Suriname.

This separation has led over the years to enormous problems and internal strife, and the country today still faces huge economic problems, with an annual GDP in the range of $1.5 billion, somewhat on a par with Chad and Togo. Bauxite mining for aluminum represents a whopping 70 percent of the county's for-

eign reserves and is almost exclusively dominated by Alcoa. It's one of the least populated and poorest countries in the world.

A Dutch colony until 1954, Suriname became independent in 1975 and lurched into a dysfunctional pattern of military regimes, obligatory corruption, rebellion, civil war, and economic stagnation. The civil war lasted from 1986 until 1995, the infrastructure was torn apart, the national spirit crushed and confused, and most of the middle class was forced by economic necessity to leave the country, many for Holland. Suriname now seems to have stabilized and is trying to right itself after so many years under colonial sway and conflict.

Tourism was stopped dead in its tracks until 1995 and has only recently begun to build itself back on the margins, though it remains almost 80 percent confined to the Dutch. The northern coast is no more than a series of extensive mangroves and shallow mud flats, the few sandy beaches are known primarily for their aggressive black flies and leatherback sea turtles, and the interior, during the rainy season, is considered to be dangerously malarial. The capital itself is decidedly third-world, teeming and loud, with all of the questionable charm and rhythms of a loosely wrapped Caribbean culture.

The real question then is why Vera and I would ever want to go there. The answer lies in the fact that 80 percent of the land mass of Suriname is pristine lowland rainforest and represents one of the richest and most beautiful sections of such habitat on the continent. It is also ripe with unique and exotic birdlife. Under the guidance of the Suriname Forest Service (STINASU), extensive tracts of wilderness have been made accessible to birders and naturalists, and during the 1970s the country was actually one of the first in South America to attract birders from around the world—specifically because one of the first field guides on South American birds happened to be the extravagant publication in 1968 of *Birds of Suriname* by François Haverschmidt and G. F. Mees. More important today is the fact that Suriname has become known for hosting the largest Guianan Cock-of-the-rock lek on the planet. So Vera and I decided to gear up and go see it.

Our old running mate, David Ascanio, joined us in Paramaribo from Caracas in late January 2003, and we checked into the Residence Inn, which had been the old Soviet Embassy during a time when Suriname was the Soviet's only foothold in South America. The next morning our little team was fleshed out as we added Sean, our local guide from the tour operator METS, and Ganesh, our cook from STINASU. The five of us would live together for nine days, joined for our stay in Voltzberg by "Raymond the Maroon."

Sean was an extremely bright and handsome Paramaribo product from an Indian-Hindu father and Creole-Christian mother. Without any formal education, he had learned to speak four languages simply from watching Brazilian TV. He also played guitar, sang, and had mastered the hobbies and enthusiasms of card tricks, knot tying, puzzles, and astronomy. He was understandably our principal source of entertainment while in Suriname.

Ganesh, the cook, was a delicate city boy from Guyana who hated the bush, preferring the bright lights and buzz of city life instead, but he was a superb field chef who could effortlessly squeeze inspired meals from challenging circumstances. He alternatingly wore T-shirts which read "Lucky Strike" or "Oklahoma Football." We liked him a lot, too.

The next morning we headed two hours south on a red-rutted dirt road to the Brownsberg Nature Reserve, a section of rich primary forest on an 1,800-foot-high table plateau. The lodge compound there overlooks the immense W. J. Bommestein Lake, a 600-square-mile reservoir created by the Afobaka hydroelectric dam built by Alcoa and the Suriname government back in the early 1960s.

The lodge accommodations were rustic, and the service sharply laced with attitude. Brownsberg was staffed with Saramacca maroons, many of whose families had been displaced when the dam below flooded their community, and the promised replacement housing had only recently been delivered—some forty years later. Additionally, over the last couple of years, the Chinese had moved aggressively into their "protected" homelands upstream along the Suriname River, armed with timber concessions granted by the government big dogs in Paramaribo, and were in the process of clear-cutting and gutting much of the acreage that had been in the families of these maroons for several hundred years. It's little wonder the locals were sometimes surly, though some of the women seemed friendly enough and often giggled and waved to Vera, obviously amused by her combination of green field clothes, camouflage gloves, and bright red lipstick.

The setting, however, was splendid—one of the most impressive we had seen in the Neotropics—and the sun-pierced clouds silvered the reservoir below like the side of a giant shad, providing a stunning backdrop to the green forest that swept down the hills to its shores. We saw only two boats on this immense expanse of water during the entire time we were at Brownsberg, and this added measurably to the unspoiled feel of the area. Even the distant lights from the dam at night represented but a thin orange thread that was, in turn, substantially subordinated to the giant skies and blanket of bright stars above. Red Howler Monkeys and Spider Monkeys lounged in the trees next to our quarters, and Keel-billed Toucans and Green Aracaris strafed the airways running to the shore. Background music from the ubiquitous Thrush-like Antpitta and the joyful Musician

Gray-winged Trumpeter (109), Suriname, 2003

Wren served to round out the aesthetic tone of the experience.

As for the birds, there were a number of special ones, and we got lucky with a couple the first morning we were there. The first was a Gray-winged Trumpeter (no. 109), a hunched-backed guineafowl type with a high-gloss, violet-purple feathering on its foreneck and breast. Vera and I had observed the species before in southern Peru, but we weren't able then to get close to one because of the bird's extreme wariness. At the first signs of trouble, trumpeters lower their heads and slink away quickly as if ducking gunfire. We were fortunate, however, to jump several small groups seeking small fruits that had fallen to the ground, and we ambushed one of the birds as it edged out of the woods that first morning.

The second win that first day came from a particular antpitta, which is extremely difficult to see anywhere, although its hollow whistle is one of the common sounds of the local woods—the Thrush-like Antpitta (no. 110). We were lucky. Without realizing it, we seemed to have hit Suriname at the apex of its breeding season, and this unusually secretive bird was now calling from everywhere and, more important, was proving to be extremely responsive to tape. Even when calling back, however, the bird tends to stay low to the ground, furtive, hidden completely from view. But not this day. One jumped up on a mossy log and actually sang back to us for several minutes. Vera tagged it. We were off to a good start.

The next several mornings we focused on a couple of celebrated antbirds of the lowlands here: the handsome Ferruginous-backed Antbird and the Wing-banded Antbird. Our strategy was simple—get off the trail and drill deep into the forest where the birds were singing, play back their songs, and then wait quietly, frozen, for the birds to move curiously close for a possible shot. This always sounds far easier than it ever turns out to be because the interior of the forest floor is very dark and both birds tend to creep silently through the tangles and shadows toward the source of the sound—if they decide to come at all. Then there's

Thrush-like Antpitta (110), Suriname, 2003

Ferruginous-backed Antbird (111), Suriname, 2003

Wing-banded Antbird (112), Suriname, 2003

Red-and-black Grosbeak (113), Suriname, 2003

the issue of the thick web of vines and creepers blanketing the ground, which can flare the camera's flash, creating an image that looks as if it had been processed through soft gauze. A sure throwaway.

We nevertheless had good opportunities with both birds, which, after some work, yielded acceptable photographs. The Ferruginous-backed Antbird (no. 111) was the easier of the two, as this elegantly handsome little guy, with his rich chestnut body and bright blue face, would unsuspiciously tiptoe toward the playback on little cat feet, sometimes singing as he did so. I eventually managed a crisp shot, up close.

The Wing-banded Antbird (no. 112) was far more skittish, almost rail-like, and tended to station himself at a safe distance from where we were hiding, nonchalantly kicking up leaves like a leaftosser looking for food or either an enraged bull pawing the dirt. But just once he jumped up on a log to sneak a sideways look, and we were able to capture him also.

We spent time on two other birds of note at Brownsberg: the first, the much-coveted and elusive Red-and-black Grosbeak (no. 113), a gorgeous bird with a syrupy-sweet whistle of a song that we saw on several occasions moving through the woods in feeding flocks. This stunner is endemic to the Guianan Shield and is one of the most sought-after birds of these forests. On our last morning we got lucky with a rogue male that had worked fearlessly close to where we were standing. The second bird was a lustrous White Bellbird singing high at the top of a dead forest tree. But this little guy, with his long black wattle flapping every time he swung his head to throw his song in yet another direction, happened to be perching far too distant, at 100 feet, especially when viewed against a chalk-white sky, to offer any meaningful opportunity for photography. He's a great bird, however, and we were hoping we might have another shot at him somewhere down the road. But it didn't happen.

After Brownsberg, we headed to the local airport where we met our pilot for the day, an impressive Surinamese black named Otto, clear-eyed, self-assured, and seemingly more tightly wrapped than his flying machine of choice—a tatty, twin-engine Islander BN2B. But on a crisp sunny morning in early February, as Paramaribo's finest were strolling smartly through the marketplace, showing off their caged birds in a manner no less prideful than manicured matrons escorting Park Avenue poodles, and with old Fefe, the lodge superintendent, and his Saramacca buddies brooding in shadowed solemnity on creaky porches at Brownsberg, awaiting further grievances, Otto lifted off. He pointed us due west in the direction of Foengoe Island and our scheduled rendezvous with the Raleigh Boys, "Raymond the Maroon," and the beautiful Coppename River. The chances were pretty good that, at that precise moment, our little team of five represented the only ones in the entire country who were penetrating Suriname air space.

We banked sharply over the Suriname River and five minutes later were flying over an uninterrupted green carpet of primary forest for as far as the eye could see. For the next hour we would spot only one small break in this sea of green, an ugly peach-colored scar of a working gold mine manned by Brazilian miners who had crossed illegally into the country to set up shop, yet who, for reasons hard to comprehend, had been left unchecked by the Surinamese government.

The forests we flew over were simply immense, and although we've all done the math and realize that at the present pace of habitat destruction, with its inadequate rates of regeneration, the great rainforests will be gone in fifty years or so, it's nevertheless hard to believe. There simply seems to be too much green for the mind to process its pro forma elimination. So conservationists trying to make the case for the imminent destruction of the rainforest would be well advised to avoid small planes flying over Suriname; they need to cruise the skies over Haiti instead. It's been stripped to the bone in one generation—there's no forest left standing at all—and from the air the entire country looks like a civilization scattered along the top of a stark mountain range, high above the tree line.

We dropped down on a dirt strip cleared from the forests on Foengoe Island, an actual island one mile long and 500 yards wide in the middle of the iodine-colored Coppename River. Foengoe Island is the headquarters of the Raleighvallen-Voltzberg Nature Reserve, and from the cabins on the bluff overlooking this black river, studded with giant boulders that resembled charcoal dumplings, emerged yet another attractive Suriname campsite. Raleigh Falls itself, however, misnamed and upstream from Foengoe Island, is but an insignificant riffle of small rapids.

The Raleighvallen-Voltzberg reserve was superintended by a group of Kwinti maroons, whom we found to be friendly and helpful and—for reasons most likely related to a less aggrieved recent history—of a disposition different from that of the surly Saramaccas of Brownsberg. Several of the Kwintis had formed an ad hoc music group, styled "the Raleigh

Boys," and they were fawned-over celebrities up and down the Coppename River. They even had a CD of their music for sale at the station.

One of the leaders of the Raleigh Boys, "Raymond the Maroon," was to be our chief porter and guide for the three days we were in Voltzberg, and we found his sense of humor and knowledge of the forest to be impressive. Raymond had grown up in Paramaribo, where his family had fled during the civil war, and in addition to the local languages he had developed a surprisingly good working English. He had a big warm smile, bare feet, and twinkling eyes. He also had a habit of speaking of himself in the third person, which would have come across as annoyingly affected in anyone else, but carried a certain lyrical charm when coming from him—as in, "Raymond thinks it's going to rain" or "the snakes run away when they see Raymond coming." Tribal custom also permits Raymond to have up to four wives—but only if he is able to provide equally for all four. Raymond allowed as to how he was perfectly content with just one, but his wink left the indelicate impression that if his tips for the season were robust enough, he might well be able to afford another. The sidekick shared with Raymond her feelings that if she were ever picked to be one of four wives, no one would be happy. Raymond didn't want to hear that.

We stowed some of our gear at Foengoe, packed a few essentials, and boarded a 30-foot canoe to maneuver upstream to the trailhead, which led to a secluded forest camp five miles away at the base of an enormous quartzite mountain, the Voltzberg. The trail is wide and flat, snaking through lowland primary forest with an open understory dominated by giant palms. The habitat isn't as rich with wildlife as those marvelous forests of southern Peru because Suriname sits on a massive geological formation called the Guianan Shield, and its thin soils—and the black rivers laden

with the tannic acids that feed them—don't provide the nutrients found in the Amazon Basin, which is nourished by the white waters draining the Andes. Whereas Manu National Park, for example, might have thirteen species of monkey, Suriname has but eight; the birdlife here is also less diverse.

Vera and I had been warned that the trail into Voltzberg was long and tough and might take most of the day, so we sent our three porters on ahead of us with our food and gear. But the hike wasn't bad at all. Dawdlers and dreamers might well struggle seven hours on the trail, as well as serious birders trying to identify each member of every feeding flock, perhaps five—but Vera and I, moving right along at a comfortable clip, managed the trail in three and a half hours. The Raleigh Boys, barefoot and even carrying a small load, can do it in about an hour.

The Voltzberg Lodge rests among large granite outcrops, blackened by oxidation, in the middle of a rich section of lowland forest. But the structure is less a lodge than it is a rustic shelter with a couple of rooms; there are no wash basins (a rain barrel outside sufficed), no beds (we slung hammocks), and no showers (Vera and I bathed and splashed naked like California hippies in a foot-deep, tea-colored stream nearby).

As for the hammocks, they weren't bad at all once we learned how to use them. If you avoid conforming your body to the banana shape of the rig, but position yourself instead at a 30-degree angle to its curve, maintaining a straight back as you do so, it's surprisingly comfortable. With our mosquito net tightly secured, Vera and I stayed snugly cocooned throughout the night and slept better than at any other time on our trip. I can't speak for the others.

Around breakfast the next morning, it was argued (but never, as I recall, fully resolved) which of the six of us, shoe-horned together, snored the loudest. The preliminary read suggested it was more or less a tie between me and "Raymond the Maroon." But it was unanimously agreed that Vera made no sound at all and that Ganesh, the cook, was the only one who talked in his sleep.

At Voltzberg not only were the facilities rustic, but the menagerie of resident wildlife was not altogether friendly. And nighttime was when these creatures were on the move. A large tarantula had a web-protected hiding place on the tree next to the kitchen, bats blew in and out of the open windows in the early morning, chatting furiously and billowing our mosquito netting with their beating wings, and a three-foot Fer-de-lance stalked small frogs around the wooden outhouse in back. We obviously tried to take care of our business before dark.

But the chiggers and ticks weren't as bad as they might have been, and since this was the dry season, we were also blessed with superb weather for the entire time we were in the interior. It could have been different—and nasty. Had we camped here during the rainy season, another concern would have surfaced: malaria, for the *Anofeles* mosquito happens to be a real issue in this part of the world. You contract malaria when this particular mosquito bites you just after it has bitten someone else who is a carrier of the disease (read: all locals who live in the interior of Suriname). So if you happen to stumble into the forested heart of Suriname during the peak of the rainy season, be sure you have appropriate malaria medication—and try to avoid late-afternoon lawn parties down by the river with Amerindian natives, Brazilian miners, and malarial maroons.

There was other interesting and colorful wildlife around the lodge: White-throated Toucans ("yelpers") and Channel-billed Toucans ("croakers"), punctuating the point that you never have two "croakers" or two "yelpers" in the same section of for-est. In addition, antthrushes and antpittas and howler monkeys thoroughly charmed us with their songs and whistles and roars throughout the day and night. We even saw a tight little tribe of 1,000 bats fly over us early one evening like a little puff of windblown smoke on their way down to the river to hunt. The six of us were all lying prone on a flat granite outcropping near the lodge, soaking up the heat absorbed there during the day, taking in deep dusk and the approaching night, until it finally turned pitch black and the stars reached down to grab us.

But Vera and I hadn't come to Suriname to earn a merit badge in "wilderness experience," nor were we there to see more toucans and monkeys. We had come to witness and photograph the largest Guianan Cock-of-the-rock lek in the world, and we took off early the next morning for an hour's walk through the forest to get to it. It was also the beginning of the breeding season for this cotinga, so we hoped our timing would reward us with lots of these big orange birds in action.

The Guianan Cock-of-the-rock, which we had first encountered, and even photographed, in eastern Venezuela in the spring of 2000, is indigenous to the rocky outcrops and cliffs of the Guianan Shield. While the females make their nests on the sides of boulders and cliffs, the males hang out together not far away in an open understory of small saplings. At this lek site, the males continually spar with one other in ritualized posturings directly above a series of cleared dirt arenas on the ground, each about six feet across. The dominant males, having perfected their claim on these display stages, will perform there when the female comes into the area to choose a mate. Although there is always a lot of head bobbing and beak clicking, as the birds caw and squawk at each other off and on, these cocks-of-the-rock are strangely low-key and restrained when compared with the continual

Guianan Cock-of-the-rock (114), Suriname, 2003

raucous carnival of noise generated by their Andean cousins during their own ritualized performances.

Late the next morning we sneaked quietly to the edge of this forest sanctuary, just as the high sun was beginning to fully illuminate the lek area. Here we witnessed a number of birds already clinging to saplings above their arenas, and quite a few more were maneuvering a bit higher in the trees above. We counted an unbelievable twenty-seven crayon-orange cotingas in our field of vision, contrasting violently against a vibrant green background dappled by sunlight. The impact was immediate and powerful. It was as if we had stumbled upon an oriental tableau of mango-colored Chinese lanterns festively sprinkled on low limbs throughout some green glen. Or else startled a fanciful field of feathered pumpkins that

had all flown to the trees to just sit and stare back at us. "Raymond the Maroon" said he had once counted up to fifty birds at this one spot. To put that arithmetic in perspective: the largest other cock-of-the-rock lek we knew of boasted only about fifteen males. This one here in Suriname is considered by many to be the mother of all leks.

Vera and I, dressed in camouflage and face netting, crouched quietly on our stools, unblinkingly still for over an hour before even attempting our first shot. We saw several males drop to their cleared arenas from time to time when a female would drift through the area, but the action was sporadic and episodic and didn't last very long. Pairs of males would leave to feed throughout the day, and others would fly in to replace them. The lek population al-

Guianan Cock-of-the-rock, Suriname, 2003

Yellow-billed Jacamar (115), Suriname, 2003

ways seemed in a state of flux; there was a lot of coming and going.

About three in the afternoon, just as we were considering calling it a day, a female suddenly swept in low and attached herself to a sapling three feet above the ground. Then, of the nearly thirty birds stationed in the trees around us, an unbelievable twelve of them suddenly dropped in unison to their arenas on the ground like giant oranges simultaneously shaken from a tree. Though there had been some half-hearted sparring and turf squabbles throughout the day, it was now clear—once the game had officially begun—that the hierarchy had already been validated, each dominant bird the undisputed lord of his own arena. There was

no confusion once the signal was given, but it was unclear just which bird had given it. Possibly the female, or a designated alpha male, or simply all the worthy contenders instinctively reacting at the same time to her arrival. We never figured it out.

The female soon began to alternate her attention among four males—they had made the playoffs—and the remaining eight conceded their elimination and drifted back into the trees. The displaying males would fan out their rump feathers like a spreading skirt while at the same time flattening and depressing their tails. Then they would crouch, freeze for a while, sometimes up to a minute, and suddenly tilt their heads sideways so that their crests would lie in a

White-plumed Antbird (116), Suriname, 2003

horizontal plane. Periodically they would bounce up and down, several times in succession, and then freeze again. It was both spellbinding and radically different from the rituals of the Andean Cock-of-the-rock, to which they are so closely related.

The female then narrowed the field of her affections to two, each competing male performing right next to the other. On a couple of occasions she actually dropped to the ground between the two of them for a close-up inspection, and we were sure that at any moment she would peck one on the back, or at his fringe feathers, to signal her final selection of a mate. But she never did. Either she couldn't make up her mind or we, by our presence, had somehow intimidated her.

But no matter. Even without witnessing full consummation of this colorful romance, the extravaganza represented a once-in-a-lifetime experience. To be sure,

Vera and I had, on other occasions, encountered glorious flocks of colorful birds, from gaudy macaws and parrots at clay licks to hundreds of ibises spiraling into their roost at dusk. But the spectacle that yielded this photo of a Guianan Cock-of-the-rock (no. 114) was different, and the day not only exceeded our wildest expectations but turned out to be the most spectacular wildlife experience that Vera and I encountered in the Neotropics. We would rank it number one.

On our way out of Voltzberg the next day, heading back along the trail to Foengoe Island, and after first hearing its piercing whistle, Vera picked up a handsome Yellow-billed Jacamar (no. 115). It was perched in a beautiful setting near a small creek on a arching vine, and we enjoyed watching it dive to capture a bright orange butterfly on one of its successful sallies. It was the third jacamar we had photographed during our time in the Neotropics.

And then finally, as the trail was narrowing on our approach to the Coppename River, we saw an army antswarm crossing in front of us as it sliced its way through the forest. It looked to be a good one, but it was hard to say from simply observing the two-inch band crossing the trail. To determine whether it had any real scale—and whether any notable antbirds or other camp followers were in attendance—we would have to move into the woods and get out ahead of where the swarm was advancing, and spreading, and reeking havoc among the understory.

As it turned out, it was an enormous swarm, with several hundreds of thousands of ants on the move, second only to the one we had encountered years before in the Darien of Panama. But oddly enough, Vera and I identified only four separate species of birds in attendance: two woodcreepers and two antbirds. The Darien swarm had boasted from ten to twelve species, including a big antpitta and the great ground-cuckoo. This one was anemic by comparison.

Of the two antbirds we jumped that day, one was the common Rufous-throated Antbird—the obligate sentinel of South American antswarms. Nothing so special there. The other one, however, just happened to be the most coveted antbird of them all, the glorious White-plumed Antbird. Practically the only time you see this superstar is at antswarms, and here it was, bouncing among the small saplings, hovering over the most seething section of the forest, looking for prey. We had our chance.

Over the next couple of hours, we tried time after time to maneuver close to where this energetic little bird was hunting to manage some kind of shot. Vera, who was working an especially heavy section of the seething swarm, had to beat a panicked retreat on several occasions when the ants overtook her and worked above the tops of her shoes. We weren't wear-

ing rubber boots, so we tried as best we could to stay out their way, but this was tough to do since the swarm was a large one, with several advancing and encircling columns, and since we were fully absorbed with trying to get some kind of bead on our target.

The light was also bad, the brush at times too thick to shoot through, and we simply couldn't work in a clean shot. It was like chasing a little chestnut ghost with a white wizard's hat through the tangle: when we zigged, he zagged; when we focused, he moved; when we fired, he was gone. And just when we were beginning to think it was all slipping away, and as the fading afternoon was starting to throw the understory into killing shadow, the bird suddenly darted to a vertical stem just twelve feet away. And he paused just long enough to allow a shot, just one shot—and I got him. The White-plumed Antbird (no. 116) had been on our hit list from the very beginning, but this was the only one we were to see. We felt proud and lucky to have him.

Arriving back at Foengoe Island in the late afternoon, elated with our victories of the day, we found our evening meal already prepared by Ganesh, and the Raleigh Boys well into their cups. After dinner, as Vera and I went off to bed to sleep like babies on clean sheets and real beds, they played and sang and beat their drums well into the night. It was a fitting last night in Suriname, and the sound of those drums and the lubricated chants of the Raleigh Boys, led by "Raymond the Maroon," remain with us to this day.

Would we go back? Perhaps. But only to track down a spectacular and almost mythical bird known to be found somewhere in the savanna and interior forests of Suriname—the brilliant Crimson Fruitcrow. It's huge like a raven and a deep crimson-red. And it's very rare. The sidekick wants it badly and once even insisted that we needed to photograph one for our book—until I finally convinced her that only two people we knew, Andy Whittaker and Phoebe Snetsinger, had ever seen one. And that was fifteen years earlier from a tower in Brazil. And then only once. The great ornithologist Steve Hilty, who has been to Suriname twenty times or so, has yet to encounter it.

But we know it's out there somewhere where the roads don't go and only black rivers run, and if we think we have a legitimate shot at this great cotinga, we'll go back. Even now, David Ascanio and Sean are putting out the word along the Suriname and Coppename rivers that they are interested in finding it. Incentives are involved. Sean said his uncle had spotted one of the birds the previous year in the Amerindian village of Palumeau down on the Tapanahony River. What he failed to mention, however, was that this particular village is also known for its high number of malarial deaths each year. Just another little obstacle to consider. So we'll have to see.

Postscript

Our SURINAME ADVENTURE was our last major excursion into the rainforests of the Neotropics, and the White-plumed Antbird and Guianan Cock-of-the-rock represented the last of the special birds we had targeted for photographs. Of course, other star birds like the Crimson Fruitcrow still called to us seductively from afar, and stunning habitats in Bolivia and Amazonian Brazil continued to intrigue us. But for the most part we had accomplished what we had set out to do—we had photographed a representative sampler of the exotic birds that inhabit the Neotropics, and we had probed multiple habitats in eleven different countries off and on over fifteen years to do it.

Along the way, Vera and I had become increasingly energized by the scope of the adventure and charmed by the special magic of the Neotropical forests. The experience had also served to substantiate the premise that many of us need regular doses of wild things and wild places to maintain our balance. That we desperately hunger for the nature-fix of exotic creatures and ancient trees, of wild skies and raging rivers, the chirring of birdlife, the smell of the forest floor. We feel deprived and edgy when we go awhile without them. Especially those of us who live in the city. We've even come to acknowledge that silence is a welcomed, if not a compulsory, respite from the roar of urban life, and that the quietness of the rainforest punctuates the privilege of solitude.

But along the way, a more overarching principal of life became validated, at least for Vera and me, that irrespective of what metropolitan enclave had captured our adult lives, there still lived within each of us a certain childhood sense of curiosity and adventure—

of kicking through mud puddles and lifting rocks to look for little creatures, of climbing trees and exploring crooked creeks. And that the rainforest experience was more than just an escape from city noise; it represented a laboratory for wonder, where one can dream dreams of seeing something enchanting, or rare, or exciting—for the very first time, where magic may be lurking around the bend, a fresh marvel just over the next rise, or perhaps whispering softly from the trees above, awaiting discovery. Where astonishment is cocked and ready to be engaged. Thoreau said as much. He knew: one can't find wonder in the cities but in "the impervious and quaking swamps."

That's where Vera and I had just been, and it had felt good.

Family Album

FAMILY NAME	BIRD NUMBER	FAMILY NAME	BIRD NUMBER
Violet Sabrewing	7	*Antshrikes*	
Violet-tailed Sylph	106	Barred Antshrike	17
White-necked Jacobin	45	Rufous-winged Antshrike	103
		Western Slaty-Antshrike	83
Trogons		*Antbirds*	
Resplendent Quetzal	8	Bicolored Antbird	37
Baird's Trogon	4	Chestnut-backed Antbird	39
Black-headed Trogon	73	Ferruginous-backed Antbird	111
Collared Trogon	20	Spotted Antbird	38
Slaty-tailed Trogon	48	White-plumed Antbird	116
		Wing-banded Antbird	112
Puffbirds		*Antpittas*	
White-eared Puffbird	102	Black-crowned Antpitta	40
White-whiskered Puffbird	85	Chestnut-crowned Antpitta	32
		Thrush-like Antpitta	110
Jacamars		*Manakins*	
Great Jacamar	82	Band-tailed Manakin	93
Rufous-tailed Jacamar	14	Blue Manakin	68
Yellow-billed Jacamar	115	Club-winged Manakin	105
		Helmeted Manakin	97
Barbets		Long-tailed Manakin	77
Toucan Barbet	107	Orange-bellied Manakin	24
Versicolored Barbet	90	Orange-collared Manakin	15
		Red-capped Manakin	9
Toucanets		Wire-tailed Manakin	60
Emerald Toucanet	79	*Motmots*	
Saffron Toucanet	67	Blue-crowned Motmot	78
		Broad-billed Motmot	13
Aracaris		Keel-billed Motmot	50
Collared Aracari	47	Tody Motmot	44
		Turquoise-browed Motmot	1
Toucans			
Chestnut-mandibled Toucan	81	*Nunbirds*	
Keel-billed Toucan	46	Black-fronted Nunbird	33
Plate-billed Mountain-Toucan	108		
Toco Toucan	96	*Tityras*	
		Masked Tityra	12
Woodpeckers			
Yellow-tufted Woodpecker	22	*Cotingas*	
Red-crowned Woodpecker	57	Three-wattled Bellbird	76
		Blue Cotinga	86
Ovenbirds			
Rufous-capped Spinetail	62		
Woodcreepers			
Red-billed Scythebill	98		

FAMILY NAME	BIRD NUMBER	FAMILY NAME	BIRD NUMBER
Capuchinbird	72	Blue-winged Mountain-Tanager	53
Andean Cock-of-the-rock	87	Golden Tanager	30
Guianan Cock-of-the-rock	114	Golden-hooded Tanager	51
Handsome Fruiteater	54	Saffron-crowned Tanager	89
Bare-necked Umbrellabird	80	Scarlet-rumped Tanager	11
		Silver-beaked Tanager	31
Flycatchers		Speckled Tanager	29
Cinnamon Flycatcher	58		
Ruddy Tody-Flycatcher	71	*Grosbeaks*	
		Red-and-black Grosbeak	113
Honeycreepers			
Green Honeycreeper	19	*Euphonias*	
Purple Honeycreeper	16	Orange-bellied Euphonia	55
Dacnis		*Blackbirds*	
Blue Dacnis	66	Red-breasted Blackbird	28
Chats		*Orioles*	
Gray-throated Chat	49	Spot-breasted Oriole	75
Tanagers		*Finches*	
Bay-headed Tanager	88	Coal-crested Finch	104

Advice Lab

A CARDINAL RULE of rainforest travel is to carry along only the absolute essentials. The goal is to travel light, make do. That's good advice, but Vera and I mostly chose to ignore it. We had lots of gear, and we wanted it with us—equipment and clothing we knew we would need and other stuff as a standby. The following items we found to be particularly useful in the field. Some are photography-specific, some general and preferential, others simply nice to have along.

PHOTOGRAPHY GEAR

Camera/Flash. We used a basic Nikon 8008, primarily in its manual mode. Also a Nikon SB-28 flash, which, when enhanced with flash extensions, added another two to three f-stops of light to our game. Nearly 90 percent of our pictures were taken with a flash; only larger birds in weak light, and at distances over 40–50 feet, were taken with the use of a tripod at low shutter speeds. Plus we always carried a spare body, lens, and flash with us for backup insurance.

Lens. Nikon 300mm F4, with Nikon 1.4x and 2.0x teleconverters. The F4 is a *slow* lens, but it's also a very light one and can be hand-held with excellent maneuverability. The extra weight of the faster F2.8, and the tripod required to effectively manage it, wasn't a good tradeoff. The 300 F4 was well suited for a thick, tight rainforest environment, although we often missed the extra f-stop of ambient light that the F2.8 provides. We opted for maneuverability.

In addition, we never used the lens's automatic focus feature. Successfully photographing a bird demands that its eye and beak be tack-sharp, and the reads from automatic focusing were never fast enough or reliable enough, we felt, to outweigh manual focusing. Automatic focusing is also especially limiting in trying to capture fast-moving small birds in thick brush. After continually using manual focusing over the years, we finally got pretty good at it.

Film. The quality of the film improved substantially from the time of our first trip back in 1987, increasingly permitting the use of higher-speed films that once would have been unthinkable because of excessive graininess. Light/film-speed tradeoffs are always driving issues in a rainforest environment, where light is a scarce commodity and the aesthetic reach for a warm, ambient backdrop for the bird image is a top priority. Balancing all elements into a pleasing composition, while at the same time avoiding "closet shots," was always our goal. Constantly experimenting with new films, we finally settled on Fujichrome Provia 100F ASA, which we pushed to 200, and Fujichrome Provia 400F ASA, which we shot straight. The color was well saturated, the grain tight enough. Sure, we might have wished to use a Velvia 50 ASA, but we simply couldn't afford to surrender the three to four f-stops. Velvia may work just fine on sun-drenched flowers with a tripod and no wind, but not chasing small birds through the dark tangles of a Neotropical woods.

To protect the film when moving through airport X-ray machines, we would carry our film canisters in X-ray shield bags—but only if we had first been unsuccessful in getting the film hand-checked. According to the party line at most airports, films with speeds less than 800 ASA will not be damaged by the carry-on X-ray machines, even if sent through naked.

We were never confident enough, however, with the consistency of that application, airport to airport, to ever risk it. And there was no need to. So request a hand check when you can, bag it when you can't. And never send your film through with *checked* luggage. Never.

Tripods. We used substantial but light-weight carbon fiber tripods from Bogen with pistol-grip ball heads for quick tracking, although, quite frankly, only a few of our birds were taken this way—most, as mentioned, were captured with a flash. The tripod stakeouts we did set up were made easier by light-weight, three-legged aluminum stools, which we often carried with us in the field for that purpose. These were essential for sitting quietly and calling in an antpitta or remaining inconspicuous and motionless at a manakin lek. When we needed to sit still and wait, sometimes draped in camouflage netting, we were prepared.

Binoculars. For birders, excellent binoculars are 100 percent essential; for photographers, maybe 20 percent. We scoped most of our birds by simply looking through the long lens of our camera and primarily used binoculars for long-distance verification. If a bird was so far away we needed binoculars to see it well, it was certainly too far away for a meaningful photograph of it. That said, we had good ones: Zeiss 10×40s. As for bird identification, we didn't take heavy reference materials to the woods. Instead we cannibalized our field guides by extracting the plates, which we then had rebound for a lighter carry in the field. We would keep the residual text back in the room for later reference.

This also serves to make another point: that bird photography and birding are, for the most part, mutually exclusive; they are two separate things. Vera and I were always so completely absorbed with the process of photographing the bird—sneaking within range, working on ambient light, keeping a moving target in focus, etc.—that our observation and identification scores suffered measurably. Bottom line: we came away from our Neotropical bird-photography adventure having become only average Neotropical birders. C+ or maybe B-. We didn't even maintain a list.

Tape Recorders. One of the most useful techniques for luring furtive birds from the shadows of the forest, or from the canopy of tall trees, is the playback of its song. The bird simply thinks the song is the seductive and bold invitation of a competitor male that has invaded his territory to woo away his girl. He doesn't like it, and many times will dart in closer to the source of the sound for a better look. Although many professional guides use heavy-duty recording equipment for this activity, we carried lightweight and relatively inexpensive cassette tape recorders from Radio Shack, which we would sometimes rig to miniature amplifier-speakers for the field.

As for the songs themselves, we had bird tapes made for us by Cornell's renowned Library of Natural Sounds or else we recorded the actual song of the bird in the field with a Sennheiser ME88 shotgun microphone, an 18-inch-long wand with a foam cover. This worked reasonably well and enabled us at times to maneuver far closer to our targeted birds than we would otherwise have been able to do.

Over the last several years, as the technology became available, we also began to use prerecorded songs on compact discs (CDs), which were particularly efficient with their digital sound clarity and random track access.

BAGS

When you have lots of gear, you need good bags. We had them:

Duffels. Large, water-resistant "Black Hole Bags" from Patagonia constituted our workhorse luggage. These were great for throwing on the back of a truck or boat, and they proved to be rugged and durable. In each one we would also carry a soft-plastic sweater bag from the Container Store for our clothes to protect them from the inevitable grit that built up in the duffels along the way. This way, we separated things we wanted to keep clean and fresh from things we didn't care about, like shoes and tripods and stools and such.

Camera Bag. Rather than a traditional, shoulder-strapped camera bag, we used a standard-size airplane carry-on with wheels to transport all of our camera gear. It was critical to have a bag with wheels simply because of the weight involved, and yet one of "carry-on" size that was small enough to stow topside in overhead compartments when traveling by plane—so we wouldn't have to check it through.

Day Pack. Required for long hikes while carrying camera equipment, tripods, and stools. A better idea is to get someone to carry the gear for you, but if you can't swing that, a day pack or small backpack is essential. Ours were from North Face.

Shell Bag. This turned out to be our most useful piece of gear of all. The three-pouch shell bag is waist-cinched and can be purchased in any hunting store. In lieu of a camera vest or backpack, we strapped a shell bag on every time we went to the field and stuffed the three pouches with our binoculars, water, flashes, snacks, batteries, film, umbrella, flashlights, and ponchos. We even buried the snout of the camera-mounted lens in the right-side pouch, which served to transfer the weight of the camera—as well as all of the other stuff we were carrying—from our shoulders and neck down to the hips. We could then move lightly and quickly along forest trails for long hours without wearing down. This is a really good idea; check it out.

Another use for the shell bag was to simply drape it over the telephoto lens when mounted to the tripod, giving it extra weight to further stabilize against camera shake at low shutter speeds.

Flyer's Helmet Bag. Sounds peculiar, but its design makes it perfect for transporting a full day's gear—camera, shell bag, hat, stools, food, etc.—from room to truck to boat to trailhead and then back again. The nylon flyer's helmet bag is padded and water resistant, has strong handles, and zips shut at the top. Purchased at any army-navy store.

Ziploc Bags and Plastic Garbage Sacks. Never leave home without lots of them. They're light and useful, from transporting muddy shoes, to protecting camera gear from rain, to storing food and medicines. Excellent all around.

APPAREL

Clothes. We found that the high-neck vest by Patagonia provided as much warmth, when layered, as we needed in the tropics. If one is staying in the High Andes, perhaps a light windbreaker could be added. Dark, crushable hat. Three wash-and-wear field changes, dark green, long-sleeve shirt/pant combinations by Ex Officio. Serious rainforest birders and wildlife photographers inevitably wear dark

green in the field, but the guides, strangely enough, all seem to show up in white T-shirts. Curious. Only freshly washed clothes should be worn each day in the field to prevent "chigger carry-over." Plus, carry one change of clothes for travel and one change for dinner at night.

Footwear. Vera and I started out wearing rubber boots in the field. They were great for slogging through the mud and wading small creeks, and they also provided some psychological comfort in the form of protection against things that crawled. But they were also impractical: they were hot, they afforded no traction at all on muddy inclines, and they offered limited foot support for long, rough hikes through the woods. We graduated early on to high-ankle hiking shoes, appropriately Gore-texed for water protection. They provided extraordinary comfort and support, and no matter how heavy the deluge, they would be manageably dry by the next day. Terrific product. There are a lot of good brands.

We also would bring along one pair of travel shoes, one pair of sneakers—as a backup if the hiking shoes didn't dry, but they always did—along with a pair of sandals for night wear and rubber thongs for the shower. We were clearly shoe-heavy, but we preferred it that way.

When it comes to socks, go for the "Smart Wool" ones, not cotton. They breathe, they hold their shape, and they feel good. Dry wool socks at the end of a long, wet day in the field is one of life's little pleasures.

Raingear. Rainforests are known for rain, so you have to deal with it and come prepared. The most essential "rain" item for the rainforest—hands down—is the small umbrella. It is indispensable. Rain suits and ponchos don't work well on narrow, brush-clawing forest trails. They also sweat a lot. Ponchos can be useful, though, on wet boat rides along fast, big rivers; they are great for protecting camera equipment; and they can serve as useful lean-to shelters in torrential downpours when fastened with clothespins to surrounding saplings. We always carried both: umbrella and poncho.

To further protect our camera equipment from the elements, we came armed with rain-proof bags, garbage sacks, and Ziploc bags filled with desiccant moisture-absorption packets.

Bug Protection. In addition to wearing long-sleeved shirts, long pants, and hats, we did other things to protect ourselves from the insects of the forest. We first tucked our pant cuffs into our socks and then sprayed the feet and lower legs and seat bottom with a bug spray that contained at least 25 percent Deet. We sensibly used a milder Cutter's lotion for face and hands. We also wore camouflaged gloves with the tips of the fingers cut off—to retain feel—which further served to protect the hands. The gloves also prevented alarming flashes of white skin, which could spook a bird if we quickly raised our cameras to photograph it.

In addition to these routine measures, we always carried with us bug netting or a mosquito mask for the face, which we found essential for those times when we were required to sit stone-still in "buggy" areas. We wouldn't have survived without them.

OTHER ESSENTIALS

Food. For openers, you don't go to the rainforest for the cuisine. This isn't Italy or southern France. Nutrition and basic health are the only concerns, with a distant nod toward tolerable taste. This said, Vera and I worked to avoid those situations in which we couldn't feel comfortable with the hygiene of the food preparation process. We relied, when we could,

on those lodges and camps that were part of the regular circuit of established birding groups, and found the food quality to range from "excellent" at the Clearwater Lodge to "quite good" at the Lodge at Pico Bonito, the Canopy Tower in Panama, and El Pescador Punta Gorda in Belize down to "comfortably acceptable" at most of the other lodges. Whenever we were in doubt as to food safety—and sometimes we found ourselves in some strange places— we went for beans and rice, cooked chicken, no salad, and Coke out of a can.

In the field we always had our little plastic bottle filled with purified water and an ample stash of trail mix to tide us over until we could get back to camp for a regular meal. One should never be without water and snacks, and there's no need to be. We also carried a thermos with us on most trips. We filled it with coffee made the night before for those times when we had to get up especially early, before the morning coffee became available. This assured that we were able to properly kick-start the new day.

Medicine. We always came prepared for as many things as we could imagine. Of course, we were current on all our requisite inoculations—tetanus, yellow fever, typhoid, and Hepatitis A. We also used the constantly improving malaria medications, but would take them only when traveling to areas where we knew there was a problem.

Additionally, we came armed with antibiotics, painkillers, sunscreen, Nuperin and aspirin, Robitussin, Flumadine, Imodium, Pepto-Bismol tablets, Band-Aids, Neosporin (an anti-infection ointment), an anti-itch medication (we liked After Bite, The Itch Eraser) for chiggers and insect bites, and a magnifying glass and tweezers for possible ticks.

Supplemental Toiletries. A supply of Kleenex in Ziploc bags (local tissue products are inadequate and dissolve with even the slightest humidity). Washcloth, favorite bar of soap, spare sunglasses, reading glasses, and contact-lens cleaners. Anti-bacterial hand-wipes for handling food in the field.

MISCELLANEOUS

(1) A *down pillow* went with Vera wherever she went, a small touch of comfort for rough places and long truck rides. It weighed nothing and could be compressed to nothing, and with the "travel calculus" of benefit-per-ounce-of-weight-carried or per-cubic-feet-of-bulk-stuffed, this ranked surprisingly high in value. An *inflatable neck brace* was the emergency pillow I used.

(2) We always carried *flashlights* and *extra batteries.* In addition, we became attached to our Petzl L.E.D. *headlamps,* which, with its white light and wide-angle reach, was particularly suited for both night walks and nighttime reading. It weighs only nine ounces. We always packed one with us in the field for returning through the woods in the late afternoons; the sun drops fast in tropical latitudes, and it's neither fun nor safe to walk forest trails in the dark.

(3) An *alarm clock.* For obvious reasons. Four o'clock in the morning comes early.

(4) *Earplugs.* Some people snore; some don't like the roar of howler monkeys at dawn.

(5) *Items for the hard core:*
   (a) Aluminum "signal" mirror to reflect sunlight back into the shadows to illuminate the bird enough to focus on it properly.
   (b) Small pair of gardening clippers, which are helpful in cutting through small creepers and vines to allow a silent approach to the bird or a shooting view through the tangle.
   (c) SOG Powerlock utility tool, with pliers blades, scissors, and such.
   (d) Garmin GPS tracking system to pinpoint an exact spot in the forest for a pre-located bird or a bivouacked antswarm or even to help find your way back to camp.

(6) *Items for the soft core:*
   (a) Chocolates for your pillow at night.
   (b) The right marmalade for your morning toast.

Resource Center

ECOTOURISM COMPANIES SPECIALIZING IN NEOTROPICAL BIRDING

The following birding companies have excellent reputations and take groups of from six to fifteen to substantially all of the lodges and destinations that Vera and I visited in the Neotropics. They have experienced guides who know the wildlife and terrain, and they've mastered the logistics. Their brochures describe specific trips, birds seen, preferred seasonal dates for travel, and general price information. Joining one of these companies for a birding tour is an excellent way to first experience the exotic birds of the Neotropics.

Field Guides, Inc.
9433 Bee Cave Road
Building 1, Suite 150
Austin, TX 78733
Telephone: 800-728-4953, 512-263-7295
fieldguides@fieldguides.com

Victor Emanuel Nature Tours, Inc. (V.E.N.T.)
2525 Wallingwood Drive, Building 10
Austin, TX 78746
Telephone: 800-328-8368, 512-328-5221
Info@ventbird.com

Wings
1643 N. Alvernon, Suite 105
Tucson, AZ 85712
Telephone: 888-293-6443, 520-320-9868
wings@wingsbirds.com

DESTINATION HIGHLIGHTS: OUR PICKS

Best Accommodations:
The Lodge at Pico Bonito, Honduras
El Pescador Punta Gorda, Belize
Canopy Tower, Panama
Chan Chich Lodge, Belize

Most Photographic Opportunities:
Henri Pittier National Park, Venezuela
Pantanal, Brazil
Asa Wright Nature Centre, Trinidad
Canopy Tower, Panama

Most "Star Quality" Birds:
Tandayapa Valley, Ecuador
Eastern Venezuela
Monteverde Cloud Forest, Costa Rica

Best Primary Forest:
Manu National Park, Peru
Suriname
Corcovado National Park, Costa Rica

DESTINATIONS

Belize

Chan Chich Lodge
P.O. Box 37
Belize City, Belize
Telephone: 011-501-223-4419
www.chanchich.com
E-mail: info@chanchich.com

El Pescador Punta Gorda
P.O. Box 135
Punta Gorda, Toledo District, Belize
Telephone: 011-501-722-0050
E-mail: jscott@elpescadorpg.org

Brazil

General Guide

Birding Brazil Tours, Inc.
Andy Whittaker
Manaus, Brazil
Telephone: 011-55-92-644-3792
E-mail: birdingbraziltours.com

Pantanal

Fazenda Santa Teresa
Rodovia Transpantaneira
Km. 67 Pocone
Mato Grosso, Brazil
Telephone: 011-55-65-624-6255

Pousada O Pantaneira
Rodovia Transpantaneira
Km. 110 Pocone
Mato Grosso, Brazil
Telephone: 011-55-65-721-1545

Pousada Penhasco
Av. Penhasco s/n Bom Clima
Chapada Dos Guimaraes
Mato Grosso, Brazil
Telephone: 011-55-65-624-1000
Fax: 011-55-65-301-1555

Southeastern Brazil

Itatiaia National Park

Hotel Do Ype
Booking Agent: Blumar
Telephone: 011-55-438-759300, 011-55-243-521453
www.blumar.com.br
E-mail: Erik@blumar.com.br

Costa Rica

Local Booking Agent

Explore Costa Rica
300 Meters W, 100 Meters South U.S. Embassy
P.O. Box 818-1200
Pavas, San José, Costa Rica
Telephone: 011-506-220-2121, 011-506-232-3321
www.explorecr.com
E-mail: explore@explorecostarica.net

San José

Hotel Herradura
Autopista General Cañas
Cruce San Antonio de Belén
Frente a Mall Cariari
Heredia, Costa Rica
Telephone: 011-506-239-0033
Fax: 011-506-293-2713
www.hotelherradura.com
E-mail: gventas@hotelherradura.com

Pacific Coast

Carara Biological Reserve

Tarcol Lodge
Telephone: 011-506-430-0400, 011-506-297-4134, 1-800-593-3305, 1-888-246-8513
www.ranchonaturalista.com/tarcol.html
E-mail: mark@ranchonaturalista.com
Fax: 011-506-297-4135

Gulf of Nicoya, Puntarenas

La Ensenada Lodge
Telephone: 011-506-289-3921
Fax: 011-506-289-5281
www.laensenada.net
E-mail: letresa@acsa.co.cr

Manuel Antonio National Park, Quepos

Hotel Mariposa
Telephone: 1-800-416-2747
www.hotelmariposa.com
E-mail: hotelmar@san.rr.com

Corcovado National Park

Sirena Biological Station
Telephone: 011-506-735-5282, 011-506-735-5440
506-735-5076
www.nps.gov/centralamerica/costarica/
http://uts.cc.utexas.edu/nelsong/sirena/staying-in-
sirena.html

Tilaran Mountains

Monteverde Cloud Forest
http://www.costa-rica-monteverde.com/monteverde-
activities-cloud-forest.htm

Hotel Belmar
Telephone: 011-506-645-5201, 1-800-566-7616
Fax: 011-506-645-5135
www.hotelbelmar.com
E-mail: info@hotelbelmar.com

Hotel Montaña Monteverde
Telephone: 011-506-645-5046, 011-506-645-5338
Fax: 011-506-645-5320
www.ticonet.co.cr/monteverde
E-mail: monteverde@ticonet.co.cr

Caribbean Lowlands

Puerto Viejo de Sarapiqui

La Selva Biological Station
Telephone: 011-506-766-6565, 011-506-240-6696
Fax: 011-506-766-6535
E-mail: laselva@sloth.ots.ac.cr

Selva Verde Lodge
Telephone: 011-506-766-6800, 1-800-451-7111
Fax: 506-766-6011
E-mail: selvaver@racsa.co.cr

Ecuador

Río Napo

La Selva Lodge
La Selva
Av. 6 de Diciembre 2816 y Paúl Rivet
Quito, Ecuador
Telephone: 011-593-2-550-995, 011-593-2-554-686
Fax: 011-593-2-567-297
www.laselvajunglelodge.com
E-mail: laselva@uio.satnet.net

Sacha Lodge
Julio Zaldumbide 397 y Valladolid
P.O. Box 17-21-1608
Quito, Ecuador
Telephone: 011-593-25660909
www.sachalodge.com
E-mail: sachalod@pi.pro.ec

Mindo Valley/Tandayapa Valley

Guide
Tony Nunnery
E-mail: Pilgrim82@hotmail.com

Bellavista Lodge
Telephone: 011-593-211632
E-mail: info@bellavistacloudforest.com

Clearwater Lodge
Fausto Valencia Vallejo
E-mail: Truchav@punto.net.ec

Séptimo Paraíso
Telephone: 011-593-22-893-512
E-mail: info@septimoparaiso.com

Guatemala

Tikal

Camino Real Tikal
Lote 77, Parcelamiento Tayasal
17002 Petén
Petén, Guatemala
Telephone: 011-5023683680
Fax: 011-5023683687

Honduras

Guide
Robert Gallardo
E-mail: rgallardo32@hotmail.com

The Lodge at Pico Bonito
Telephone: 011-504-440-0388
Fax: 011-504-440-0468
www.picobonito.com

Panama

Southern Darien Province
Cana

Booking Agent
Field Guides or Wings. V.E.N.T. no longer goes to the Darien.

Soberanía National Park

Canopy Tower
www.canopytower.com
E-mail: stay@canopytower.com

Peru

Southern Peru
Manu National Park

Booking Agent
Inkanatura
P.O. Box 1065
Alachua, FL 33616
Telephone: 011-51-144002022
1-877-8881770
www.inkanatura.com
E-mail: travel@tropicalnaturetravel.com

Lodges
Cock-of-the-Rocks Lodge (book through Inkanatura)
Manu Wildlife Center (book through Inkanatura)

Suriname

Booking Agent
METS
E-mail: Mets@sr.net

Trinidad

Booking Agent
Caligo Ventures
E-mail: denise@caligo.com

Asa Wright Nature Centre
Reservations Office
P.O. Box 4710
20 Farfan Street
Arima, Trinidad
Telephone: 1-868-667-4655

Venezuela

Guide
David Ascanio
E-mail: morphos@telcel.net.ve

Andes

Barquisimeto (foothills)

Barquisimeto Hilton
Cr 5 entre Cl 5 y 6 Nueva Segovia
Barquisimeto-Lara, Venezuela 3002
Telephone: 011-58-251-2564111
Fax: 011-58-251-2544365
www.hilton.com/en/hi/

Barinas

Bristol Barinas
Avenida 23 De Enero
Barinas, Venezuela
Telephone: 011-58-7320911

Santo Domingo

Hotel Los Frailes
Mucabaji, Santo Domingo
Mérida, Venezuela
Telephone: 011-58-414-7412986

Hotel Moruco
Carretera Trasandina, kilómetro 79
vía a Santo Domingo
Santo Domingo
Mérida, Venezuela 5130
Telephone: 011-58-73-88070

Coastal Cordillero

Henri Pittier National Park

Rancho Grande Biological Station
Carretera Nacional Maracay-Ocumare de la Costa
Parque Nacional Henri Pittier
Aragua, Venezuela

Maracay

Hotel Italo
Av. Las Delicias
Urb. La Soledad 6ta. Avenida
Maracay
Aragua, Venezuela
Telephone: 011-58-43321576
www.hotelitalo.com.ve

Llanos

Hato Piñero
Municipio Giraldot
Carrebera El Tinaco, via El Baúl
Distrito El Baúl
Cojedes, Venezuela
Telephone: 011-58-862000
www.hatopinero.com

Hato El Cedral
Av. La Salle, Piso 5 PH. Los Caobos
Caracas, Venezuela
Telephone: 011-58-212-781-8995, 011-58-212-793-6082
Fax: 011-58-212-793-6082
www.hatocedral.com
E-mail: info@hatocedral.com
011-58-42940249

Eastern Venezuela

Río Grande Reserve

Parador Taguapire
Colina de la Ceiba
Via Río Grande
El Palmar
Bolívar, Venezuela
Telephone: 011-58-088811196

La Escalera

Barquilla de Fresa
Telephone: 011-58-212-923268
Fax: 011-58-212-9516226
Serranía de Lema, cerca del pueblo Las Claritas
Gran Sabana
Gran Sabana, Venezuela

Chalet Raymond
Ruth Carrero and Ramón Rojas
Telephone: (0415) 212-04-33

Bibliography

Ayensu, Edward S., ed. *The Life and Mysteries of the Jungle.* New York: Crescent Books, 1980.

Beebe, William. *High Jungle.* New York: Duell, Sloan, Pearce, 1949.

Bonta, Mark, and David Anderson. *Birding Honduras: A Checklist and Guide.* Tegucigalpa, Honduras: EcoArte, 2003.

Caufield, Catherine. *In the Rainforest.* New York: A. A. Knopf, 1985.

Chapman, Frank. *My Tropical Air Castle.* New York: Appleton and Company, 1929.

Croat, Thomas B. *Flora of Barro Colorado Island.* Stanford: Stanford University Press, 1978.

Dorst, Jean. *South America and Central America: A Natural History.* New York: Random House, 1967.

Dunning, John Stewart. *South American Land Birds.* Newton Square, Pa.: Harrowood Books, 1982.

Emmons, Louise, and François Freer. *Neotropical Rainforest Mammals: A Field Guide.* Chicago: University of Chicago Press, 1990.

Fogden, Michael, and Patricia Fogden. *Costa Rica: Wildlife of the National Parks and Reserves.* San José, Costa Rica: Fundación Neotrópica, Editorial Heliconia, 1997.

Forsyth, A., and K. Miyata. *Tropical Nature: Life and Death in the Rainforests of Central and South America.* New York: Charles Scribner's Sons, 1984.

Forsyth, Adrian, and Michael Fogden. *Portraits of the Rainforest.* Camden East, Ontario: Camden House, 1990.

Fjeldsa, Jon, and Niels Krabbe. *Birds of the High Andes.* Svendborg, Denmark: Apollo Books, 1990.

Goodwin, Mary Lou. *Birding in Venezuela.* Caracas: Sociedad Conservacionista/Audubon de Venezuela, 1987.

Haverschmidt, François, and G. F. Mees. *Birds of Suriname.* Paramaribo, Suriname: Vaco N.V., 1994.

Hilty, Steven L. *Birds of Tropical America.* Shelbourne, Vt.: Chapters Publishing Ltd., 1994.

Hilty, Steven L. *Birds of Venezuela.* Princeton: Princeton University Press, 2003.

Hilty, Steven L., and W. L. Brown. *Guide to the Birds of Colombia.* Princeton: Princeton University Press, 1986.

Hudson, W. H. *Green Mansions.* New York: Airmont Publishing Company, 1956.

Isler, Morton L. and Phyllis R. *The Tanagers: Natural History, Distribution, and Identification.* Washington, D.C.: Smithsonian Institution Press, 1987.

Janzen, Daniel H. *Costa Rica Natural History.* Chicago: University of Chicago Press, 1983.

Kricher, John C. *A Neotropical Companion: An Introduction to the Animals, Plants and Ecosystems of the New World Tropics.* Princeton: Princeton University Press, 1989.

Macquarrie, Kim (text) and Andre Bärtschi (photographs). *Peru's Amazonian Eden: Manu.* Introduction by John Terborgh. 2d ed.. Barcelona: Francis O. Patthey and Sons, 1998.

McCullough, David. *A Path between the Seas.* New York: Simon and Schuster, 1977.

Meyer de Schauensee, Rodolphe. *A Guide to the Birds of South America.* Wynnewood, Pa.: Livingston Publishing Co., 1970.

Meyer de Schauensee, R., and W. H. Phelps, Jr. *A Guide to the Birds of Venezuela.* Princeton: Princeton University Press, 1978.

Richards, P. W. *The Tropical Rain Forest: An Ecological Study.* Cambridge: Cambridge University Press, 1952.

Ridgely, Robert S., and Paul Greenfield. *The Birds of Ecuador.* Ithaca: Cornell University Press, 2001.

Ridgely, Robert S., and John A. Gwyne Jr. *A Guide to the Birds of Panama,* 2nd ed. Princeton: Princeton University Press, 1989.

Ridgely, Robert S., and Guy Tudor. *The Birds of South America,* Volume I, *The Oscine Passerines.* Austin: University of Texas Press, 1989.

———. *The Birds of South America,* Volume II, *The Suboscine Passerines.* Austin: University of Texas Press, 1994.

Sick, Helmut. *Birds in Brazil.* Princeton: Princeton University Press, 1993.

Snetsinger, Phoebe. *Birding on Borrowed Time.* Colorado Springs, Colo.: American Birding Association, 2003.

Snow, D. W. *The Web of Adaptation: Bird Studies in the American Tropics.* New York: New York Times Book Co., 1976.

Stap, Don. *Parrot without a Name.* New York: Alfred A. Knopf, Inc., 1990.

Stiles, F. Gary, and Alexander F. Skutch, *A Guide to the Birds of Costa Rica.* Ithaca, N.Y.: Comstock, 1989.

Terborgh, John. *Where Have All the Birds Gone?* Princeton: Princeton University Press, 1989.

Wheatley, Nigel. *Where to Watch Birds in South America.* Princeton: Princeton University Press, 1995.

Index